Borges and Kafka, Bolaño and Bloom

D1519125

Borges and Kafka, Bolaño and Bloom

Latin American Authors and the Western Canon

JUAN E. DE CASTRO

Vanderbilt University Press
Nashville, Tennessee

Library of Congress Cataloging-in-Publication Data
Names: De Castro, Juan E., 1959– author.
Title: Borges and Kafka, Bolaño and Bloom : Latin American authors and the
  Western canon / Juan E. De Castro.
Description: Nashville, Tennessee : Vanderbilt University Press, [2022] |
  Includes bibliographical references and index. | Summary: "How modern
  and contemporary Latin American writers and critics have approached and
  defined the Western canon"— Provided by publisher.
Identifiers: LCCN 2021046161 (print) | LCCN 2021046162 (ebook) | ISBN
  9780826502483 (paperback) | ISBN 9780826502490 (hardcover) | ISBN
  9780826502506 (epub) | ISBN 9780826502513 (pdf)
Subjects: LCSH: American literature—Appreciation—Latin America. |
  American literature—20th century—History and criticism. | Spanish
  American literature—20th century—History and criticism. | Canon
  (Literature) | LCGFT: Literary criticism.
Classification: LCC PS159.L38 D4 2022 (print) | LCC PS159.L38 (ebook) |
  DDC 809—dc23/eng/20211110
LC record available at https://lccn.loc.gov/2021046161
LC ebook record available at https://lccn.loc.gov/2021046162

Para Magdalena

CONTENTS

ACKNOWLEDGMENTS

AS HAS BEEN the case with my recent books, Ignacio López-Calvo and Nicholas Birns read the manuscript and made many valuable suggestions. Maria Rosa Olivera-Williams provided me with advice on the bibliography on Gabriela Mistral. The book is infinitely better thanks to their knowledge and friendship. I am also grateful to the editors at Vanderbilt University Press, in particular Zachary Gresham, for shepherding this project and helping improve it. Obviously, all remaining flaws are my responsibility. I also want to thank Gorica Majstorovic and Ignacio for their generous blurbs. Finally, Carolyn Vellenga Berman, chair of literature, and Federico Finchelstein, director of the Janey Program in Latin American Studies, helped create the environment that has made my research possible.

This is a book written during the recent lockdown. As such, it would have been impossible to write without the loving support of Magdalena, my wife.

INTRODUCTION

THERE IS SOMETHING conservative about most books about "the canon," something musty in their lists of dead white men, in their celebration of works often read more as part of course syllabi than out of passion or curiosity. They seem irrelevant in their frequent claims about the perennialness and universality of the authors included in their honor rolls. This conservatism even applies to those studies that work to open the canon by arguing for the inclusion of authors from marginalized groups, be they women, queer authors, writers of color, novelists, poets, or dramatists from the Global South, or studies that vindicate those who write so-called minor genres, such as romance, science fiction, or fantasy. Though worthy efforts that often bring attention to forgotten or marginalized authors, these critical works still aim to expand the canon rather than question it. They uphold the division between two tiers of authors: those worthy of inclusion in the canon and those who, for whatever reason, are seen as not having enough merit to be included. Thus, the canon remains.

Despite its title, *Borges and Kafka, Bolaño and Bloom: Latin American Authors and the Western Canon* is not a book *about* the canon, either Western or Latin American. The book does not aim to provide qualitative definitions of what constitutes a canonical work. Instead, it traces how the concept of canon (partially) displaced analogous terms, such as *classic* and *tradition*, used throughout Spanish America. Nor does this study propose a comprehensive list of authors who compose the canon, whether regional, Western, or global. It is true that Franz Kafka is a central figure of the Western canon, and for many people, Harold Bloom, before he died in 2019, had become something like its incarnation. Furthermore, if Jorge Luis Borges is the most solidly established Latin American member of the Western canon and, for many, the core of the Latin American canon, then Roberto Bolaño is the newest member of both. Nevertheless, this book studies how these two authors, together with a third and established member of all canons, Gabriel García Márquez, think about the canon. In other words, how these authors, from Latin America, the periphery certainly, attempt to define, *for their own practical purposes,* their relationship with the major authors of the Western literary tradition.

In addition to analyzing how three major writers—surely (from the view of the center) the three major Spanish-language Latin American writers of fiction—have thought about Western canon and the Latin American canon, this book also studies the region's tradition of women writers, from Sor Juana Inés de la Cruz, arguably the founder of the Spanish American literary tradition, to Gabriela Mistral, to date the only woman to have won a Nobel Prize in Literature from the region. Another chapter analyzes the uses made of Kafka's work by Borges, as well as such important writers as Argentina's Ricardo Piglia, Peru's Nobel Prize winner Mario Vargas Llosa, and Mexico's Guadalupe Nettel. The book concludes by looking at the works of two indigenous authors—Rigoberta Menchú and Lurgio Gavilán—whose writings serve as a counterpoint to the mainstream writers analyzed in the rest of the book.

Borges and Kafka, Bolaño and Bloom thus traces the diverse manners in which Latin American authors and critics have imagined and practiced their connection with the major Western writers—that is, with the Western canon—and by implication Western culture.

THE WEST VERSUS THE GLOBAL SOUTH

The use of the term *Western* can be problematic. After all, the "defense of the West" has become code for white supremacy and white nationalism in academic and political discourse. Even though we know that ancient Greece was marked by the influence of Egypt and Mesopotamia, and that Rome itself was multicultural and multiethnic, contemporary racism tends to imagine a homogeneously white past for Europe and its offspring in North America. In fact, the defense of the Western canon—or at least Western masterpieces—by authors, listed according to their politics from right wing to liberal, such as Dinesh D'Souza, Allan Bloom, E. D. Hirsch, and Harold Bloom, is connected, at best, to a defense of Eurocentric culture against putative multicultural threats (Hirsch and Harold Bloom) and, at worst, to an intellectual justification of racism. *Western civilization* has become a term used by Europeans and North Americans to deny the cultural achievements, and even the personhood, of Africans, Asians, and Latin Americans, and their diasporas.

Without denying the obvious fact that claims to Western culture are not in themselves incompatible with the affirmation of whiteness on the part of Latin Americans, one must note that intellectual figures across the political spectrum—Mistral to Borges, and García Márquez to Bolaño— have stressed their participation in Western culture and its classics, whether ancient or modern. Mistral calls Europe "old mother" ("vieja madre") in a poem (*Poesía y prosa* 181). Borges famously claimed, "I believe that our tradition is the whole of Western culture, and I also believe that we have a right to this tradition, a greater right than that which the inhabitants of one Western nation or any other may have" ("The Argentine Writer and Tradition" 426).[1] Along these lines, García Márquez decried that "the novel, undoubtedly and fortunately influenced by Joyce, Faulkner or Virginia Woolf has not yet been written in Colombia. I say fortunately, because I don't believe that Colombians can now be an exception to the flow of influences" ("¿Problemas de la novela?" 213).[2] Likewise, Bolaño stated, "Basically, I'm interested in Western literature, and I'm fairly familiar with all of it" ("Roberto Bolaño by Carmen Boullosa" n.p.).[3]

This interest on European literature and culture on the part of Latin American authors responds to a history of settler colonization and its impact on the constitution of new societies and nations. After all, Spain invaded the Americas in the sixteenth century, destroying existing indigenous written traditions, such as the glyph writing of Mesoamerica and the Andean *quipu*, without erasing all indigenous cultures or languages. Moreover, the struggle for independence was mostly led by descendants of the colonizers and left many of the colonial institutions, practices, and mores in place. Yet no matter how Western Latin American societies, inhabitants, and writers consider themselves, Latin America is also part of the Global South. Latin America participates in a parallel history of conquest, imperialism, exploitation, and unequal economic and cultural exchanges to those of Asia and Africa. And this tension is present in the region's literature. Ignacio Sánchez Prado provides an accurate description of the region's contradictions when he notes its "paradoxical status as belonging both to the Global South (or the Third World, or the postcolonial world) and to Western culture. Both legacies exist in a history of dialectical conflict and engagement with each other" (8).[4] Given this "dialectical conflict," it is not surprising that Borges stresses the participation of Latin America in a world culture that, by definition, includes what today we call the Global South and that of the West: "We must believe that the universe is our birthright and try out every subject; we cannot confine ourselves to what is Argentine in order to be Argentine because either it is our inevitable destiny to be Argentine, in which case we will be Argentine whatever we do, or being Argentine is a mere affectation, a mask" (427).[5]

Borges's rhetorical relocation from the West to the world reflects the fact that authors from Africa or Asia must pass through European and North American publishing gates. In the same way that García Márquez became a world writer primarily through the English translation of *Cien años de soledad* (*One Hundred Years of Solitude*, 1967), authors such as Rabindranath Tagore, to mention one of the few non-Western writers widely read in Latin America during the 1920s, including by Borges,[6] became well known in the region thanks to their previous success in Europe and the United States.

WOMEN AUTHORS AND WORLD LITERATURE

One of the main difficulties in dealing with issues regarding the canon is that the culturally entrenched sexism that excluded female authors from the canon can easily nudge a study to reproduce this inequality. Not only is the Western canon patriarchal, but bias against women is also found in the Latin American canon and other regional ones. The global and Latin American republics of letters are patriarchies, but so are the political and social republics. Therefore, Latin American women writers have dealt with barriers to education, gendered social expectations, pressures against intellectual activity, and marginalization of their works. It was only in the 1940s and 1950s that women throughout much of the region won the right to vote.

Given the structural discrimination throughout the region, it is no accident that the most characteristic genre of essayistic writing associated with women authors is what Mary Louise Pratt denominates "the gender essay, "whose topic is the stature and reality of women in society . . . it is a contestatory literature that aims . . . to interrupt the male monologue" (90). According to Pratt, the gender essay is at the core of "a women's countercanon" (90). Pratt compares the gender essay to the Latin American "identity essay" (e.g., José Martí's 1893 "Nuestra América" ["Our America"], Octavio Paz's 1950 *El laberinto de la soledad [Labyrinth of Solitude]*), often considered the core of the region's essayistic tradition. Despite these challenges, women writers have produced important works of literature— Mercedes Cabello de Carbonera, Clorinda Matto de Turner, and Julia Gorriti played a central role in the development of the novel in the Andean region and in Argentina—and also have produced a significant body of criticism, even during the nineteenth century, when writing about literature was not the norm for authors of any gender.

As Pratt also notes, in addition to the gender essay, women authors produced historical catalogs that listed "examples of women who have made significant contributions to society and history" (92). These catalogs, already found in Sor Juana Inés de la Cruz's "Respuesta a Sor Filotea de la Cruz" ("Response to Sor Filotea de la Cruz," 1692), have canonical connotations. Because women writers compile these catalogs, it is no surprise that they often include writers "who have made significant contributions" to literature. They frequently constitute supplements to the patriarchal canons or even (proto)feminist countercanons.

While a detailed analysis of these feminist genres is beyond the scope of this study, *Borges and Kafka, Bolaño and Bloom* looks at texts by women authors from Sor Juana to Gabriela Mistral as a way of tracing their implications regarding the relationship of Latin American literature, Western literature, and the Western canon. These texts provide an alternative view to this problematic relationship.

STRUCTURE OF THIS BOOK

As mentioned earlier, this book is not a study of the Western canon per se, or even primarily of the authors who Latin American writers have privileged as members of such canon. Instead, the study looks at how these writers have "theorized" the canon and at their relationship to it.

The first chapter, "Harold Bloom in the Hispanic World: From Classic to Canon," looks at Harold Bloom's work as a catalyst for consolidations and changes in the understanding of literature among Spanish-language scholars. Earlier critics such as Borges studied questions of literary quality and permanence using terms such as *tradition* or *classic*, but over the past couple of decades, the term *canon* has become widely used. While this meaning of the word derives from earlier uses of *canon*, it also responds to the influence of one of the most widely read and discussed works of cultural criticism published over the past few decades. That book, of course, is Bloom's *The Western Canon: The Books and School of the Ages*, first published in English in 1994 and in translation a year later. Despite Bloom's mistakes in, for example, considering Pablo Neruda an influence on César Vallejo (the latter was older and had published earlier), or his surprising devaluation of Borges, who, by 1995, was clearly situated at the center of the modern Hispanic canon, his ideas rapidly acquired a key position in literary discussion, even for otherwise iconoclastic readers and writers such as Bolaño. This chapter therefore studies the impact of Bloom's *The Western Canon* on Latin American and Spanish critical discussion, and it situates his proposal of a clearly established canon of major authors within earlier discussions on what constitutes a "classic," the preferred concept for discussing works of excellence in the Spanish-speaking world to that point. Moreover, this chapter examines the cultural moment and discussions of the late 1990s that facilitated the widespread influence of the North American critic.

Chapter 2, "Latin American Women Writers and Western Literature: On Sor Juana, Gabriela Mistral, and Others," briefly looks at the evolution in the relationship between literature of the region and of the Western center from the seventeenth century to the 1920s. In this period Latin America went from participating, if subordinately, in a pan-Hispanic and pan-Catholic cultural space centered in Madrid, to inserting itself in the nineteenth century into a Western literary space centered in Paris, to establishing connections with other centers of Western culture during the twentieth century. This chapter begins by studying the catalogs found in Sor Juana's "Response" and the implications of the cultural relationship between Mexico and Madrid, implicit in her "Loa al *Divino Narciso*" ("Prologue to the Mystery Play *Divine Narcissus*"). It continues by looking at the criticism written by Cabello and how her work reflects critically, rather than merely epigonally, the debates on the novel taking place in Paris in the last third of the nineteenth century. The chapter then analyzes a historical catalog of women writers provided by Matto. Finally, it examines Mistral, the most celebrated modern woman writer in Spanish. Mistral's criticism provides a (proto)feminist countercanon to that being developed in the 1920s by the first generation of professional critics, both academic, as in the case of Pedro Henríquez Ureña, and anti-academic, as in that of José Carlos Mariátegui.

"Borges and the Canon," the third chapter of this book, looks at ideas the Argentine writer expressed on the "Western tradition." Borges is arguably the first Latin American narrative writer to be incorporated into the Western canon, after being awarded the Prix Formentor in 1961 together with Samuel Beckett. His penchant for reusing characters and topics from the European and North American classics has permitted him to be seen by such noted critics as Paul de Man, John Updike, or George Steiner as something akin to a European writer who was accidentally born in South America. However, in essays such as "Quevedo" (1948), "Kafka y sus precursores" ("Kafka and His Precursors," 1951), "El escritor argentino y la tradición" ("The Argentine Writer and Tradition," 1951), and "Sobre los clásicos" ("On Classics," 1965), among others, the Argentine writer develops his ideas on how a writer born in the periphery of Western culture can make use of the European and world classics. Furthermore, this embrace of the world canon is far from acritical. Instead, by denying chronological precedence as determining canonical worth, Borges imbues with agency writers who from other perspectives could be seen as epigonal. In fact, in "Sobre los clásicos," Borges rejects, avant la lettre, Bloomian notions of the canon as based on "aesthetic value," no matter how agonistic, by placing the canonizing role on the reader rather than the writer or even the critic (as differentiated from the lay reader). By deconstructing hierarchies based on precedence, by purposefully undermining the aura of the classics, ancient and modern, and by rejecting any conceivable "anxiety of influence," Borges showed later Spanish-language writers from the Americas how to use the canon with freedom and irreverence.

The chapter "Rewriting Kafka in Latin America" studies the uses made of Franz Kafka's narrative by some of the key authors in the region. While the influence of William Faulkner on Spanish-language Latin American authors who came of age in the 1950s and 1960s has long been acknowledged by both critics and writers themselves, Faulkner is far from the only modernist master who made an imprint on the region's literature. If the North American novelist became, as Pascale Casanova argued, a "temporal accelerator" used by writers from peripheral regions to break free from nineteenth-century narrative models and make their works readable as modern literature by critics in Paris, New York, and London, then Kafka became not only a stylistic model for writers from Latin America but also a thematic and even allegorical resource. Borges, especially in stories like "La biblioteca de Babel" ("The Library of Babel," 1941) and "La lotería en Babilonia" ("The Lottery in Babylon," 1941), found in Kafka the starting point for new and original works of literature that nevertheless reflect characteristically Borgesian concerns, such as the paradoxes of textuality or the dangers of mob government. Borges is far from alone. In *Respiración artificial* (*Artificial Respiration*, 1980), Ricardo Piglia also found in Kafka the means for representing and understanding the history of his country and the world from the 1940s to the (then) present. In *El hablador* (*The Storyteller*, 1989), Vargas Llosa used Kafka's *The Metamorphosis* as a thematic device for exploring the tensions between orality and writing, indigenous and Western cultures, and cultural preservation and modernization. *The Metamorphosis* also serves as a recurring intertext for Guadalupe Nettel's autofiction *El cuerpo en que nací* (*The Body Where I Was Born*, 2011), as a sign of the difficulties her fictionalized self experienced growing up female in Mexico, as well as of the problematic relationship she developed with her body. Borges, Piglia, Vargas Llosa, and Nettel exemplify the ways some Latin American writers in Spanish have approached a modernist Western classic not as an untouchable monument but as a resource for understanding local reality and creating new works of literature that are respectively Argentine, Peruvian, or Mexican and also universal.

The chapter "Gabo's Canon: Gabriel García Márquez and the World Canon" explores the Colombian author's relationship with the Western modernist classics (James Joyce, Franz Kafka, Virginia Woolf, and William Faulkner). For many writers and readers throughout the world, García Márquez's *One Hundred Years of Solitude* (*Cien años de soledad*, 1967) is the central example of a literature of the Global South—even if that "South" is located mostly north of the equator (also the case for all of Asia and much of Africa). The foundational importance of García Márquez's masterwork to contemporary narrative from that Global South is evidenced by the effusive acknowledgments of his influence by such major contemporary writers as the Anglo-Indian Salman Rushdie and the Mozambican Mia Couto, as well as theorists like the Indian Homi Bhabha. Given the influence of García Márquez throughout Asia and Africa, it may surprise readers to find that the intertextual threads with which he weaved his now-classic novel are nothing less than the modernist canon. Gabo's canon—meaning a list of great books, but also meaning, in its original sense, works that serve as models for the artist to follow and as measuring sticks for judging new works—is composed precisely of the European and North American masterpieces of the first half of the twentieth century. By being both a quintessential Colombian and Caribbean writer and the keystone of a new world canon, García Márquez continues and develops the literary practice exemplified and proposed by Borges.

The chapter "Roberto Bolaño on/in the Canon" explores the Chilean master's writings on the topic. Bolaño is justifiably seen as a literary innovator, and his work has had significant influence on current US, European, and Latin American narrative. Moreover, he is capable of such antiestablishment gestures as questioning the literary value of García Márquez. Given his apparent radicality, his work has been seen as congruent with the Global North's most radical modes of reading. That said, despite his justified reputation as a literary revolutionary, Bolaño presents a very traditional view of the Latin American and Western canon that is surprisingly rooted in the works of Harold Bloom. In addition to studying essays such as "Literatura y exilio" ("Literature and Exile," 2000) and "La traducción es un yunque" ("Translation Is an Anvil," 2003), this chapter analyzes the manner in which Bolaño depicts such major authors as the Chilean Pablo

Neruda in the story "Carnet de baile" ("Dance Card" 2001) and the Mexican Octavio Paz in the Chilean novelist's instant classic *Los detectives salvajes* (*The Savage Detectives*, 1998).

The final chapter, "Indigenous Authors and the West," is meant to serve as a counterpoint to the Latin American mainstream analyzed in this rest of the book by highlighting two of the main indigenous autobiographical writers of the past forty years. *Me llamo Rigoberta Menchú y así me nació la conciencia* (*I, Rigoberta Menchú: An Indian Woman in Guatemala*, 1983), Menchú's *testimonio*, edited from interviews by the anthropologist Elizabeth Burgos-Debray, marked for many the irruption into the world republic of letters (and perhaps even the Western canon), of the unmediated voice of those marginalized by Western culture. Although the chapter looks at the polemics generated by the rapid inclusion of Menchú's (and Burgos-Debray's) text into college syllabi, it also analyzes the tensions found in the text between its belief that indigenous culture cannot be fully communicated to Western readers and the text's own international impact. In contrast with Menchú (and Burgos-Debray), Lurgio Gavilán's *Memorias de un soldado desconocido* (*When Rains Became Floods: A Child Soldier's Story*, 2015) assumes a common cultural background when telling the first-person narrator's surprising evolution from child soldier for the Shining Path, to being saved from execution at the hands of communal militias, to becoming a soldier and then a priest, to leaving the Franciscan order to study anthropology. While from the beginnings of colonial times, there have been indigenous authors who have written in Spanish, Gavilán's work is representative of the current boom in indigenous authors in Spanish, as well as in indigenous languages.

Borges and Kafka, Bolaño and Bloom analyzes the intersection of the Western canon—with all its changing aesthetic ideologies—and the literature of Spanish-speaking Latin America, within a diachronic framework that ranges from Sor Juana (seventeenth century) to Gavilán (beginning of the twenty-first century).

The writers studied in this book, with the possible exception of those included in the last chapter, can be seen as struggling with simultaneously belonging to Western culture, seeing the Western canon as theirs and as a resource, and the unavoidable reality of being part of the Global South. Despite points in common, *Borges and Kafka, Bolaño to Bloom* does not share the world literature perspective recently exemplified by such influential volumes as Mariano Siskind's *Cosmopolitan Desires: Global Modernity and World Literature in Latin America* (2014), Héctor Hoyos's *Beyond Bolaño: The Global Latin American Novel* (2015), and Sánchez Prado's *Strategic Occidentalism: On Mexican Fiction, the Neoliberal Book Market, and the Question of World Literature* (2018). In a way, it looks at the issue from the opposite perspective—rather than exploring Latin American *deseo de mundo* (cosmopolitan desire), that is the world "as a signifier of abstract universality" or "a finite set of global trajectories" (Siskind, *Cosmopolitan Desires*, 3), it limits itself to studying how the region's writers have thought about the Western canon, their relationship to it, and the uses that they have made of it. These authors clearly express "cosmopolitan desires," but this study looks at those only in terms of their relationship with the Western classics.

Borges and Kafka, Bolaño to Bloom also differs from the kind of critique Hoyos identifies in the region's "global novels" by authors such as Bolaño, the Mexican Mario Bellatín, and the Chilean Diamela Eltit. It is difficult not to agree with the following statement of principle by Hoyos: "I believe that Latin Americanism, which has indeed a rich political tradition to draw from, could invigorate world literature debates, especially because it does not sacrifice close reading or attention to the specific forms of works of art in the name of politics. In this way, Latin Americanizing world literature entails both politicizing that paradigm and bringing it closer to texts themselves" (10). However, rather than political readings of the novels, what is original about *Borges and Kafka, Bolaño and Bloom* is its stress on the ideas about the canon expressed by these authors and their use as a key to reading their fiction.

Likewise, one could also see Borges, García Márquez, Bolaño, and others as practicing what Sánchez Prado has called "strategic occidentalism":

The way in which specific writers . . . adopt a cosmopolitan stance to acquire cultural capital within their national tradition. This cosmopolitan stance is "Occidentalist" because it focuses fundamentally on the appropriation of Western literature, but always in a strategic form: through the translation and vindication of marginal traditions and authors and the formulation of literary aesthetics, poetics, and politics that do not replicate hegemonic waves of influence, but instead seek to reconstruct networks of cosmopolitan works through practice. (18–19)

However, this study does not concentrate on these authors' creative use of alternative "traditions." Instead, it is the question of the central tradition, that is the Western canon, and the way Latin American authors have made use of it that is studied.

Despite the more traditional nature of *Borges and Kafka, Bolaño and Bloom*'s author-centered approach, it is not lacking in a political dimension, given the intellectual subalternity assigned to authors and intellectuals writing from Latin America. This study attempts to contradict the tendency in US and European "theory" to ignore critical writings from the region, even those produced by its best-known representatives. Needless to say, in culture as in production, Latin America is almost always seen as a source for raw materials, even if named Borges, García Márquez, Bolaño, or Mistral. Underlying this disregard for Latin American critical thinking is, as Hosam Aboul-Ela notes, the result of "the old epistemological core/periphery divide, which retained Europe and Anglo-America's status as the exclusive domain of ideas and theory" (11). By contrast, *Borges and Kafka, Bolaño and Bloom* sees Latin America as a domain of ideas.

Today Latin America is described across the political spectrum of the United States as a distinct "other." The ever-growing right wing in the United States sees the region as threatening. To Donald Trump we are nothing but criminals. Tony Ivy League professors, such as the late Samuel P. Huntington, fretted about "the Hispanic challenge." Legions of racist politicians, commentators, and even militia groups see marginalization, internment, and deportation as the solution to the alleged danger posed by migrants from the region. In contrast, liberals often reify Latin America. Not only is magical realism still the lens through which many view the region, but liberal, even radical, political hopes have often been pinned on Latin America and its population, as if there were an innate progressiveness to its diaspora, regardless of country of origin and reason for emigration, as if the region were not home to many a right-wing regime, and in several cases with significant popular support.[7] Both the Right and the (alleged) Left often see the region and, in particular, immigrants from Latin America from a simplistic and essentialist perspective.

Given these stereotyped views of Latin America and its population as a clear "other" that is differentiated from, if not opposed to, Europe and the United States, it is of use to look at the fiction and essays of some of the most representative and important writers from the region. Against these (US) American views, Latin American writers across stylistic and political divides—from the "conservative" Borges to the "revolutionary" García Márquez—see their work as framed within the confines of a globalized Western literary tradition. However, even if they reject the position of "other," their work is often subversive rather than epigonal. Latin American authors subvert both the Western canon and the ideas held in the United States and Europe about the region, its cultures, and its population.

1

Harold Bloom in the Hispanic World

From Classic to Canon

IN 2013, THE Spanish-language translation of Ted Gioia's *The Jazz Standards: A Guide to the Repertoire* was published by Editorial Turner, a press that specializes in books on the arts. Gioia's work is fascinating, but what is here of interest is the title given to the translation: *El canon del jazz: Los 250 temas imprescindibles.* Ignoring the Spanish title's obvious poetic license,[1] what is most surprising is that the word *standards* is rendered as *canon.*[2] Also surprising: the meaning of canon implied in Gioia's title was only added to the Real Academia Española's *Diccionario de la lengua española* in 2014, just a year later.[3]

One can easily assume that just few years earlier instead of canon, Gioia's book would have included *clásico* (classic) in its title, since this is the word most widely used in Spanish for works of great excellence before

14

the mid-1990s.[4] Despite the differences between *canon* and *clásico*—the first refers to a catalog or group of masterpieces, the second to individual works—a title such as "Los clásicos del jazz" would have been as inexact as Editorial Turner's actual choice. The decision to use a word that twenty or so years earlier would have been incomprehensible in this context, and that had still not been included in the official dictionary of the Spanish language, rather than *clásico*, reflects the dissemination of a new meaning for *canon*, one that must have made the title more appealing to the reading public. The term *clásico* has become devalued by its overuse, but the Spanish-language version of Gioia's book is also trying to bring to mind one of the few works of literary criticism that became a best seller during the 1990s and 2000s: Harold Bloom's *The Western Canon: The Books and School of the Ages* (1994). Translated as *El canon occidental: La escuela y los libros de todas las épocas*, Bloom's book was published only a year after it came out in English, by Anagrama, perhaps the most prestigious Spanish-language book publisher.[5] Unlike in the United States, where *The Western Canon* was published by a popular press—Houghton Mifflin Harcourt—and marked a central moment in its author's distancing of himself from academia, Anagrama published Bloom's study in a series that included such authors as René Girard and Michel Foucault.[6]

REDEFINING CANON

The relative novelty of this use of the word *canon* in Spanish—previously most often understood in its nonliterary meaning of tax—is implied in the novelist, poet, and critic Vicente Molina Foix's review of the English original of Bloom's book, published in late 1994 in *El País*, the most widely read Spanish and Hispanophone newspaper. (The fact that a book in English would be reviewed before it came out in translation is an early example of the impact of *The Western Canon* in the Hispanic world). In his review, Molina Foix provides a definition of Bloom's use of *canon*: "norma de aquellas obras y autores que 'el mundo no querría dejar morir'" ("rules [or standards] of those works and authors the world wouldn't want to see die"). While this definition is confusing in that it seems to refer to the earlier meaning of *canon* as rule or standard rather than to the books that have made it into the canon, throughout the review, Molina Foix refers to "hit parade" (in English) and list, thus (sort of) making clear to the reader what is meant by Bloom's use of canon.

A brief perusal of the cultural journal *Vuelta* (1976–1998), founded by no less a figure than Mexican poet and Nobel Prize winner Octavio Paz, serves as a further example of how the word *canon* came to replace the older *clásico*, and of the role played by Bloom's book in inserting this word and concept into popular vocabulary. The first use of *canon*—in any of its meanings—in *Vuelta* came in 1996, twenty years into the publication of this cultural journal and, not surprisingly, in a review of Harold Bloom's *El canon occidental*. Also written by a Spanish man of letters, in this case Juan Malpartida, the review provides something like a definition of canon: "El canon, esa vara para medir, puede servir también para golpear, y a eso se arriesga cualquier obra que, como la de Harold Bloom, quiere establecer la jerarquía que ocupan los autores en la cultural occidental" (The canon, that measuring stick, can also be used to hit, and that is a risk run by any work, such as Harold Bloom's, that aims to establish a hierarchy for authors within Western Culture) (42). Here we see a slippage from the classical (ancient Greek) meaning of *canon* as a measuring stick to the newer, at least in Spanish, Bloomian meaning of canon as a catalog of model masterpieces or master authors. Malpartida's and Molina Foix's reviews show how earlier definitions of the word *canon* were easily transposed into the meaning popularized by Bloom.

Of course, the use of *canon* in its earlier, best-known meanings—whether as a corpus of specific related texts, such as the "Cervantine canon," or in the sense of aesthetic criteria used to evaluate and classify works, such as "the canons of *modernismo*"—were widely used in Spanish-language literary studies.[7] Moreover, in the Hispanic cultural world, issues related to the Bloomian sense of the canon had been long discussed using terms such as *classic* or *tradition*. As Susana Cella notes: "The idea of canon can be confronted with comparable terms that are in an opposed or synonymic relationship, among which one can consider tradition, classic, margin and center. These considerations represent the intention of not limiting the discussion to what could be considered the Bloom effect derived from his hyperbolic title *The Western Canon*" (8).[8] As we will see, Jorge Luis Borges discussed what today we would call the canon by means of the concepts of classic and tradition.

THE CANON DEBATES IN THE US

In English, the word *canon* had been used much earlier, though sporadically, in this later "Bloomian" sense.[9] For instance, as early as 1918, Van Wyck Brooks referred to "the accepted canon of American literature," contrasting it with "those of the literatures of Europe" (338). That said, it is not fully clear whether Brooks is using *canon* in its meaning in *Merriam-Webster's Dictionary* of "a sanctioned or accepted group or body of related works"— that is, as a sense of works belonging to a clearly differentiated American tradition—or in its sense as a catalog of masterpieces. The latter meaning is, however, clearly present in Carl Van Doren's 1932 "Toward a New Canon." Unlike Bloom, Van Doren notes the mutability of the canon—"The canon of American literature refuses to stay fixed"—as writers such as Melville and Dickinson are described as toppling Bryant, Longfellow, Lowell, and Holmes from what once seemed "secure" and "solid thrones" (429). Van Doren's insistence on the role of presses and professors in the development and maintenance of this earlier canon led Jan Gorak to argue that "Van Doren makes the current canon debate look rewarmed" (67).[10]

The "rewarmed" debate raged in (primarily) the United States during the 1980s and 1990s. As John Guillory noted in 1990, "In recent years many literary critics have become convinced that the selection of literary text for 'canonization' (the selection of what are conventionally called the 'classics') operates in a way very like the formation of the biblical canon. These critics detect beneath the supposed objectivity of value judgments a political agenda: the exclusion of many groups of people from representation in the literary canon" ("Canon" 233). New critical perspectives (e.g., deconstructionist, feminist, queer, Afro-centric) contradicted the values (e.g., heteronormative, Eurocentric, patriarchal) long associated with mainstream academia.[11] Given the intensity with which these debates were held, it is not surprising that such important works as Gorak's *The Making of the Modern Canon* (1991) and Guillory's *Cultural Capital: The Problem of Literary Canon Formation* (1993) were published during the early 1990s, before Bloom's *The Western Canon* came out.

While these discussions had their first home in academia—Guillory has argued that "the problem of the canon is a syllabus and curriculum" ("Canon" 240)—they rapidly spilled into the public sphere. It may surprise contemporary readers, given the current embrace of a (pseudo)populist anti-rationalism and anti-academicism on part of the US Right, that conservatives such as Allan Bloom in his *The Closing of the American Mind* (1987)[12] and Dinesh D'Souza—then considered a serious cultural interlocutor rather than right-wing hack—in his *Illiberal Education: The Politics of Race and Sex on Campus* (1991) publicly denounced the loss of interest in traditional high culture within academia. To these two names one must add the liberal E. D. Hirsch, who in *Cultural Literacy: What Every American Needs to Know* (1988), chimed in with his two cents to this decrying of the popularization of cultural knowledge. While the three were concerned with what they saw as the negative impact of then "progressive" critical, theoretical, and political concerns on what was being taught in colleges, only D'Souza showed a particular interest in issues directly related to the literary canon.[13] In fact, D'Souza's attacks, albeit lacking sophistication, against those seeking to open up the canon prefigure Harold Bloom's complaints against the "School of Resentment." As D'Souza notes, "Ironically some of the same people who most stridently oppose a great books canon seem most active in devising their own consciously ideological and highly exclusive canon for race" (213). Despite the intellectually elitist bias exhibited by these books, found precisely in their attempts to debunk the supposedly populist then-current state of academia, they played a role in the rejection of knowledge, including that found in the "classics" they purportedly aimed to defend, that characterizes today's Right.

According to Harold Bloom, this defense of the "Western canon" underlies a preoccupation with "the academic-journalistic network I have dubbed the School of Resentment, who wish to overthrow the Canon in order to advance their supposed (and nonexistent) programs for social change" (4). Elsewhere he further identifies this network's academic tendencies: "Feminists, Afrocentrists, Marxists, Foucault-inspired New Historicists, or Deconstructors—of all those whom I have described as members of the School of Resentment" (20). Certainly not all members of this "School" would see themselves as comrades—a "deconstructor" and a Marxist wouldn't consider themselves as representing compatible viewpoints, and second-wave feminism implies a belief in an identity that resists deconstruction—but Harold Bloom's list of villains is not too dissimilar from the ones previously identified by D'Souza, Hirsch, and Allan Bloom

It is true that Harold Bloom decried conservative political uses of the "canon" and was far from being a right-winger.[14] However, given that his work and Harold Bloom himself achieved a level of popularity beyond that of his conservative or liberal predecessors—according to Marc Redfield he became "the representation of the canon in the American media" (103)—*The Western Canon* must be placed within this genealogy of works that—even if written with diverse purposes in mind—ultimately played a role in discrediting "really existing academia" and learning itself.

Despite the presence of some of the most important Latin American critics in US universities and the concomitant influence of US cultural debates on their work, one still wonders about the relevance of these debates to the Latin American public cultural sphere. It may be no accident that Allan Bloom's *The Closing of the American Mind* (curiously translated twice into Spanish in 1989),[15] Hirsch's *Cultural Literacy*, and D'Souza's *Illiberal Education* (the latter two never translated) have exercised little or no influence on Latin American or Spanish cultural discussions. It is true, though, that Latin American scholars, often ensconced in US academia, included discussions of the canon in their wrings. For instance, Beatriz Pastor, writing in the *Revista Casa de las Américas*, the once-iconic cultural journal of the Cuban Revolution, noted in 1988 that "the debate on the canon is in fashion" ("La discusión en torno al canon está de moda" 78). However, these concerns would break into the Hispanic public sphere only with the publication of Bloom's *The Western Canon*.

THE RECEPTION OF *THE WESTERN CANON* IN THE SPANISH-SPEAKING WORLD[16]

Several of Harold Bloom's works had been translated into Spanish before *The Western Canon*. Seix Barral, home of such Latin American Boom movement classics as Mario Vargas Llosa's *La ciudad y los perros* (*Time of the Hero*, 1963), had published the Spanish translation of *The Visionary Company: A Reading English Romantic Poetry* (1961) in 1974. In 1976, the Venezuelan press Monte Ávila had done the same with *The Anxiety of Influence* (1973), perhaps the most important of all Bloom's works, at least within academia. However, according to Genara Pulido, Bloom's influence in Spain (and Latin America) was limited, although his works' translation is a sign of a persistent, if not widespread, interest in his works before 1995.[17] Thus, Bloom's impact in wider cultural circles is directly connected to the publication of the Spanish-language version of *The Western Canon*.

What makes this influence surprising is that, rather than showing great appreciation for the literatures of Spain or Latin America, Bloom's canon comprises primarily English-language authors, as most early Spanish-language reviews of the book pointed out. Molina Foix's notes in colorful soccer-inflected idiom that, "in the championship of languages, Bloom is shamelessly in favor of the home team: out of the 26 [authors] classified [into the canon], half wrote in English" ("en el campeonato de las lenguas, Bloom es un árbitro descaradamente casero: de los 26 clasificados, la mitad escribieron en inglés"). Christopher Domínguez Michael, perhaps Mexico's best-known literary critic and an admirer, with caveats, of Bloom's *The Western Canon*, writes about the absence of Spanish-language authors such as Quevedo, Góngora, and Calderón: "A canon without the Golden Age is inconceivable" ("Es inconcebible un canon sin el Siglo de Oro") (58). After pointing out the similar omission of major French authors, such as Flaubert, Stendhal, and Balzac, Domínguez turns his attention to Bloom's evaluation of Latin American literature:

> The chapter dedicated to Hispanic-Portuguese [*sic*] literature is a disaster. Advised by a specialist in Carpentier—Professor Roberto González Echevarría—Bloom assures the reader that the Cuban novelist is the most important writer of the century. Afterward, he gets rid of Borges, Neruda and Pessoa as diligent students of Walt Whitman. A critic who ignores the golden age is obviously incapable of appreciating Darío, García Lorca, Neruda, Vallejo or Paz, not to speak of the Spanish American novel, absent from *The Western Canon*. (58)[18]

Despite these lacunae, the Hispanic cultural establishment (as well as the region's general readers) ultimately embraced Bloom. As Ignacio Sánchez Prado noted in 2021, "*El canon occidental* turned Bloom into a household name in the Spanish-speaking world" ("On Cosmopolitanism and Love").

Less than a decade later, Bloom received the Premi Internacional Catalunya (2002) from the Generalitat de Catalunya and the Premio Internacional

Alfonso Reyes (2003) from the Mexican Ministry of Culture. He was even a finalist for the Premio Príncipe de Asturias (2010), granted by the Spanish monarchy. Moreover, Bloom will be embraced as a master—arguably, *the* master—critic by some major contemporary Spanish American authors, such as Juan Villoro and Juan Gabriel Vásquez.[19] As we will see in a later chapter, for no less a figure than Roberto Bolaño, Bloom was "probably our continent's best literary critic" ("The Book That Survives" 200) ("es probablemente el mejor ensayista literario de nuestro continente") ("El libro que sobrevive"186). By the time of Bloom's death, he was hailed in *El País* as "the most influential critic" ("el más influyente crítico literario") by the respected Spanish novelist Eduardo Lago, who also noted the (US) American critic's "portentous wisdom" ("sabiduría portentosa").

Given Bloom's Anglo-centrism and the many problems found in his actual comments made about Spanish and Spanish American literature, his enormous influence and the support he found in the Spanish-speaking world is strikingly mysterious. One way of unveiling this mystery, then, is to look at what was going in Latin American culture and society at the time of the publication of *The Western Canon*.

TRAVELING THEORY

The 1960s saw the rise in the Spanish-speaking world of an adventurous high-modernist literature—the so-called Boom—that produced such innovative and popular works as Vargas Llosa's *The Time of the Hero* (*La ciudad y los perros*, 1963) and Gabriel García Márquez's *One Hundred Years of Solitude* (*Cien años de soledad*, 1967). But by the 1980s and especially the 1990s, the most characteristic works were "'light,' easy literature, which, without any sense of shame, sets out to be—as its primary and almost exclusive objective—entertaining" (Vargas Llosa, *Notes on the Death of Culture* 26).[20] As Roberto Bolaño, the most lauded Latin American writer of the past two decades, asked in 2002, precisely as he declared himself "not to be in any way an inheritor of the Boom": "Who are the official descendants of García Márquez? Precisely Isabel Allende, Laura Restrepo, Luis Sepúlveda, and others" ("Entrevista con Roberto Bolaño").[21] Bolaño's list included authors whose works were character-

ized by a watering down of the Boom's innovations and their incorporation into market-friendly narratives.

The publication of the *Spanish*-language version of *The Western Canon*,
then, took place during the hegemony of this post-Boom literature that popularized techniques characteristic of the Boom and of earlier high-modern
writers (Jorge Luis Borges, Juan Rulfo), such as magical realism, telescoping
dialogues, and interior monologues. This was also a time characterized by
the "expansion of the Spanish book industry into Latin America as a publisher of books by Latin American and non-Latin American authors" (De
Castro, *The Spaces of Latin American Literature* 96) as a result of the region-
wide process of neoliberal reorganization and incorporation into global markets. While there were always important creative authors, including Bolaño
himself, the commercial success of this renewed pan-Hispanic book market
was built on the publication of these new best-selling authors and on older
but still well-known and marketable names, such as the then-living Boom
masters Vargas Llosa, García Márquez, and Carlos Fuentes.

In 1996, only a few months after the Spanish translation of Bloom's *The
Western Canon* came out, the purported generational change and development of a literature more in tune with the cultural and commercial winds of
the time were made explicit with the publication of *McOndo*, an anthology
of short stories by young Latin American and Spanish writers, compiled by
the Chilean novelists Alberto Fuguet and Sergio Gómez. In that same year,
a group of young Mexican writers—Jorge Volpi, Ignacio Padilla, Pedro Ángel
Palou, and others—published the *Manifiesto del Crack*, but those writers
explicitly positioned themselves against commercial literary tendencies of
the time and as representative of a high-modernist aesthetic: "to the super-
ficiality of what is disposable and ephemera, the Crack novels oppose the
multiplicity of voices and the creation of autonomous worlds" (Palou).[22]
However, the editors of the *McOndo* anthology, Fuguet and Gómez, saw
their narrative as in tune with then contemporary cultural tendencies: "As
an aside, let's say that *McOndo* is *MTV Latina*, but in black and white letters" ("De paso, digamos que McOndo es MTV latina, pero en papel y
letras de molde") (16). *McOndo* presents itself as promoting a literature
different from the Latin American best sellers of the time, without in the
least rejecting the novel's role as a merchandise in a growing pan-Hispanic
business and rapidly globalizing cultural markets.[23]

Given this context in which the old Boom lions were no longer produc-
ing the kind of ambitious works they made their name by—Cortázar died
in 1984, and in 1993 and 1994 Fuentes published *Diana, the Goddess Who*
Hunts Alone (*Diana, o la cazadora solitaria*, 1994); Vargas Llosa, *Death in*
the Andes (*Lituma en los Andes*, 1993); and García Márquez, *Of Love and*
Other Demons (*Del amor y otros demonios*, 1994)—and the younger generations were writing works more attuned to market and cultural tendencies,
in Latin America, Bloom's paean to the canon represented a defense of the
values of high literature, which were threatened in a cultural environment
progressively being taken over by commercial considerations. Moreover,
from 1995 to the present, this hegemony of commercial versus aesthetic
value has become more apparent, as even some of the most prestigious literary awards for Spanish works have been given to books that seem closer to
best sellers than works of aesthetic ambition.[24]

Against this apparent hegemony of commercial *literature*, Bloom begins
The Western Canon by noting: "This book studies twenty-six writers, necessarily with a certain nostalgia, since I seek to isolate the qualities that made
these authors canonical, that is, authoritative in our culture. 'Aesthetic value'
is sometimes regarded as a suggestion of Immanuel Kant's rather than an
actuality, but that has not been my experience during a lifetime of reading"
(1). For Bloom, unlike for many contemporary Latin American and Spanish
book award committees or national academies,[25] market success, celebrity,
and literary value were clearly distinct, if not in opposition to one another.
Bloom's defense of high literature and his belief in the need for critics to
evaluate and discard "inferior" literature became a useful critical levee for
those critics attempting to keep the commercial literary ocean from flood-
ing the Hispanic Republic of Letters.

Similarly to the examples of such earlier conservative defendants of
"high culture," Latin American criticisms of "light literature" lead to per-
formative contradictions. For instance, Vargas Llosa is one of the region's
most respected writers, even winning the Nobel Prize in Literature in 2010,
but he is also an intransigent defender of the free market. In other words,
despite his criticisms of "light" literature, he is a main proponent of the
full implementation of the radical free-market policies that have helped
create the conditions that make possible the identification of marketabil-
ity with artistic quality.

THE SCHOOL OF RESENTMENT SOUTH OF
THE (MEXICO-US) BORDER

Somewhat counterintuitively, the main reason many Latin American critics give for embracing Bloom is not his implicit defense of high-modernist literature when it was under commercial siege, but his attack on "the School of Resentment." According to Jean Franco in 1996, precisely when *The Western Canon* began to leave its imprint on Hispanic culture, "'Literatura *light*'... is most often written by women—Laura Esquivel, Ángeles Mastretta, Sara Sefchovich, and Isabel Allende—some of whom are best-selling authors, the sales of whose books are only rivalled by those of García Márquez" (97). As Franco notes, "women writers figure prominently in what is sometimes called the neo-avantgarde and have nothing but scorn for 'literatura *light*'" (97). However, the criticism of "light literature" incorporates the rejection of some of the best-known women writers, and through them of a key "branch" of a Hispanic version of the School of Resentment.

Domínguez Michael, for instance, correctly identifies the (US) American character of Bloom's criticisms, even if he shows clear antipathy toward culturally progressive movements: "The School of Resentment is the offspring the authoritarian egalitarianism of 1968 and of the importation into North American universities of France's logocidal thought" (57).[26] And: "Multiculturalism, the core of the School of Resentment is not only a postmodern version of Zhdanovism, but the very late cultural victory in the university of the once and present failed North American left" (57).[27] Despite its vitriol—and his dependence on US right-wing propaganda—Domínguez Michael's statement identifies the specifically local character of Bloom's polemics. However, for Domínguez Michael, Bloom's theories do travel. Thus, in a tendentious manner, Domínguez Michael resituates Bloom's writings in his Mexican cultural context. After noting that in postrevolutionary Mexico the state saw itself as the incarnation of political correction, a role inherited after 1968 by "civil society," the Mexican critic argues about the main local version of the School of Resentment: "is not *indigenismo* from Manuel Gamio to Subcomandante Marcos a lyrical and primitive version of multiculturalism?" (58).[28] He concludes his diatribe by noting: "In a Mexican clef, Bloom's battle is the one fought by [Alfonso]

Reyes, *los Contemporáneos* [a group that included poets Xavier Villaurrutia, José Gorostiza, and Gilberto Owen], and Octavio Paz" (58).[29]

For Domínguez Michael, as was the case for many of Bloom's admirers throughout the Hispanic world, *The Western Canon* and its author became a weapon for attacking left-wing or localist versions of culture—as if these were necessarily synonymous.[30] As Sánchez Prado argues—in an essay that qualifies, without fully rejecting, his early admiration of Bloom's work— about Mexico's cultural circles, as "a place in which his [Bloom's] defense of literature as a product of an elite and of individual genius is very relevant" (103).[31] However, the embrace of Bloom's *The Western Canon* is the result not only of a belief in a canon made up of masterworks composed by "individual geniuses," but also of the belief that Mexico participates fully in Western culture.

CONCLUSION

Bloom became the living representation of the Western canon for US media. Redfield, perhaps with some postmodern excess, writes of the Yale critic:

> By the mid-1980s, Harold Bloom . . . became a unique figure in the Ameri-can higher-brow mass media: the critic as genius, who personified the internalization of the Western canon. Bloom was the critic as cyborg— almost as monster, insofar as his ingestion of the canon required preter-natural reading speed and memory; but he also stood for the embodiment of an aesthetic judgment that, at once omnivorous and discriminating, knew how to ingest, specifically, *the canon*. (10–11)

The variety and prestige of the popular print media that embraced this identification between Bloom and the Western canon—Redfield men-tions *Newsweek, Time, New York Magazine,* and especially *New York Times Magazine* and the *New Yorker*—and the impact of US media in the His-panic world, also helps explain why the region's cultural networks would see Bloom as the living representative of the Western canon, despite his lack of knowledge about most Spanish-language literature.[32] Moreover, his status as a best-selling author added to a visibility that ultimately over-shadowed more thoughtful thinkers like Gorak or Guillory, whose books predated Bloom's.[33]

According to Bloom, "The Canon, once we view it as the relation of an individual reader and writer to what has been preserved out of what has been written, and forget the canon as a list of books for required study, will be seen as identical with the literary Art of Memory, not with the religious sense of canon" (17). This is a perplexing definition, since it embraces an individualistic framework that seems to contradict the notion of the canon as "a book and school of the ages," in other words, as constituting a kind of unit capable of withstanding fashions and other vicissitudes. However, what Bloom ultimately brings to the discussion of literature is precisely the idea of great books that also belong to a series, of "the strangely intimate family romance of the great writers, who are influenced by one another without regard for political resemblances and differences" (526). For Bloom, "a poem, play, or novel is necessarily compelled to come into being by way of precursor works, however eager it is to deal directly with social concern" (11). Thus, the view of literary works as a continuum is imbricated with the rejection of any social or political concern as alien to literary writing and reading.

It is true that a related idea is already found in T. S. Eliot's "Tradition and the Individual Talent":

> The existing monuments form an ideal order among themselves, which is modified by the introduction of the new (the really new) work of art among them. The existing order is complete before the new work arrives; for order to persist after the supervention of novelty, the *whole* existing order must be, if ever so slightly, altered; and so the relations, proportions, values of each work of art toward the whole are readjusted; and this is conformity between the old and the new. (526)

However, Latin American reflections on the region's literature have often delinked the idea of tradition from the classics. For instance, the Peruvian José Carlos Mariátegui, a foundational Marxist thinker and one of the region's first professional literary critics,[34] saw tradition as disconnected from the idea of masterwork, at least until César Vallejo.[35]

The reference to classics, in contrast, stressed the individual traits of a literary work rather than its belonging to a constellation of interrelated masterpieces. Continuing with Mariátegui, it could be argued that he sees the poetry of José María Eguren, one of his favorite authors, as constituting a classic, even if he is presented as delinked from the Peruvian tradition: "In Peru, Eguren does not understand or know the people. He is remote from the Indian's history and alien to his history. He is spiritually too Western and foreign to assimilate indigenous orientalism" (*Seven Interpretative Essays* 245).[36] Ironically, Eguren is presented as clearly belonging to Western literature, less so to that of his native country.

Bloom's concept of the canon may have become influential given the vagaries of the market, the conservatism of the Hispanic world's cultural arbiters, the dependent—regarding capital and cultural capital—character of its literary world, and the breakdown of national cultural frontiers as a consequence of globalization. But it also provided a (partially) new way to think about the relationship between books, authors, and Spanish, Latin American, and Western literatures more generally.

2

Latin American Women Writers and Western Literature

On Sor Juana, Gabriela Mistral, and Others

MANY PEOPLE ASSOCIATE Latin American literature with its great male writers, like Jorge Luis Borges, Gabriel García Márquez, Vargas Llosa, and more recently Roberto Bolaño, to limit ourselves to authors studied in this book. Without denying the stature of these writers, we must note that patriarchal structures limited the access of women to education, literacy, and even the public sphere, not only in Latin America but throughout Western culture as a whole. Thus, the preponderance of male Latin American writers in the Western canon is partly a result of patriarchy in the region and outside it, due to the conditions mentioned above, and to the bias often present in the selection of authors considered "of worth." The Spanish republic of letters, as well as the world republic of letters, to use Pascale Casanova's terminology, was (and perhaps still is) mostly male. And of course the Western canon is primarily made up of dead white men.

Despite this, we can posit a countercanon of Spanish-language women writers of comparable worth. For instance, the early modernist novelist María Luisa Bombal (Chile, 1910–1980), author of such pathbreaking novellas as *La última niebla* (*The Final Mist*, 1931) and *La amortajada* (*The Shrouded Woman*, 1938), was a younger contemporary and friend of Borges. The 1960s saw the Mexican novelists Elena Garro (1916–1998), author of the modernist and proto–magical realist *Recuerdos del porvenir* (*Recollections of Things to Come*, 1963), and the novelist, poet, playwright, and second-wave feminist thinker Rosario Castellanos (1925–1974), author of *Balún Canán* (1957). While well known and widely read, these two Mexican novelists are often excluded from discussions of the Boom of the 1960s. Moreover, beginning in the 1980s, a slew of women novelists, from Elena Poniatowska (Mexico, b. 1932) to Marcela Serrano (Chile, b. 1951) to Fernanda Melchor (Mexico, b. 1982), have taken the reins of the region's narrative, gaining equal, if not greater, reputation than most of their confrères. Finally, the list must include the Chilean poet Gabriela Mistral (1859–1957), Nobel Prize winner in 1945 and the one modern woman writer who made it not only into the Hispanic canon but, arguably, also those of the West and the world.

This chapter briefly looks at the evolution of the relationship between Latin American literature and the so-called world republic of letters through the writings of major women writers. It attempts to briefly map the evolution of this relationship from colonial days, when the region participated (even if subordinately) in a pan-Hispanic and pan-Catholic space centered in Madrid; to the nineteenth century, when these cultural borders opened in particular to French culture; to the 1920s, when the region's critics and writers began to consider what today we would call national canons and the relationship between these local authors and Western classics.

SOR JUANA INÉS DE LA CRUZ

What makes male-centered genealogies particularly problematic is that the founder of the Spanish-language Latin American literary tradition, if such a thing exists, is a woman: Sor Juana Inés de la Cruz (1648–1695), née Asbaje Ramírez de Santillana. Born in San Miguel Nepantla, Mexico, in the Viceroyalty of New Spain, Sor Juana is the first major "Spanish American" author and also the last of the great Hispanic writers of the Golden Age. This lineage begins with Garcilaso de la Vega (1501–1536), who transplanted the sonnet from Italy to Spain, and reaches its zenith with Luis de Góngora (1561–1627) and Francisco de Quevedo (1580–1645), the latter two generally considered the greatest poets in the Spanish language. Equally important, she is also seen as the precursor of the region's feminism, thanks to her defense of the ability of women and their right to education, scholarship, and creation in her 1691 "Respuesta a Sor Filotea de la Cruz" ("Response of the Poet to Sor Filotea de la Cruz").

The "Respuesta" already implies discussions about the canon. After all, Sor Juana creates genealogies of women scholars and writers, including actual persons (Hypatia, St. Paula, and Queen Christine of Sweden) as well as mythical characters (Athena, the Sibyls, the Queen of Sheba).[1] However, her lists of authors reveal a basis from which to refute the accusations leveled against her intellectual activity, rather than a canon proper—at least in the Bloomian sense that has become prevalent in thinking about literature. (Of course, she wrote not long after the birth of the Western literary space, when the existence of vernacular classics was only beginning to be acknowledged).[2]

Among the names listed by Sor Juana, exemplary women scholars and authors, is a figure like Hypatia, particularly congenial to the author of the "Response." After all, Hypatia was a polymath like the Mexican nun, although she mainly concentrated on mathematics and philosophy rather than literature and was a victim of religious patriarchy at its very worst, martyred by a Christian mob in 415 CE. However, it is highly unlikely that Sor Juana ever read, or had the possibility of reading, the Alexandrian scholar.[3] Moreover, the inclusion of legendary figures as precursors, though examples of how the classical world and the Bible have imagined female intellectual agency, undermines the usefulness of Sor Juana's lists as a potential feminist canon. However, the lists are an early "historical catalogue, in which the writer enumerates examples of women who have made significant contributions to history and society" (Pratt 92), a genre characteristic of much writing by women in Latin America. As we will see, these lists will acquire a canonical dimension, as they begin to incorporate women not only as role models or predecessors but also as concrete examples of exceptional authors on par with the very best male ones.

Other writings by Sor Juana take up the issue of the relationship between writing in Mexico and the literature produced in Madrid, the literary center for writers throughout the Spanish-speaking world. As is well known, her *Primero sueño* (*First Dream*, 1692) is prefaced by a brief epigraph: "as titled and composed by Mother Juana Inés de la Cruz, in imitation of Góngora" (*Sor Juana Inés de la Cruz: Selected Works* 77).[4] In fact, as Octavio Paz notes: "*First Dream* is a Gongorist poem. It is Gongorist also in the repeated use of inversion, which reverses the normal order of phrases in an attempt to accommodate them to the pattern of Latin. And there are traces of Góngora in certain passages. This said, we must add that the differences are greater and more profound than the similarities" (358).

Of course, Sor Juana is not alone in her embrace of a baroque aesthetic that perhaps reached its highest expression in Góngora's poetry. According to Michael J. Horswell, "An integral element of the Counter-Reformation in Europe, the Baroque traveled to the Americas to become one of the central literary and artistic expressions of the new identities being forged in the viceregal capital cities and as well as on the more remote frontiers of the Spanish and Portuguese empires." By being a Gongorist, and more precisely a baroque writer, Sor Juana evidences her belonging to the Counter-Reformation Hispanic world, what we could call the Hispanic Republic of Letters.[5] Notably, she is far from being an epigonal Gongorist baroque poet. As Paz notes: "We must underscore Sor Juana's absolute originality; nowhere in all of Spanish literature of the sixteenth and seventeenth centuries is there anything like *First Dream*. Neither do I find precedents in earlier centuries" (361). Nevertheless, she achieves her originality within the frameworks prescribed by the Counter-Reformation culture in which she flourished and against which she struggled.

A similar, though much more explicit, reference to the differences between areas of cultural production can be found in the concluding moments of her "Loa al *Divino Narciso*" ("Prologue to the Mystery Play *Divine Narcissus*"). What makes the "Loa" exceptional is that it deals with the Conquest and the cultural and military confrontation between Aztecs and Spaniards. In this text, Sor Juana provides an ideological—that is, imaginary—solution to the real-life contradictions generated by the Spanish invasion about 160 years earlier. This brief "prologue," then, is an early exploration of cultural and historical traits that would later be seen as determining Mexican and regional difference vis-à-vis Peninsular and more generally Western societies. As such, it proposes *in nuce* what has come to be known as *mestizaje* (in the play this mixture is portrayed exclusively within the field of religion).[6] However, in a metatheatrical dialogue, Sor Juana also acknowledges the possible impact of differences in locations of cultural production and consumption.

After being informed by Religion, the female character who represents the missionary activities of the Catholic Church, that the play would be performed in Madrid, Zeal, the character who allegorizes the conquistadors and the more general violence of the Conquest, transmuted in the "Prologue" into religious fervor, asks: "Do you see impropriety in writing it in Mexico and performing it in Madrid?" (*Sor Juana Inés de la Cruz: Selected Works* 137).[7] Religion responds: "Do you mean you have never seen a thing created in one place that is of use in another?" (138).[8] After additional questioning by Zeal, Religion concludes that "nothing must be denied or changed although I take them to Madrid: for an intelligent species no distances are a hindrance and no oceans an obstacle" (139).[9] Sor Juana, then, posits what we might call a flat cultural space in which what is produced in the "Indies" can be fully understood and appreciated in Madrid, and vice versa.

It is possible that the publication and dissemination of Sor Juana's works throughout the Spanish-speaking world during her lifetime and for a few years after her death serve as proof of her belief in the perfect translatability—being understood outside the original location of production—of her writing and, more generally, of all intellectual production in Spanish of the time. As Margo Glantz notes: "It is not an exaggeration to note that, while she lived, her fame reached the confines of the immense Hispanic world, and that her fame lasted for many years, as evidenced by the successive editions of her work . . . in the poems her contemporaries dedicated to her, during the period between her death and the first third of the eighteenth century" (xiii).[10] This "fame," or perhaps influence, corresponds to that of Góngora on writers throughout the Hispanic world and in the Indies; although, as Glantz also points out, after the 1730s, "her works begin to fall into oblivion, like those of Góngora, and although she is still mentioned, it's almost commonplace to see her referred to not as a poet but as learned, erudite, and great woman" (xiii).[11]

Still, it is important to note that, as Paz argues in his examination of Sor Juana's library, the boundaries of the Hispanic cultural space had narrowed by her time:

The examination of Sor Juana's library reveals a world very distant from our own. The intellectual movement that began in the Renaissance with the new science and the new political philosophy is not represented in that collection of books. . . . Sor Juana's library is a mirror of the massive failure of the Counter Reformation in the sphere of ideas. This movement presented itself as an answer to Protestantism and as a moral and intellectual renewal of the Catholic Church. Its not inconsiderable first fruits were sublime works of poetry, painting, music, sculpture, and architecture. Neither would it be fair to ignore the work of the Jesuits in humanistic studies or in the sciences. But based on its very suppositions, the movement was destined to ossify. If any society has merited the designation "closed society," in the sense given it by Karl Popper, that society was the Spanish empire. (260)

This closing of the "Hispanic mind," underlies the delinking of Spanish-language writers, male and female, from the Americas, from the burgeoning world literary space. As Casanova notes:

The highpoint of the Golden Age had passed by the mid-seventeenth century, however, by which point Spain entered upon a period of slow decline that was inseparably literary and political. This "vast collapse, this very slow sinking" created a growing gap between Spanish literary space and that of the French and the English, now poised to assume their place as the leading literary powers in Europe. (55)

Therefore, since independence, women writers and all other writers navigate very different international cultural frameworks than Sor Juana did. For them, the literary canon, in all meanings of the word, is no longer composed primarily of Spanish-language works, and rather than being characterized by perfect communication and translatability in which a writer from New Spain can be easily read and understood in Madrid, the new international literary space is hierarchical and, with few exceptions, its evolution determined by French- and English-language works.

THE LIMA GROUP AND NINETEENTH-CENTURY SPANISH WOMEN WRITERS

The main issues that concerned Sor Juana—the rights of women to participate in cultural activity, including the right to education—continued to be at the core of women writers' concerns, even if Sor Juana's own works were mostly forgotten. As Pratt has noted, women writers during the nineteenth century (and arguably beyond) continued providing historical catalogs of women authors who prove the equality of women when it comes to their roles as producers of culture and literature, but they also "generated a tradition which could accurately be called the *gender* essay" (90). While a study of this essayistic tradition is outside the purview of this study of the "theory and practice" of Latin American authors regarding the Western canon, both the catalogs and the gender essay highlight the fact that the region's women writers were preoccupied with a political feminist or proto-feminist aim that served to think through what constituted the Western canon, as well as the relationship of their writing to it. However, as we have seen, there is potential overlap between catalog and canon, especially because the former often also comprises writers who are seen as being exceptionally relevant.

After Latin America's independence from Spain, sealed with the Battle of Ayacucho in 1824, the literary space was no longer limited to the Spanish-speaking world, and it grew to include authors from Europe and North

America. Ronald Briggs, for instance, argues for the ideological influence of the French feminist writer Madame de Staël and Harriet Beecher Stowe on the region's women writers during the nineteenth century, citing the Peruvian Aurora Cáceres (1877–1958) and the Colombian Soledad Acosta (1833–1913). According to Briggs, Madame de "Staël argued that women writers would need to destroy the arbitrary boundary between the literary and the 'real' world in order to bring their writings to bear on the dominant discussions from which they were excluded" (14). Briggs adds: "Like Harriet Beecher Stowe, she [Madame de Staël] remained a polestar for Spanish American feminists seeking to link literary production and political power" (14).

Both authors were read and known (especially Stowe) in nineteenth-century Latin America. For instance, Juana Gorriti (1818–1892), an Argentine writer who helped create the Veladas Literarias de Lima (Literary Soirees of Lima) that brought together the country's elite female and male writers of the 1860s and 1870s,[12] gave Angélica Palma (1838–1935), who was the daughter of her friend Ricardo Palma, the nickname of "Madame Staël" (del Águila 48).[13] Stowe's *Uncle Tom's Cabin* (1852), originally translated into Spanish as *La cabaña del tío Tomás*, and published first in Mexico in 1853 and then throughout the continent—was also published in Lima in serial form in 1853. The popularity of *La cabaña del tío Tomás* was such that it circulated in print and also shortly thereafter became a play widely performed throughout the world, including in Spanish-speaking Latin America.[14]

However, the presence of a (US) American author and a French one (Staël) in nineteenth-century Latin America shows how the old Hispanic literary space had opened up to include authors from throughout the central Western countries, including the former colony turned world power. In the nineteenth century, Spanish-speaking Latin American women authors exhibit familiarity not only with writers from the region and Spain but also with those from throughout the Western center. Despite this cultural opening, the number of women authors actually translated into Spanish from other languages is relatively small. While many intellectuals were fluent in French, fewer were able to read English and even fewer German, not to speak of Russian or other more exotic (from their perspective) languages. In addition to local translations and publications, as well as those made in

Spain, French culture and publishing were the main mediators for other Western literatures.

However, the best writers, specifically the best women writers, did not merely accept an epigonal role in relation to French literature; instead, they subjected it to a critical examination based on their cultural locations and traditions. A case in point is the critical writings of the Peruvian novelist Mercedes Cabello de Carbonera (1845–1909), a key participant in the Literary Soirees, and one of the few nineteenth-century Latin American woman writers who produced a significant body of literary criticism in addition to proto-feminist gender essays.[15] Thus, in her essay "La novela moderna" (The Modern Novel, 1891), Cabello presents a critical review of the novel in the twentieth century as based on the presence of two "opposing schools that have maintained a long and furious struggle ... Romanticism ... [and] Naturalism" (4373).[16] Early in the essay, she concludes that "the definitive triumph belongs to Naturalism," adding that "its rules, principles, doctrines are followed not only by the novelists in Old Europe, but also by those in Young America" (4373).[17] While her context and examples are almost exclusively French—Victor Hugo, George Sand, Balzac, Stendhal, Paul Bourget, Renan, Lemonier, Flaubert, the latter misread as a Naturalist, de Kock, Goncourt—Cabello ends up rejecting both schools: "In the same way that Romanticism created a world where one doesn't see the reality of human life, Naturalism created a human being in whom one doesn't see the reality of sentiments and affects that agitate the human soul" (4373).[18] Even if the actual arguments of the article are of limited interest for this study, what truly matters is that Cabello shows knowledge of and engagement with the works of many of the best-known and influential French authors.

If the core of Cabello's intellectual influence is French, she also shows a real (if limited) knowledge of other non-Hispanic literary traditions. For instance, she mentions Anglophone authors such as "Longfellow and "Miss Stowe" (4015), and she lavishes particular praise on Walter Scott. Moreover, her criticism of naturalism and her proposal to surpass it, while assimilating what is best in the novelistic school led by Zola, is ultimately based on her high opinion of Scott—an opinion that was very widespread during the nineteenth century.[19] According to Cabello: "We, today, with our analytical and positivist spirit need the novel that sets Walter Scott in Emile Zola. Antithetical one to the other, but both symbolic and magnificent" (5055).[20]

And: "Walter Scott and Zola, representing one the moral being, the other the material being, will complete realist art" (5055).[21] However, the references to Scott, despite having long been translated into Spanish, are mediated by French literature, as evidenced by the fact that she acknowledges developing ideas proposed by Victor Hugo (5055).

This Franco-centrism was of her time and place. After all, no less a figure than the Nicaraguan Rubén Darío, almost unanimously considered the greatest Spanish-language poet of the nineteenth century, described his innovatory verses as characterized by "thinking in French and writing in Spanish" ("pensando en francés, y escribiendo en castellano") (163). As Mariano Siskind notes in *Cosmopolitan Desires*, for most of the region's writers, "France is not another particular culture, or even a cultural primus inter pares; it is the linguistic and cultural body of the universal itself, the condition of possibility of culture as humanity's shared patrimony" (195). Obviously without denying the impact of French culture on their writing, Cabello and the other women writers of the Lima circle, such as Clorinda Matto de Turner (1852–1909), best known as author of the proto-*indigenista* novel *Aves sin nido* (*Torn from the Nest*, 1889), were far from mere followers of French literary trends. Instead, they subjected them to a scrutiny rooted in their local realities.

Moreover, this Franco-centrism did not necessarily imply a turning away from Spanish-language literature. Thus, in "La novela moderna," Cabello finds in the Spanish novel a solution to the contradictions in the world narrative (i.e., French narrative) she studies. She argues that novelists "such as the illustrious Leopoldo Alas, Picón, Palacio Valdés, Pereda, Ortega Munilla . . . will be the one to transform Naturalism, converting it into psychological and philosophical realism." And she adds: "At the head of this school is Emilia Pardo Bazán" (4015).[22] With the exception of Emilia Pardo Bazán and Leopoldo Alas "Clarín," these are novelists generally considered minor, but for Cabello, even if French culture is the dynamic center of world literature, it is in Spain, the old colonial center, where the synthesis between Naturalism and "nature and truth" ("naturaleza y verdad" 5055) actually takes place.[23]

This critical distance from French culture is also expressed by Matto. Writing after the death of Gorriti, Matto places her friend in "a new constellation next to that in which shine the immortal names of George Sand,

Fernán Caballero, Gertrudis Gómez de Avellaneda y Carolina Coronado" (184).[24] In this manner, Matto creates a feminist literary catalog of dead writers that includes the Argentine Gorriti, the French Sand, the Spaniard Fernán Caballero, the Cuban-Spanish Gómez, and the Spaniard Coronado. This catalog includes writers who, much more clearly than Sor Juana's fanciful lists or Cabello's less gender-specific references, are concrete examples of what a woman novelist can be. Moreover, this list is one in which gender seems to cut across political considerations: Sand was a well-known progressive, though her positions regarding women's suffrage were surprisingly complex, if not ambiguous;[25] Caballero, a monarchist and Catholic; Gómez de Avellaneda, the archetypal Hispanic romantic whose sentimental novel *Sab* (1841) criticized slavery and questioned the institution of marriage under patriarchy; and Coronado, another romantic feminist and novelist. Despite these differences, all these writers explored women's lives and celebrated emotion and sentiment as precisely defining the female experience. As has often been pointed out, the celebration of sentiment and its potential political impact was a central trait of nineteenth-century literature written by women within and without the Hispanic world. While Matto, like Cabello, was critical of romanticism and shows an awareness of realism and even naturalism, her work never fully rejected the literature of sentimentality that often characterized women's writing in their time.[26]

Of course, to these names, Matto adds Gorriti, the main animator of the Literary Soirees, whose own *La quena* (*The Quena*, 1848) signaled the beginning of the novel in Argentina and arguably Peru, given her participation in Peru's culture. But it must be noted that Matto clearly presents this catalog as having canonical implications: the writers are described as belonging to "the literary heaven" ("cielo literario") and as "immortal names" ("nombres inmortales) (184).[27] Matto's list shows that, for Spanish-language Latin American writers of the nineteenth century, the canon is no longer exclusively classical or Hispanic, as was the case during Sor Juana's time.

GABRIELA MISTRAL, ROSARIO CASTELLANOS, AND WORLD LITERATURE

As Cabello's comments about Walter Scott show, Paris was both the literary meridian and the clearinghouse for world literature[28]—though there were some exceptional cases like *Uncle Tom's Cabin* that jumped directly into Latin American cultural markets and literary circles. However, by the 1920s, without necessarily contradicting the cultural centrality of France, there arose in the region a concern with national canons. Grínor Rojo, for one, has noted that Dominican critic Pedro Henríquez Ureña "was the first among us who worked to give a space to the problematics of the canon."[29] As Rojo insinuates, the fact that this renewed interest takes place when "we had already walked a century of Republican life (Ayacucho was fought in 1824 and Henríquez Ureña is publishing the essay in question in 1925), connects it with questions about national identity that were in the air during the Centennial."[30] An early instance of this process of revaluating earlier regional and national authors and literatures is the rediscovery of Sor Juana Inés de la Cruz as a major poet, which began in earnest with Amado Nervo's *Juana de Asbaje: Contribución al centenario de la independencia de México* (Juana de Asbaje: Contribution to the Centenary of the Independence of Mexico 1910), which was part of this centennial process of literary reevaluation.[31]

Be that as it may, this concern with determining and evaluating local literary tradition was intimately connected to a growing awareness of the relations between national literatures and European literature, in particular French, but also in some isolated cases non-Western literatures. In part, this opening occurred because, with ever-growing celerity, the literature of the nineteenth century and its new modernist and avant-garde writing began to be translated into Spanish. The literary criticism of José Carlos Mariátegui, an author who helped establish the Peruvian canon—by stressing the centrality of his contemporary César Vallejo—can serve as an example. In addition to presenting a very critical revision of Peru's literature from the colony to the 1920s, he also wrote about books as diverse as Mariano Azuela's *Los de abajo* (*The Underdogs*) (1915), James Joyce's *Portrait of the Artist as a Young Man* (1916), and Fyodor Gladkov's *Cement* (1925). Mariátegui's febrile activity "as one of Latin America's first practicing literary critics" (Unruh 45) responded to the availability of these books in Spanish. It was no longer necessary to read the world's literature in French.

The writings and activities of Gabriela Mistral—possibly the one woman author to have entered the Western and world canon—can serve as further examples of a (proto)feminist version of the revaluation of national, regional, and world literatures promoted by Henríquez Ureña and Mariátegui.

Mistral's *Recados para América* (1978), translated in an expanded version as *Women* (2000), is a case in point.[32] Even if anthologized by other hands, and despite including gender essays such as "On Mexican Women" and "On Chilean Women," *Women* is a book-length version of the historical catalog described by Pratt. For instance, among the exemplary women are such disparate figures as Catherine of Siena and Isadora Duncan; Mistral describes the Italian saint and the founder of modern dance as embodiments of Christian and classical virtues, respectively. The list also includes Norah Borges, praised in a way that curiously reflects the stereotype created around Mistral as a maternal poet and painter of children.[33]

In its totality, the book can also be seen as reflecting the tendencies described above, but from a feminist or proto-feminist perspective:[34] a revaluation of local literature, in this case Spanish-language Latin American women writers, and those of the world. In other words, *Women* presents a canon of women writers from Latin America and the world, even if stylistically and structurally, Mistral's essays are a step back to belletristic, early nineteenth-century criticism and distant from Cabello's more informed literary criticism. Her *recados* (messages) concentrate on biography as well as anecdote and psychological and physical description, including an emphasis on race, rather than attempting in most cases to analyze or describe the writers' works. Regardless, *Women* includes articles on writers from Latin America. There are poets: Sor Juana,[35] Alfonsina Storni, Luisa Luisi, and María Monvel; novelists: Teresa de la Parra and Marta Brunet; a writer in Portuguese: Carolina Nebuco; a memoirist: Victoria Ocampo; writers from Spain: Carmen Conde and Blanca de los Ríos; and authors from non-Spanish-speaking Europe: Emily Brontë and Selma Lagerlöf. Curiously, no French women writers, not even George Sand or Colette, were included in her informal canon.

It is possible to see in Mistral's list a kind of feminine countercanon to the lists of both Spanish American and world writers being produced by male authors in the region during the first decades of the twentieth century. In particular, this is a canon that shows how women writers in the early twentieth century were revaluing Spanish American writers,[36] looking at the literature of Brazil, and expanding their world literature gaze beyond France. For Spanish American writers, in the twentieth century the literature of the world finally became available, despite lacunae and biases in publishing and distribution.

The incorporation of world literature into the daily reflection of women writers has continued in the works of more recent authors. For instance, it is fully evidenced in the works of the Mexican author Rosario Castellanos, who comes closest to Sor Juana in the depth, scope, and mastery of the diverse world of letters among modern writers. For instance, her essay on Virginia Woolf, already read by Mistral,[37] exhibits her deep knowledge of the Anglophone novel and British cultural history. Castellanos includes in her analysis of the author of *Mrs. Dalloway* informed references to Jane Austen, the Brontë sisters, and George Eliot, as well as to the Bloomsbury milieu. She writes with equal depth and ability about Eliot's *Murder in the Cathedral* and the British author's theories about poetry, about Simone de Beauvoir, Thomas Mann, and the Japanese novelist Ryūnosuke Akutagawa. Castellanos is exceptional in the spread of her interests; however, she developed the opening to world literature seen in the writers of the start of the twentieth century.

CONCLUSION

There is no denying that women writers have had innumerable hurdles to overcome both inside and outside Latin America. In fact, to the usual lament about "mute, inglorious, Miltons" justly made by critics decrying the impact of illiteracy and poverty on silencing potential literary talents,[38] one could juxtapose "mute Sor Juanas": the legions of genius women who have been silenced not only by illiteracy but also by the limited educational and publishing opportunities available to women. To these factors we can add repressive social expectations and obligations that make it even more difficult for women to become published writers. Given these socially imposed difficulties, it is truly amazing that the writers in this chapter were able to produce so much.

Unlike Borges, Bolaño, or the male authors studied in the rest of this book, women authors from Cabello to Castellanos have had other concerns beyond purely literary ones. Perhaps one of the main reasons they so rarely have written on issues related to literary theory, including those related to the canon, is that women authors have had to justify and theorize their own practice as writers, and have had to examine their relationship to society as women. None of the male authors studied here ever had to attempt to understand or justify his role as a male author or a man. Thus, what Pratt calls the gender essay is a constant from Sor Juana and her "Response" to Cabello and Matto, Mistral, and Castellanos, herself a major second-wave feminist.

Despite all this, the canons of Spanish-speaking Latin American authors developed in the 1920s by authors such as Henríquez Ureña and Mariátegui tended to underrepresent, if not ignore, women authors.[39] Beyond them, world and Western canons also tend to marginalize Spanish American women authors. Outside Latin America, perhaps even more than in the region itself, the region's male authors have often been seen as representative. In fact, despite winning a Nobel Prize in 1945 and being translated by such renowned figures as Langston Hughes and Ursula Le Guin, Mistral could be seen as at the margins of the Western canon, much further from its core than, for instance, her compatriot Pablo Neruda.

A brief perusal of key canonizing instances in the Anglophone world serves as proof of this marginalization. Thus, the 2018 edition of the *Norton Anthology of World Literature* includes only three Spanish-language Latin American women writers in its list of world classics: Sor Juana Inés de la Cruz, Gabriela Mistral, and the contemporary novelist Isabel Allende.[40] Harold Bloom, the subject of the previous chapter, lists only Sor Juana in the polemical appendix to his widely read *The Western Canon* (1994). Even a more recent attempt at developing a world canon, such as Ken Seigneurie's *A Companion to World Literature* (2020), has only one chapter on a woman author, Sor Juana, despite including articles on such unexpected texts as the Mayan *Popol Vuh* and Colombian Jorge Isaacs's sentimental 19th century novel *María*, not included in any of the other Anglophone versions of the world "canon."[41] So the view from the center is also patriarchal. This is why I have decided to begin this study proper by looking at the history of the relationship between Latin American authors and world literature, or the way in which authors of the region have thought about world literature, by looking through the writings of women authors.

3

Jorge Luis Borges
and the Canon

NO LATIN AMERICAN writer is more identified with the Western canon
than Jorge Luis Borges. Borges's narrative presents an imaginative history
of the Western literary and cultural tradition. He begins with Homer, in
"El inmortal" (The Immortal") (1947) and "El hacedor" ("The Maker")
(1960); includes Cervantes in "Pierre Menard, autor del *Quijote*" ("Pierre
Menard, Author of the *Quixote*") (1939), the story he often considered his
first mature work; and touches on Shakespeare in "La memoria de Shakespeare" ("Shakespeare's Memory"), his last published *ficción* (1983).[1] In fact,
the list of Borges's textual engagements with the mainstream and marginalia
of Western literary culture is easily expanded if we consider his essays and
poetry, as well as the many intertextual connections established in his stories.[2] There is a kind of poetic justice, then, in the fact that, after he shared
the International Formentor Award—granted to the most important living writer in 1961, with Samuel Beckett—Borges was welcomed into the
canon. As Beatriz Sarlo notes, during her stay in England in the early 1990s,

she discovered that Borges was "considered universal," a fact that "received further verification when I found the paperback editions of Borges, alongside the ancient and modern classics, in all the bookshops that I visited in Britain, without exception" (1, 2).

As any active reader of contemporary fiction knows, after the 1960s, Borges's stories became a major intertextual source for writers in languages other than Spanish.[3] For many later readers, admirers or detractors, Borges became the most Western of Latin American writers. In the words of Lucille Kerr, many saw in him "perhaps the most European of the Spanish American writers . . . whose eye has been fixed on European literature and philosophy for over fifty years now" (*Suspended Fictions* 3). This view of Borges as linked to European literature, though now often without any reference to his Argentine context, dominated the first Anglophone responses to the translations published after the Formentor Award. In fact, three widely read English-language reviews by major critical and literary voices—Paul de Man in 1964, on the brink of his deconstructionist turn in the *New York Review of Books*, John Updike, already considered a major US novelist in 1965, and George Steiner in 1970, both in the *New Yorker*—stressed in different manners Borges's participation in the Western tradition.

De Man's essay "A Modern Master" can be read as a proto-deconstructive interpretation of Borges's stories, but it also presents him as a kind of deconstructionist avant la lettre.[4] However, what matters for our purposes is that one could easily imagine a similar title being used for Joyce, Kafka, or Beckett. As with these other "modern masters," there's no need to add another adjective to the title. *Modern* may not be identical to *Western*, but it's contained by it in this context. Updike presents a similar take on Borges in his article "The Author as Librarian": "He is European in everything except the detachment with which he views European civilization, as something intrinsically strange—a heap of relics, a universe of books without a central clue" (181).[5] Finally, Steiner, while acknowledging the presence of Argentine topics in Borges's personal trajectory and in his works, argues that "there is a sense in which the director of the Biblioteca Nacional of Argentina is now the most original of Anglo-American writers. This extraterritoriality may be a clue" (26). Leaving aside Steiner's "Anglocentrism," this clue leads him to deduce Borges's "universality" (26). For Steiner, the universe is delinked from "territoriality," that is, the sense of belonging to a local tradition, and is implicitly Western.

While Borges may have been accepted into the Western tradition and its canon, his essays posit a radical challenge to the notion of canon, be it national, Latin American, Western, or universal, even if he does not use the term *canon* himself. In this chapter, I briefly look at several essays by Borges, in particular "Quevedo" (1948), "Kafka y sus precursores" ("Kafka and His Precursors"), "El escritor argentino y la tradición" ("The Argentine Writer and Tradition"), both first presented in 1951, and "Sobre los clásicos" (On the Classics) (1965). Through analysis of these essays and a few other pieces, I trace the diverse manners in which Borges's writings undermine the monumentality and stability of the Western canon and all canons.

QUEVEDO AND THE WESTERN CANON

Borges ends his essay on Francisco de Quevedo, the seventeenth-century Spanish poet and prose writer as follows: "Like Joyce, like Goethe, like Shakespeare, like Dante—like no other writer—Francisco de Quevedo is less a man than a vast and complete literature" ("Quevedo" 42).[6] One cannot help but assume that the inclusion of Quevedo in this august list would surprise more than one non-Spanish-speaking reader. For instance, that best seller among literary studies, Bloom's *The Western Canon*, has only three brief references to Quevedo: including two mentions while writing about Neruda.[7] Even if Quevedo's *Visions* and "Satirical Letter of Censure," make it into Bloom's "Appendixes," which lists the works that he thought merited inclusion in the Western canon, unlike all the other names mentioned by Borges, the Yale professor does not include a chapter on the Golden Age author.

One must note that Borges's brief list includes authors often seen as defining their national and linguistic traditions. Shakespeare and Dante are, perhaps, the two main rivals for the position of greatest author in the Western canon, while Joyce is often seen as the major modernist.[8] One can classify these writers, without exception, as being at the core of the Western canon. Even if Borges does not use this terminology, it is clear that in 1948, the date of first publication of the essay,[9] he saw Quevedo as belonging to this core. However, the Baroque Spanish writer, whom Borges describes as being "a vast and complete literature," does not occupy a similar position outside the Spanish-speaking world.

That said, the apparent contradiction of a writer whose literary achievements would seem to merit inclusion to the highest reaches of the Western canon, but who is in practice excluded from it, is at the center of the essay. It begins by noting: "Like the history of the world, the history of literature abounds in enigmas. I found, and continue to find, none so disconcerting as the strange partial glory that has been accorded to Quevedo. In the censuses of universal names, his is not included" (36, translation adjusted).[10] Perhaps one way of rephrasing the enigma identified by Borges in Quevedo is that it implies the discovery that quality is only a necessary condition, not a sufficient one, for incorporation into the world and, in principle, any canon. Or: in Quevedo, Borges identifies that inclusion in a specific linguistic or national canon, even at its core, does not guarantee inclusion in higher-level canons, be they linguistic, Western, or global. Quevedo, for Borges in 1948, occupies the central position in the Spanish-language canon.[11] However, as his marginal position in Bloom's work exemplifies, he is generally seen as occupying a secondary position within world literature.

To Borges's example of Quevedo, one can add that of other writers who, though occupying central positions in the Spanish-language canon, are often excluded from the Western canon, as compiled by critics of the Global North. The case of Rubén Darío is pertinent. According to Borges, *modernismo*, the poetic movement Darío founded, "is and continues being the most important movement in Hispanic letters," but also "aurally [Darío] has not been superseded or even equaled" ("Dario" 125–26).[12] However, the Nicaraguan poet is not particularly well-known outside the Spanish-speaking world. To belabor a problematic case, Bloom includes Darío only in his "Appendixes."[13] There are other examples of major writers within local "canons" who have had limited impact outside a national or linguistic sphere, but limiting ourselves to Argentine writers, consider Domingo Faustino Sarmiento, the author of *Facundo* (1845), or José Hernández, the author of *El gaucho Martín Fierro* (1872 and 1879). While both authors and works are at the core of Argentine literature, they are barely known outside the Hispanic world. Even within it, Sarmiento and Hernández are basically known for these, their most representative works.

In "Quevedo," Borges assays an answer to this issue: the exclusion of a great writer, central to a linguistic canon, from the Western or world canon. According to the Argentine writer, all writers in the Western canon have found "a symbol that captures the popular imagination": "Dante, the nine circles of hell and the Rose of Paradise; Shakespeare, his worlds of violence and music" (36).[14] While he gives no "symbols" for Joyce or Goethe, the frank description of sexuality, as exemplified in Molly Bloom's famous monologue that concludes *Ulysses*, or the selling of Doctor Faust's soul to Mephistopheles in *Faust*, can be seen as equivalent to those he identifies in Dante and Shakespeare.[15] Borges notes: "No writer has attained universal fame without coining a symbol; but that symbol is not always objective and external . . . Whitman endures as the semidivine protagonist of *Leaves of Grass*. But all that endures of Quevedo is a caricature" (37).[16] Instead, Quevedo is the case of a writer whose works in fiction, didactic prose, or poetry "are verbal objects, pure and independent like a sword or a silver ring" (42). Given that Quevedo's "greatness is verbal" (37),[17] Borges concludes: "To like Quevedo one must be (actually or potentially) a man of letters; conversely, no one with a literary vocation can fail to like Quevedo" (37).[18]

The above statement—and Borges's analysis as a whole—raises important questions. The first regards the marginalization of Quevedo outside the Hispanic world. While Borges's essay explains why, for instance, *Don Quixote* and *Moby Dick* are well known throughout the "world republic of letters," it is not clear that this actually solves the questions raised by Quevedo's limited standing. After all, if "men of letters," to use Borges's obsolete phrase, exist in all languages, why hasn't Quevedo become admired throughout the world, even if only by writers? Given that Quevedo's fame is limited to the Spanish-speaking world, and that his "greatness is verbal," isn't it logical to find the key to Quevedo's marginalization in the difficulty in translating "verbal objects"? Borges famously stated in "The Homeric Versions" that "the superstition about the inferiority of translations—coined by the well-known Italian adage—is the result of absentmindedness" (69).[19] However, the case of Quevedo, as well as that of Darío, lead us to question this belief in translatability, at least in the case of writers who are primarily creators of "verbal objects."

As we have seen, Borges's reflections on Quevedo questions the relationship between canon and the quality of canonical works. If Quevedo is excluded from the Western canon despite being as great as its very greatest authors, and greater than many who are included in the canon, then the canon is no longer a reliable measure of literary quality.

"KAFKA AND HIS PRECURSORS"

"Kafka and His Precursors" was first published in 1951 and added to *Otras inquisiciones* (*Other Inquisitions*) in 1958. One of Borges's best-known essays, it details his putative evolution as a reader of Kafka: from believing the Bohemian writer was "as singular as the fabulous Phoenix" to a moment "when I knew him better I thought I recognized his voice, or his habits, in the texts of various literatures and various ages" (106).[20] The importance of "Kafka and His Precursors" is such that it has been described as "the *Discourse on the Method* in the history of the development of the canon" by no less an authority than the Argentine novelist Ricardo Piglia (157).[21] Piglia is correct that one can build an understanding of the canon from the ideas Borges proposed in "Kafka and His Precursors"; although rather than leading to a version of the canon similar to Bloom's, Borges's essay implies its deconstruction.

The authors that Borges identifies as Kafka's precursors are a heterogeneous group of writers and texts: a paradox by Zeno, a fable by ninth-century Chinese writer Han Yu, a parable by Kierkegaard, a poem by Browning, a short story by Léon Bloy. While some of these authors may be seen as potentially canonic—Bloom includes Browning and Kierkegaard in his notorious appendixes of authors and works—there is something eccentric about the conjunction of the names and titles. As we have seen, Borges takes credit for the creation of this list of precursors: "I recognized his voice, or his habits in the texts of various literatures."

Most theorizations of the canon—Bloom's, for instance—see it as rooted in the act of writing, even if that is obviously connected to the act of reading:

> The burden of influence has to be borne, if significant originality is to be achieved and reachieved within the wealth of Western literary tradition. Tradition is not only a handing-down or process of benign transmission; it is also a conflict between past genius and present aspiration, in which the prize is literary survival or canonical inclusion . . . Poems,

stories, novels, plays come into being as a response to prior poems, stories, novels, and plays, and that response depends upon acts of reading
and interpretation by the later writers, acts that are identical with the
new works. (*The Western Canon* 8–9)

This is clearly a bowdlerized version of Bloom's own theory of the anxiety of influence. However, despite its Nietzschean and Freudian trappings,
Bloom presents a traditional version of the history of literature as composed of the writing of texts and their rewritings. Influence is an objective
fact that can be verified in the "poems, stories, novels, plays" that take up
the challenge posed by earlier texts as the starting point for new composi-
tions. To give an obvious example, the canonical statuses of Homer's *The
Iliad* and *The Odyssey* are verified in the existence of works that "respond"
to these works, such as Virgil's *The Aeneid*, Derek Walcott's *Omeros*, and
even Joyce's *Ulysses*. The canon is based on a history of texts that determines what and who constitutes it.

Even though like most texts written before Bloom's *The Western Canon*,
T. S. Eliot's "Tradition and the Individual Talent" does not use the word
canon, it does stress the centrality of actual influence on the act of writing
and the constitution of what we would today call the canon:

The historical sense compels a man to write not merely with his own
generation in his bones, but with a feeling that the whole of the literature of Europe from Homer and within it the whole of the literature of
his own country has a simultaneous existence and composes a simultaneous order. This historical sense, which is a sense of the timeless as well
as of the temporal and of the timeless and of the temporal together, is
what makes a writer traditional. And it is at the same time what makes
a writer most acutely conscious of his place in time, of his own contem-
poraneity. (525–26)

Eliot's "historical sense" is obviously more than just the fact that the writer
has read Homer and other European classics: it implies a sense of belonging
to a tradition, but it is not independent of reading and influence. A writer
can be truly "contemporaneous" only if she is also "traditional"; only by

being aware of the literary past can she also be conscious of the literary present. Moreover, by being aware of the past and the present, a writer can develop a "feeling" or identification with the "whole of the literature of Europe."

In another often-quoted passage, Eliot notes:

> The existing monuments form an ideal order among themselves, which is modified by the introduction of the new (the really new) work of art among them. The existing order is complete before the new work arrives; for order to persist after the supervention of novelty, the whole existing order must be, if ever so slightly, altered; and so the relations, proportions, values of each work of art toward the whole are readjusted; and this is conformity between the old and the new. Whoever has approved this idea of order, of the form of European, of English literature will not find it preposterous that the past should be altered by the present as much as the present is directed by the past. And the poet who is aware of this will be aware of great difficulties and responsibilities. (526)

While the canon—called by the Anglo-American poet "existing monuments"—is presented as evolving thanks to "the introduction of the new (the really new work) of art" as "the relations, proportions, values of each work of art toward the whole are readjusted," it is composed of a clearly identifiable set of works. Unlike for Bloom, for Eliot it is not unthinkable that Shakespeare in the very long run be toppled from his central position in the canon, because literary evolution is, in geological terms, gradualist not catastrophist. Nevertheless, even the really new literary work of art results in a reshuffling of the "existing monuments," not necessarily their immediate demotion.

The importance of Eliot's essay is that, as John Guillory notes, it "lies behind every subsequent reflection on tradition" (*Cultural Capital* 142–43), including Borges's. In fact, in "Kafka and His Precursors," the only reference to be found is to Eliot's *Points of View*, a collection of essays that includes "Tradition and the Individual Talent." Moreover, Borges's other reflection on topics related to the canon, "The Argentine Writer and Tradition," shows the imprint of Eliot's essay in its title, even if any mention of the author of *The Wasteland* has been erased. There are, however, significant differences between Borges and then Bloom and Eliot. Underlying Bloom's canon and Eliot's tradition is a "poetics of writing." For both, it is the act of writing, of creating new literature, of responding to, or at least considering, earlier authors and works, that ultimately determines Western literature and the inclusion of works in its tradition and canon.

Unlike these Anglophone critics, Emir Rodríguez Monegal character-izes Borges's fiction and essays as "a new poetics, based not on the actual writing of a work but on its reading" (*Jorge Luis Borges* 330). "Kafka and His Precursors" shows that this "poetics of reading" also informs Borges's criticism and thinking about literary tradition, and by extension the canon. In this text, the actual recognition of key authors is ultimately left to the reader—a category that includes but is not identical to the critic—rather than the author. Even if Borges the writer was clearly influenced by Kafka, it is as a reader that he acknowledges Kafka's "uniqueness" and, therefore, canonicity. It is also as a reader that he is able to establish something like a "Kafka tradition" that includes works from diverse ages and languages. Although it is quite certain that Kafka knew some of the texts and authors mentioned in "Kafka and His Precursors," for instance, Zeno and Kierke-gaard, their designation as precursors is ultimately delinked from Kafka's personal history of readings. Instead, it is the reader of Kafka whose job it is to determine the authors who could be designated as Kafka's precursors, whether these were actually read by Kafka or not.

In contrast, Bloom identifies Kafka in *The Western Canon* as engaged in a literary agon with Goethe and the Jewish Bible, two cornerstones of the Western canon: "In terms of literary influence, Goethe was the Abraham from whom Kafka shrank; in spiritual terms, the Law or positive Judaism was incarnate in Abraham. Kafka, forsaking the Law for his own Negative, abandoned also an Abraham who had misinterpreted the world" (450). For Eliot and Bloom, the textual presence of previously "existing monuments," such as Goethe and the Bible, together with Kafka's ability to create "really new works," ultimately determines the canonicity of *The Metamorphosis* or *The Trial*. In other words, what Eliot calls the "historical sense" is imbricated with originality in the constitution of new canonical works.

Ricardo Piglia, in "Vivencia literaria," attempts to reconcile the ideas proposed by Borges in "Kafka and His Precursors" with a traditional vision of the canon as centered on *the experience of writers* . . . that illuminate and gives value to the works of the past. The essence of the concept of canon is the fact that writing in the present *transforms and modifies* the reading of the past and of tradition. It the experience of literature that decides that some texts, some books, be rescued from the sea of written words and made to function as "literature." (It also decides that some books that were in once considered great literature with the passing of time become lost and forgotten). (156)[22]

Later, he adds, "Literature produces readers and the great works of art change the way of reading. Cortázar's *Rayuela* (*Hopscotch*) made us read differently Leopoldo Marechal's *Adán Buenosayres*, helped rescue it from oblivion, and led to its inclusion in the canon" (156).[23] According to Piglia, Marechal's work is not the only one recovered from the rear shelves of the canon; he claims that the popularity of Cortázar's novel helped bring Macedonio Fernández's *Museo de la novela de la Eterna* back into print (156). To Piglia's exclusively Argentine examples, we can add a Peruvian one: the publication of Alfredo Bryce Echenique's *Un mundo para Julius* (*A World for Julius*) in 1970 led not only to the revaluation of his predecessor's José Diez Canseco's earlier novel *Duque*, originally published in 1934, but also to its reprinting in 1973. (Both novels are bildungsromans about upper-class Peruvians). Surely there are many examples from other literatures, as well.

While Borges's "Kafka and His Precursors" contains Piglia's ideas on the canon, it also exceeds them. Borges would agree with Piglia that "literature produces readers, and great works change the ways of reading" (156).[24] In fact, he said something very similar in his lecture on Poe: "The detective novel has created a special type of reader. This tends to be forgotten when Poe's work is evaluated, for if Poe created the detective story, he subsequently created the reader of detective fiction" ("The Detective Story" 492).[25] However, Piglia's supposedly Borgesian revision of the canon as still working within Eliot's paradigm that "the past should be altered by the present as much as the present is directed by the past." Moreover, given the cultural commonality among the three authors mentioned by Piglia—as well as the fact that we know Cortázar had read and commented *Adán Buenosayres* and was familiar with Macedonio Fernández's works—this vision of the Argentine canon is still within the set of ideas proposed by Eliot and even Bloom.

In other words, even if *Hopscotch* led to the revaluation of these earlier works, they themselves were part of the influences—in the most traditional sense of the word—that made the writing of *Hopscotch* possible. Rather than unrelated works, one can find in these three authors—Fernández, Marechal, Cortázar—a chain of influence from older to younger writer.[26]

"Kafka and His Precursors" has much more radical implications. Rather than finding the precursors among German-language authors whom Kafka was bound to have read, Borges's selections range far afield of European and world literature—China, France, Ireland, Denmark, Ancient Greece. Instead, it is the works of Kafka—the traits Borges identifies as characteristic of the works of Kafka—that leads him to identify these precursors: "the heterogeneous selections I have mentioned resemble Kafka's work: if I am not mistaken, not all of them resemble each other, and this fact is the significant one. Kafka's idiosyncrasy, in greater or lesser degree, is present in each of these writings, but if Kafka had not written we would not perceive it; that is to say, it would not exist" (108).[27] These are ultimately unrelated works that can be seen as precursors exclusively because Kafka initiates, as Piglia notes, a new way of reading that makes it possible to identify these earlier texts and authors as such. However, the actual determination of "Kafka's precursors" is not based on the identification of intertextualities in his texts, as Bloom does when noting that Kafka is dealing with the Tanakh or Goethe. Instead, it is based on the reader's, or more specifically, the critic's, developing what we might call a Kafkaesque gaze through the scrutiny of, let's say, *The Metamorphosis* or "The Great Wall of China." This gaze permits the identification of commonalities across works that, from the perspective of direct or indirect influence, are completely unrelated to Kafka's writing.

THE ARGENTINE WRITER AND TRADITION

One can see "The Argentine Writer and Tradition" as supplementing "Kafka and His Precursors." If "Kafka and His Precursors" primarily provides a way of looking at literature diachronically, then "The Argentine Writer and Tradition" proposes a synchronic and spatial analysis. If the former privileges the act of reading, then the latter addresses the act of writing within a specific cultural and geographical location.

A key argument made in the essay is that being an Argentine writer is not opposed to making use of or, for that matter, participating in Western culture. As Borges writes, "What is Argentine tradition? I believe that this question poses no problem and can easily be answered. I believe that our tradition is the whole of Western culture, and I also believe that we have a right to this tradition, a greater right than that which the inhabitants of one Western nation or any other may have" (426).[28] Paraphrasing Thorstein Veblen's comments on "the intellectual preeminence of Jews in Western culture," Borges argues that "Jews are prominent in Western culture because they act within that culture and at the same time do not feel bound to it by any special devotion; therefore . . . it will always be easier for a Jew than for a non-Jew to make innovations in Western culture" (426).[29] After adding that, for the Irish, "the fact of feeling themselves to be Irish, to be different, was enough to enable them to make innovations in English culture" (426), Borges concludes: "I believe that Argentines, and South Americans in general, are in an analogous situation; we can take on all the European subjects, take them on without superstition and with an irreverence that can have, and already has had, fortunate consequences" (426).[30] Unlike Eliot, for whom full participation in the Western tradition, which he described as feeling "in his bones," is at the core of the "really new work of art," Borges proposes a distance from the tradition as paradoxically what gives the Argentine writer this "greater right" to it. Sarlo had "The Argentine Writer and Tradition" in mind when noting:

> Although it could be argued that this is very seldom the case with great European writers of the twentieth century, those outside the European tradition consider that native Europeans have a close affinity with their "natural" cultures. Yet the fact that they are embedded in a culture that is, for them, inevitable, deprives them of the very freedom that Latin Americans can deploy. Freedom is our fate. (36)

Paradoxically, innovation, the result of this freedom in using and reusing, in writing and rewriting, arises not from identification but from difference.[31]

Borges's stress on the Western nature of the tradition may respond to the fact that "The Argentine Writer and Tradition" proposes a spatial view of culture. In the essay there is a center, Europe or perhaps the US, and a periphery. Moreover, as the example of British culture, which has Ireland at the periphery, this center is itself constituted by a series of national and "minor" cultures. This spatial view of culture—or more exactly, this view of a space as constituted by subspaces—also leads to one of the main novelties of Borges's essay: his stress on the national and regional identity of the writer who is described not only as Argentine but, unusually in his work, as South American. The possibility of creativity based on distance from the tradition—a distance that doesn't imply a lack of belonging, even as it problematizes it—is not exclusive to Argentine writers or culture; it applies to other South Americans as well. Moreover, one is tempted to see in Borges's reference to South America the differentiation from North America, from the United States, rather than a strict geographical identification.[32] In fact, in earlier drafts of his lecture, Borges referred to Guatemalan writers as being in an analogous position to those from Argentina.[33]

In contrast to Eliot, who saw tradition as unitary and homogeneous, Borges sees it as constituted of numerous internal differences. With only some exaggeration, the phrase "contradictory totality" can be applied to the vision of culture implied in "The Argentine Writer and Tradition," a phrase coined by Antonio Cornejo Polar to describe Peru and its multicultural and multilingual literature. Cornejo Polar notes that "the image of Peruvian literature as a unified system sufficiently integrated does not resist the weight of contradicting evidence, such as the verifiable existence of several systems and with very high levels of autonomy" (43).[34] However, unlike the Peruvian critic, Borges doesn't necessarily see these different interlocking national and regional systems as necessarily based on oppression or opposition,[35] even if a whiff of the anticolonial and antidiscriminatory remains in his writing, as when he notes the creativity of the Irish, Jews, and, of course, South Americans.

Borges ends his lecture by moving outside the Western limits he had earlier placed on his reflection: "Therefore I repeat that we must not be afraid; we must believe that the universe is our birthright and try out every subject; we cannot confine ourselves to what is Argentine in order to be Argentine because either it is our inevitable destiny to be Argentine, in which case we will be Argentine whatever we do, or being Argentine is a mere affectation, a mask" (427).[36] In the conclusion, Borges argues that Argentine writers—and presumably also South American, and by implication Latin American writers—have access to an ocean of literature that undermines borders and identities precisely as it becomes the resource from which identity is constructed. Despite the tensions between Western and "universal" birthrights, in the same way that Argentine literature is a subset first of that of South America, and then of that of the West, one could see the later as included in that of the universe. Borges's thinking always leads to the undermining of hierarchies without completely denying national or regional identities. As stated earlier, "The Argentine Writer and Tradition" can be seen as supplementing "Kafka and His Precursors." If "Kafka and His Precursors" sees the "really new work" as escaping from hierarchical determinations based on chronologically and influence, then "The Argentine Writer and Tradition" transforms the canon into a resource for creation and the peripheral location of writing into precisely the possibility of creating "really new works."

ON CLASSICS

The last text I consider here is "Sobre los clásicos" (1966), which Borges added to his collection *Otras inquisiciones* in 1969. Briefer but more radical than his earlier essays, it undermines the concepts of classic and, by implication, canon. In this text, Borges flatly states:

> Classic is that book that a nation or a group of nations or posterity have decided to read as if in its pages everything were deliberate, fatal, profound as the cosmos, and capable of endless interpretation. For Germans and Austrians, the *Faust* is a work of genius, for others, one of the most famous examples of tedium, as is the case of Milton's second *Paradise*, or the works of Rabelais. Books like *Job*, *The Divine Comedy*, *Macbeth* (and, for me, some of the Norse Sagas) bear the promise of a long immortality, but we know nothing about the future, except that it will be different from the present. Preference [for a book] can very well be a form of superstition. (773)[37]

Here his "poetics of reading" have been expanded from the individual to a collectivity. If in "Kafka and His Precursors" the "classic," represented by Kafka's works, seemed to be defined by its phoenix-like originality, even if Borges is finally able to find works that partially forecast the Czech master's writings, in this later essay, the category of classic is ultimately the product of a collective and perhaps arbitrary decision.

Furthermore, against the Blooms (Allan and Harold) or D'Souza, who see in the classic a work different in quality, even in nature, from the bulk of literary production, Borges argues:

> Thirty years ago, under the influence of Macedonio Fernández I believed that beauty was the privilege of a few authors; today, I see that it is abundant and is threatening to appear in a mediocre writer's unformed pages or in an overheard dialogue. Thus, while my ignorance of Malay or Hungarian letters is absolute, I am convinced that if I were granted time to study, I would find in them all the spiritual nourishment I require. In addition to linguistic barriers, political and geographical ones also intervene. Burns is a classic in Scotland; south of the Tweed he is of less interest than Dunbar or Stevenson. The glory of a poet therefore, depends on the excitement or apathy of anonymous readers who put it to the test in the loneliness of their libraries. (773)[38]

Even though one can question whether English readers would argue for the canonicity of Dunbar or Stevenson over their fellow Scott Burns, Borges is deconstructing the literary category of classic and undermining the absolute ability to distinguish between a great and a mediocre writer. Implicit here is the possibility that mediocre works be collectively chosen as "classics," for linguistic, political, or geographical reasons. Moreover, as the mention of Burns, Dunbar, and Stevenson exemplifies, local readers may prefer a specific Scottish author (Burns), while foreign ones may favor others— Stevenson, Dunbar—who in their original "local tradition" are considered inferior.

These arguments could also apply to the cases of Quevedo or Darío. After all, the inexistence of translations that overcome the linguistic difficulties characteristic of their poetry, together with, perhaps, the lack of recognition often accorded the Spanish-language in France or the United States, could become an explanation for their absence in the world canons. Moreover, if in "The Argentine Writer and Tradition," Borges, not without contradictions, held on to the centrality of the Western tradition, in "Sobre los clásicos" he takes his antihierarchical, anti-Eurocentric perspective to its logical conclusion. In this text, all literary traditions, including non-Western ones—whether written in Malaysia or in Europe but at the margins, like Hungary—would be capable of proving him with the "beauty" and "spiritual nourishment" found in literature.

Borges's view of literature as presented in "Sobre los clásicos" ultimately undermines any and all canons: "The emotions that literature arouses are perhaps eternal, but the means used must constantly change, even if slightly, in order to not lose their virtues. They are spent as the reader becomes familiar with them. This is why it is foolhardy to state that there are classic works and that these will remain such forever" (773).[39] While, perhaps inconsistently, Borges identifies permanence in literature, it is based on the effect and the affect of texts. There may be human needs for the stimuli—the emotions—found in and provoked by literature, but the actual works that help satisfy these needs vary. Works once considered classics may with time lose their ability to satisfy needs that are both individual and collective. Even the central classics of the Western tradition—Shakespeare, Dante—will ultimately lose their affect and fall from the canon. In fact, it is not inconceivable that the time will come—it may already have—when other means will satisfy these emotions and literature itself will be superseded.

Borges concludes this brief text by restating his definition of the classic: "Classic (I repeat) is not necessarily a book that possesses these or those merits; it is a book that generations of men, urged by diverse reasons, read with preexisting fervor and with a mysterious loyalty" (773).[40] Here he takes this relativistic view of the classic to its ultimate conclusion: the reasons a specific work has been elevated to the status of a classic vary so much as to defy a single explanation. At the same time, Borges's deconstruction of the concepts of classic and canon does not deny the existence of either, even if he relativizes both concepts. As a result, he radicalizes Eliot's view of an evolving canon by further stressing that it perpetually changes and is dependent on societal and individual conditions.

CONCLUSION

It may very well be impossible to deduce from Borges's reflections a clear intellectual proposal regarding the canon—a term he doesn't use. Nevertheless, one can trace a sort of development in these essays: from "Quevedo" and its puzzlement at the exclusion of the Spanish master from what one could describe as the "canon"; to "Kafka and His Precursors" and its delinking of excellence from precedence; to "The Argentine Writer and Tradition" and its stress on the possibilities opened by marginal cultural positions; to "Sobre los clásicos," which undermines any possible definition of the classics as intrinsically different and separate from all other literary production. That said, both "Quevedo" and "Sobre los clásicos" deal directly with the topics of classics and canons. In "Quevedo," Borges points out the deficiencies of Western and world canons: their scandalous omissions, and how even the toniest critics and writers include works based on often paraliterary criteria, such as the creation of showy symbols, or the appeal, or lack of it, of the figure of the author. In "Sobre los clásicos," the Argentine writer stresses the instability of the category of the classic, and implicitly that of the canon, as well as noting how the criteria for elevating works to these categories are both arbitrary and mutable.

"Kafka and His Precursors" and "The Argentine Writer and Tradition" are texts written to justify both Borges's own practice and his burgeoning position as a world-renowned master writer, but by doing so, he also theoretically empowers writers from the margins, from South America and from Argentina. In "Kafka and His Precursors," Borges argues that true innovators can create their own tradition, that writing after the creation of the Western canon can be innovative, not just epigonal. As Edna Aizenberg notes, "At the 'periphery,' where things have as yet to cohere, one must create a genealogy, an identity, and a place" (109). Moreover, it is the creative act of reading that makes this new genealogy and new writing ultimately identifiable and possible. "The Argentine Writer and Tradition" is analogous. If for Eliot it is a sense of belonging that makes possible literary innovation and, therefore, future classics, for Borges it is precisely difference—geographic, even cultural—that makes possible creativity, or at least, a certain kind of creativity.

Critics have long noted that Borges is a precursor of deconstruction and more generally postmodern ways of reading.[41] This explains how he became, in Ian Almond's words, the "*écrivain préferé* of Derrida and Foucault" (435). However, there is also significant difference: as Borges wrote from an Argentine and "South American" location. By presenting the canon—be it Western or global—as evolving, by rejecting chronological and spatial hierarchies, the canon loses its monumentality and can be viewed as analogous to a library, one of Borges's preferred tropes. This library is both a paradise, as in "El poema de los dones" ("Poem of the Gifts"), and a dystopia, as in "La biblioteca de Babel" ("The Library of Babel), but either way, it ideally includes all books regardless of provenance. The canon as library—with access to all knowledge—becomes a resource for writing, reading, and thinking.

4

Rewriting Kafka in Latin America

JAMES JOYCE, MARCEL Proust, and Franz Kafka are the modernist holy trinity of the early twentieth century. Kafka, despite being the last of the trinity to become widely known in Latin America,[1] arguably exercised as great an influence, or perhaps even greater, on Spanish-language Latin American fiction than his colleagues. As no less a figure than Gabriel García Márquez evidences, this was partly due to the wide dissemination of "Franz Kafka's *The Metamorphosis*, in the false translation by Borges published by Losada in Buenos Aires" in 1938 (García Márquez, *Living to Tell the Tale* 247).[2] The fact that this translation was published under the name of Jorge Luis Borges, already a cult writer throughout the region, if not yet widely acknowledged as a master, surely must have helped Kafka's circulation. (Ironically, Borges did not translate *The Metamorphosis*, only a few of the other stories in the volume).[3] Even so, Borges noted on more than one occasion the centrality of Kafka in his view—and practice—of modern literature.[4]

Needless to say, there are countless books to still be written on the influence of all three writers,[5] as well as somewhat later but equally influential modernists, such as William Faulkner. However, while a thorough analysis of Kafka's presence in Latin American literature is beyond the scope of this chapter—which would have to include such major authors as Julio Ramón Ribeyro, Carlos Fuentes, Julio Cortázar, Elena Garro, Antonio di Benedetto, César Aira, and Roberto Bolaño, not to mention writers from Brazil—here I look only at some Spanish-language Latin American texts that make explicit use of the Czech writer's works and ideas. Nevertheless, the chapter still includes some of the most important writers in the region: we begin with Borges, who, in addition to translating Kafka and writing "Kafka and His Precursors" (1951) includes a cryptic but discernible reference to Kafka in "La lotería en Babilonia" ("The Lottery in Babylon") (1941); we continue with the Argentine Ricardo Piglia, who in *Respiración artificial* (*Artificial Respiration*, 1980) found in Kafka's works a key to understanding, or at least representing, his country's history of repression and the brutal dictatorship of the 1970s; we cover Mario Vargas Llosa, who in his 1987 *El hablador* (*The Storyteller*) used *The Metamorphosis* as a framework to describe the problematic relationship between Westernized urban Peruvian culture and that of indigenous Amazonia; and we conclude with the contemporary Mexican novelist Guadalupe Nettel, who, in her award-winning autofiction *El cuerpo en que nací* (*The Body Where I Was Born*, 2016), uses the plight of Gregor Samsa, the protagonist of *The Metamorphosis*, to explore her problematic relationship with her body, family, class, and culture. Through the unavoidably superficial analysis of a handful of texts by major Hispanic writers, the chapter presents a test case of how Latin American fiction has made use of one of the key authors in the Western canon.

BORGES ON KAFKA

As we have seen, one of Borges's most important essays—"Kafka and His Precursors"—was nominally about the Czech author. This essay questioned traditional hierarchies regarding historical precedence—Kafka reshapes literary history, even the canon, rather than being determined by it—but it is also worth noting how, for Borges, unlike for some of the other writers in this chapter, Kafka is not primarily the author of *The Metamorphosis*.

In "Kafka and His Precursors," though Borges lists several precedents for the German-language fictionist, there is no consistent attempt to make a detailed description of Kafka's writing (that is, what makes Kafka "as singular as a phoenix" (106) is not the main concern of the essay). Therefore, it becomes necessary to look at the examples Borges gives in order to see how he understood Kafka's works. Borges's list of authors and texts begins with Zeno, the pre-Socratic philosopher whose parables attempted to deny the possibility of movement and change, and the list ends with two complementary stories by Léon Bloy and Lord Dunsany: the first is about travelers who, despite all the necessary accoutrements, are ultimately unable to begin their trip; the second is about an army that despite endless military successes never reaches its goal. Although Borges never puts into words what these works have in common, it is quite obvious: all, in different ways, are stories about the inability of breaking free from stasis. If we consider the other texts in "Kafka and His Precursors"—by Han Yu, Browning, and Kierkegaard—they are also about impossibility itself. Given this interpretation of Kafka, it is not surprising that Borges sees him not as the author of *The Metamorphosis* but as that of "The Great Wall of China," a story that the Argentine writer did translate, and in which the construction of a protective wall becomes an endless, explicitly Babelian project, in the sense that it can never be completed and it ultimately overwhelms the fabric of society.[6] In fact, Borges's two main Kafkaesque stories—"La biblioteca de Babel" ("The Library of Babel") (1941) and "La lotería en Babilonia" ("The Lottery in Babylon") (1941)—repeat this structural trait he identified about Kafka in "Kafka and His Precursors."[7]

Another key to Borges's understanding of Kafka's writing slips in briefly when he notes the latter's similarities to Kierkegaard: "The fact that Kierkegaard, like Kafka, abounded in religious parables on contemporary and middle-class themes" (107) ("Kierkegaard, como Kafka, abundó en parábolas religiosas de tema contemporáneo y burgués" [711]). This idea had earlier been explored in Borges's "Nathaniel Hawthorne" (1949), which attempts to introduce this classic US writer to an Argentine readership. Thus, after a long description of Hawthorne's "Wakefield"—in which the titular character leaves home, secretly moves close by to observe his wife, only to return after twenty years, as if nothing had happened—Borges declares: "'Wakefield' prefigures Franz Kafka, but Kafka modifies and refines the reading of 'Wakefield.' The debt is mutual; a great writer creates his precursors" (57), thus foreshadowing the key idea he would present two years later in "Kafka and His Precursors."[8] In "Nathaniel Hawthorne," in addition to presenting a succinct version of his innovative views on literary history, Borges adds two precursors to the list found in "Kafka and His Precursors": Hawthorne and Melville.

However, for our current purposes, the fact that "Nathaniel Hawthorne" includes a more detailed discussion of "parables" and the larger issue of the tension between modern narrative and allegory is of greater relevance.[9] In this text, Borges explains the problem he finds with the New England writer, even at his best: "One aesthetic error debased him: the Puritan desire to make a fable out of each imagining induced him to add morals and sometimes to falsify and to deform them" (51).[10] Thus, Hawthorne concludes his "Wakefield," supposedly based on a real event, by noting: "Amid the seeming confusion of our mysterious world, individuals are so nicely adjusted to a system, and systems to one another, and to a whole, that by stepping aside for a moment a man exposes himself to a fearful risk of losing his place for ever. Like Wakefield, he may become, as it were, the Outcast of the Universe" ("Nathaniel Hawthorne" 56).[11] Even if somewhat convoluted as a morale for a parable, Hawthorne is characteristically guiding the reader as to how to understand a tale and, therefore, a behavior, that on its own seems incomprehensible.

Borges notes, "In that brief and ominous parable, which dates from 1835, we have already entered the world of Herman Melville, of Kafka—a world of enigmatic punishments and indecipherable sins" (56).[12] However, the Argentine author then adds: "If Kafka had written that story, Wakefield would never have returned to his home; Hawthorne lets him return; but his return is no less lamentable or less atrocious than is his long absence" (57).[13] Without betraying Borges's arguments in the least, one can also add that if Kafka had written "Wakefield," there would have been no attempt to find a morale to the story. If there is one characteristic of Kafka's "religious parables on contemporary and middle-class themes"—where "religious" refers only to the "enigmatic" and "indecipherable" nature of the event—it is that they offer no guidance to the reader as to how they should be interpreted.[14]

While a discussion of the actual relationship between parables and allegories is clearly beyond the scope of this chapter, the fact is that Borges denies that Hawthorne wrote allegories, given his supposed inability to provide a coherent relationship between the two levels of narrative and meaning that characterizes the genre.[15] That said, the relationship between the two genres is complicated. For instance, the *Concise Oxford Dictionary of Literary Terms* defines parables as "a brief tale intended to be understood as an allegory" (Baldick 182). Some critics have noted echoes of the allegory in Kafka's writing. In fact, precisely as he criticizes allegorical readings of Kafka in terms similar to those Borges used in rejecting the notion that Hawthorne wrote allegories, Ritchie Robertson notes:

> But the religious element in the story is not expressed in any coherent way. A mode of writing that coherently relates earthly events to the timeless realities of religion is called allegory. But Kafka does not write allegory. It would be impossible, for example, to read "The Judgement" as an allegory in which Georg stands for Jesus. Yet even if literature no longer has any coherent way of representing such realities, that does not mean that they no longer exist or no longer have any claim on our attention. They therefore appear in Kafka's writing as a series of hints and allusions which fracture the surface of the text. (30–31)

Perhaps the problem with Borges, at the time, and Robertson, in ours, is that their definitions of allegory, while perfectly appropriate to medieval and early modern texts such as John Bunyan's *Pilgrim's Progress* (1678), or such obviously allegorical modern works as George Orwell's *Animal Farm* (1945), are extremely rigid.

Kafka, like other twentieth- and twenty-first century writers, makes different use of the allegory. As Robertson notes, he presents hints that the text should be read allegorically without providing any clear guide to what is being allegorized. As Nicholas Birns notes about views on allegory after deconstruction, "de Man overhauled the way the distinction between symbol and allegory had stood since Coleridge—symbol standing for the image itself, allegory for its connection to the world and to reference. Allegory became revalued in the aftermath of the deconstructive turn because, by reaching back toward reference, it acknowledges its own failure" (*Theory after Theory* 98). In the case of Kafka, by presenting allegorical hints—to use

Robertson's phrase—or offering parables without a clear morale, the stories ask to be interpreted as connected "to the world and to reference," yet at the same time, there is no way of knowing what the reference actually is. Following Birns, they are purposely failed allegories. The fact, for instance, that *The Metamorphosis* has been seen as a parable of the Jewish condition in German-speaking lands, or as allegorizing the existence of the artist in bourgeois society, or the alienation experienced by individuals under modernity— these are examples of the "allegory effect" of Kafka's works, as they generate the need for readers to try to identify "the world and reference" that is being allegorized, despite the impossibility of any clear meaning ever being found.

In fact, later in life, Borges revised his ideas about allegory and its role in Kafka's writing. In his 1982 preface to a translation of *The Metamorphosis*, he notes, "Now, Kafka's work is more than anything an allegory of the state, but with time will be an allegory of the universe, governed by an unknowable God" (qtd. in Sarah Roger 46).[16] As Roger notes, "For Borges, Kafka's stories were simultaneously temporally specific and timeless, containing hierarchies that managed to be both contemporary and everlasting, depending on how they were interpreted" (46).

A SACRED LATRINE

While Paul de Man argued, "The stories that make up the bulk of Borges's literary work are not moral fables or parables like Kafka's, to which they are often misleadingly compared, even less attempts at psychological analysis" (199–200), the fact is that in another late text on Kafka, Borges *partly* contradicted the Belgian critic by noting the influence of the Czech master on his writing: "I've also written some stories in which I ambitiously and unsuccessfully attempted to become Kafka. There's one titled "The Library of Babel" and certain others, that were exercises where I tried to be Kafka. Those stories were of interest but I realized that I had not fulfilled my purpose and needed to find another way" ("Un sueño eterno" 232).[17] Moreover, his interpretation of Kafka as an allegorist of state and universe is present in "The Library of Babel" and "The Lottery of Babylon."

Because this chapter deals only with those texts that explicitly acknowledge the imprint of Kafka's fiction,[18] I limit myself to noting that "The Library of Babel" is a clear example of "an allegory of the universe." The story begins by declaring: "The universe (which others call the Library) is composed of an indefinite, perhaps infinite number of hexagonal galleries" (112).[19] However, the episodes described in the story—bibliophilic violence, the listing of religious movements that remind readers of the heresies and convulsions of the history of Christianity, and even of the possibility of a Book-Man who bears some echoes of Christ—all serve to make the story not only into an allegory of the universe, but a history of human attempts to make sense of it and, therefore, history itself. However, as should be clear, "The Library of Babel" is much more clearly allegorical than the bulk of Kafka's stories that serve as its model—as we saw, it explicitly is presented as reflecting the human condition before a meaningless universe—as it hews closely to Borges's view of the Czech writer as a narrator of impossibility, like Zeno. As the story notes, "The Library is 'total'-perfect, complete, and whole-and that its bookshelves contain all possible combinations of the twenty-two orthographic symbols (a number which, though unimaginably vast, is not infinite)—that is, all that is able to be expressed, in every language" (115).[20] However, the option of reading the totality of books it includes, or even finding a specific one, is impossible.

If Kafka is an inspiration and intertext for "The Library of Babel"—it echoes "The Great Wall of China" in its depiction of impossibility, in the case of Borges's story, of ever fully understanding the library and, therefore, the universe—then "The Lottery of Babylon" playfully states the presence of the Czech author: "There were certain stone lions, a sacred latrine called Qaphqa, some cracks in a dusty aqueduct—these places, it was generally believed, gave access to the Company, and well- or ill-wishing persons would deposit confidential reports in them" (104).[21] In a way that simultaneously acknowledges Borges's anxiety of influence regarding Kafka—the Czech writer is a latrine, even if sacred—and makes fun of anxiety precisely by a near surrealist juxtaposition of opposites, in this case the spiritual and low body functions, this (ironic) mention highlights the importance of Kafka for Borges. Additionally, the juxtaposition of spiritual to material points to a reading of "The Lottery of Babylon" as allegory of both universe and state, or a certain variant of the latter.

Unlike "The Library of Babel," which is set apparently outside our time and space, "The Lottery of Babylon" includes numerous actual historical references such as the Roman emperor Heliogabalus (203–222 CE), the astronomer Heraclides Ponticus (390–310 BCE), Pythagoras, and Plato, that, at least in principle, situate the story in our world—and apparently during the time of the late Roman Empire. There are also corresponding geographical references, such as the Euphrates River—which crossed through Babylon—and cultural ones, like the presence of Greek letters and culture, and the cult of Baal, worshipped in pre-Roman and Roman Babylonia. However, the situation described, in which the "Lottery"—always capitalized— progressively acquires complete control of society and every individual life of this version of "Babylon," is obviously fictional. That said, "The Lottery of Babylon" can be read as both an "allegory of the universe governed by an unknowable God" and an "allegory of the state."

It is an allegory of the universe for its description of a society and world far from rational rule following. The story notes how every aspect of Babylonian society is governed by chance, paradoxically overseen by the secretive Company that runs its infinite lotteries. However, the description of Babylon progressively begins to resemble our everyday life. For instance, "No book is published without some discrepancy between each of the edition's copies. Scribes take a secret oath to omit, interpolate, alter. Indirect falsehood is also practiced" (105).[22] Even if, as all authors know, books of the same edition are rarely different, it is almost impossible to find a book without mistakes, no matter how careful the process of editing. It is tempting to read the story, then, as simply presenting a slightly distorted view of our everyday reality. The haphazard nature of our world, where our professional and personal lives seem at the mercy of accident, reminds us of Borges's Babylon. We, too, experience life as if it were being controlled by secret and arbitrary lotteries.

The story makes clear—for those readers who had not been paying attention—its allegorical character in its ending:

> The Company, with godlike modesty, shuns all publicity. Its agents, of course, are secret . . . That silent functioning, like God's, inspires all manner of conjectures. One scurrilously suggests that the Company ceased to exist hundreds of years ago, and that the sacred disorder of our lives is purely hereditary, traditional; another believes that the Company is

eternal, and teaches that it shall endure until the last night, when the last god shall annihilate the earth. Yet another declares that the Company is omnipotent, but affects only small things: the cry of a bird, the shades of rust and dust, the half dreams that come at dawn. Another, whispered by masked heresiarchs, says that the Company has never existed, and never will. Another, no less despicable, argues that it makes no difference whether one affirms or denies the reality of the shadowy corporation, because Babylon is nothing but an infinite game of chance. (106)[23]

Babylon is ultimately a version of our world that is also "nothing but an infinite game of chance," and the secretive Company, nothing but another name for God. And as is the case with God, we cannot prove its existence.

However, as Beatriz Sarlo notes, "It is not difficult to read this story allegorically, not only as a presentation of destiny, but as a presentation of totalitarianism in the order of everyday life" (76). One can also include "The Lottery of Babylon" in the series of stories that, like "Tlön, Uqbar, Orbis Tertius," or even more distant from Kafka or allegory, "Deutsches Requiem," deal with fascism and, more generally, totalitarianism. As Efraín Kristal notes, "The story is about a man escaping a dangerous place run by an organization (as ineffable as 'The Direction' in Kafka's 'The Great Wall of China')"; and: "The dangerous and life-threatening aspects of this mysterious organization are expressed by the fears of the narrator, who appears to be fleeing an unbearable and violent land where the controlling institution has apparently gone awry" (*Invisible Work* 127). Referring to the work of Adelheid Hanke-Schaefer, Kristal adds: "It is possible to read 'The Lottery in Babylon' . . . as a Kafkaesque parable about Fascist dictatorships of the 1930s and 1940s" (*Invisible Work* 127).[24]

As an "allegory of the state," perhaps better said, of the rise of a certain kind of state, "The Lottery of Babylon" presents a dire view of democracy. What is particularly surprising about the story is the manner in which this "dictatorship," if one can actually call it this, is achieved. Instead of the "Company" usurping power and destroying institutions, it is "civil society" that ultimately asks it to take over society. In its beginnings, the lottery, like our existing lotteries, simply gave away prizes. However, the Company's rise to power began when it started to give punishments as well as awards: "As one might expect, that small risk (for every thirty 'good' numbers there was one ill-omened one) piqued the public's interest. Babylonians flocked to buy tickets" (102).[25] Progressively, this led to the increase in the violence and number of the "ill-omened tickets," which included physical punishments and prison, and concomitantly to an increase in the popularity of the lottery. Finally:

> The lower-caste neighborhoods of the city voiced a different complaint. The members of the priestly class gambled heavily, and so enjoyed all the vicissitudes of terror and hope; the poor (with understandable, or inevitable, envy) saw themselves denied access to that famously delightful, even sensual, wheel. The fair and reasonable desire that all men and women, rich and poor, be able to take part equally in the Lottery inspired indignant demonstrations—the memory of which, time has failed to dim . . . There were disturbances, there were regrettable instances of bloodshed, but the masses of Babylon at last, over the opposition of the well-to-do, imposed their will; they saw their generous objectives fully achieved. First, the Company was forced to assume all public power. (The unification was necessary because of the vastness and complexity of the new operations.) Second, the Lottery was made secret, free of charge, and open to all. (103)[26]

Rather than a military coup, the takeover of institutions, or even the manipulation of democratic procedures, the Company here has progressively attained power as a result of its need to satisfy the desire of the different sectors of society: beginning with desire of the rich for risk—that helps create the Company—and ending with the desire of the poor for equal rights, here only regarding the dubious pleasure of risk. In the story, revolution— "regrettable instances of bloodshed"—is presented as leading to a dystopia that echoes both the fascism of the 1930s and the Stalinism of the Soviet Union. Given its equal rejection of Left and Right, and the role it assigns to the masses, it is tempting to read "The Lottery of Babylon" as one of the first, if not the first, textual manifestations of Borges's progressively antidemocratic turn.[27] Regardless of class, the "will of the people" helps contribute to the creation of a repressive regime. Democracy ends in dystopia.

There is, however, tension between the two main allegories proposed in the story: does it portray a "totalitarian" society run by the Company so is therefore an allegory of the antidemocratic movements of the 1930s, either fascism or Stalinism? Or is this a society that, seemingly like ours, is at the mercy of chance, so representative of all human collective and individual communities? It is a sign of Borges's literary mastery that the reader asks these questions only after having finished reading the story.

PIGLIA, KAFKA, AND ARGENTINE HISTORY

In 1980, in the midst of the brutal Argentine military dictatorship (1976–1983), Ricardo Piglia (1941–2017) published *Respiración artificial* (*Artificial Respiration*), a novel with numerous plot strands that can be chronologically unwoven into two main series: the first, set in 1850, details the life and writings of Enrique Ossorio, an obscure member of the Argentine 1837 generation, who, in addition to his diaries, is also writing a futuristic epistolary novel that takes place in 1979; the second, mostly set in 1979, deals with the (epistolary) renewal of the relationship between a nephew and his uncle—the novelist Emilio Renzi, and Marcelo Maggi, who is reconstructing the story of Enrique Ossorio—and Renzi's failed attempt at meeting Maggi in Entre Ríos. The story of this failed encounter is told through a long monologue in which Vladimir Tardewski, a failed Polish philosopher and friend of Maggi's, details his conversation with Renzi. It is Tardewski who speaks about Kafka.[28]

Critics have long described the novel it as a "national allegory," written during a time when a direct and explicit text about the horror of Argentina's present and its history would surely have been banned and almost surely have its author jailed or murdered. Even its title, whether in Spanish or English, has been read as hiding in its initials—A.R.—those of the country. Daniel Balderston notes, "The title of the novel suggests, by a sort of anagram that the theme is the Argentine Republic, in its tragic history" ("Introduction" 2). The first sentence of the novel, "¿Hay una historia?" (15) is unavoidably mistranslated as "Is there a story?" (11), given the double meaning of *historia* in Spanish as both history and story. But the sentence in Spanish correctly reads as referring to both literary and historical emplotment. However, the epigraph that opens the novel clearly states that history, rather than fiction, is the not-so-secret topic of the novel: "To Elías and Rubén who helped me to come to know the truth of history" (v).[29]

That said, the complex structure of the text, including its double historical framework—the mid-nineteenth century and 1979, which to make things more complicated are interrelated, as well as the different textual material Piglia uses in the novel, such as letters, diaries, and first-person narratives—adds to the difficulty in finding history, as well as a story, in the text. However, if *Artificial Respiration* is an allegory, it is in a different way from those exemplified by Borges's or even Kafka's narratives, which present events that appear to have an only tangential relationship with reality. Instead, *Artificial Respiration* moves in and out of the mud of the real as it brings readers flickers with which to reconstruct Argentina's historical narrative.

Referring specifically to the second chronological thread, Idelber Avelar argues: "In this game of infinite decipherments, that of Emilio Renzi takes the form of a dilemma: how to narrate the present? How to narrate Marcelo Maggi's search? What is the language with which one can narrate the relationship of Argentina with its history/histories?" (421).[30] Piglia clearly situates his narrative, insofar as it can read as an allegory, as one that refers to the Argentina of 1979—a country governed by a criminal state. In fact, while the novel is set in 1979, it actually begins in 1976: "If there's a story it begins three years ago. In April 1976, when my first book is published, he [Maggi] sends me a letter" (11).[31] The year 1976 is when the Argentine coup took place. Moreover, as the connections established with the Argentine past indicate, the Dirty War and the disappeared are the consequence of Argentine history, not an aberration. Even if the reasons for his absence are never made clear, Maggi strangely does not show up to meet his nephew in Entre Ríos. It is insinuated that he may have been killed or disappeared. The novel ends with Renzi opening again one of the folders with Ossorio's writings. He reads the nineteenth-century Argentine's suicide note: "To the one that finds my body" (216) ("Al que encuentre mi cadáver" [218]). The note reads as if it were written by Maggi. It is not accidental that Elías and Rubén, who, according to the epigraph that opens the novel, helped Piglia learn the truth of history, were among those disappeared by the Argentine military.[32] Death is presented as the hidden truth of Argentine history.

As noted, it is Tardewski, a disciple of Wittgenstein, who brings up Kafka. The conversation between Renzi and Tardewski, recounted by the latter in a hallucinatory monologue, brings together all the topics of the novel: Argentine literature and history; philosophy and its connections to Nazism; the relationship between political commitment, represented by the possibly disappeared Maggi, and commitment to philosophy, literature, and truth, represented by Tardewski and others. But it also uses Kafka and his literature to connect the Argentine horrors of the 1970s with those of Nazism.[33]

Tardewski had experienced the sideswipe of Nazism when he escaped Warsaw for Buenos Aires as the German troops invaded, while searching for a former friend of Kafka's. The reason for this meeting was to verify his theory—based on certain cryptic passages in Kafka's diaries and on the fact that Hitler had spent time in Prague—that the Czech writer and the future Führer had met and conversed at "the Arcos Café in Prague" (206) between the end of 1909 and the beginning of 1910. As Piglia puts it:

> The atrocious utopia of a world converted into an immense penal colony: that's what Adolf, the insignificant, grotesque draft dodger, talks about to Franz Kafka, the one who knows how to listen . . . And Kafka believes him. He thinks it is *possible* that the impossible and atrocious projects of that ridiculous hungry little man may come to pass and that the world may be transformed into what the words were constructing: the Castle of the Order of the Twisted Cross, the machine of evil that engraves its message on the flesh of its victims. Couldn't he hear the abominable voice of history? (207)[34]

If Borges saw in Kafka's writings a guide to creating seamless allegories about the universe and the state, his use of the Czech master's writings was based on his then-liberal political view that any and all states are ultimately repressive. Thus, in "The Library of Babel" and especially in "The Lottery in Babylon" the dystopian world depicted is not the product of "atrocious projects," but it comes into being in what almost seems an unavoidable and natural process. Piglia reads Kafka's allegories of the state as directly connected with fascism. Regardless of the fictional nature of Kafka's encounter with Hitler, the Czech novelist is to be able to read the present and imagine the horrors to come during the Nazi regime: "The word *Ungenziefer*, said Tardewski, which the Nazis would use to designate prisoners in the concentration camp, is the same word that Kafka uses to describe what Gregor Samsa has turned into on morning, when he wakes up" (206).[35] But by narrating this (imagined) encounter between Kafka and Hitler, in a novel about the Argentine Republic (A.R.), the horrors of the Holocaust are linked to those experienced in Argentina during the military dictatorship's Dirty War. As Tardewski notes, "The genius of Kafka resides in his having understood that if those words could be spoken then they could be realized" (207). And in 1979, they were being realized again by the Argentine military. Piglia's description of Kafka as "attentive to the sickly murmurs of history" (208) ("Estaba atento al murmullo enfermizo de la historia" [210]) is an alternative not only to Borges's view of Kafka as a creator of parables or allegories dealing with both the universe and the state, but also to historicizing the Czech author, even if we have to keep in mind that this bit of *literary criticism* is taking place within a hallucinatory work of fiction. If as David Damrosch notes, there has been a trend from "a universal Kafka to an ethnic Kafka" (189), that is, from Kafka as an explorer of the human condition to one ultimately writing about his local Jewish reality and experience, then Piglia presents Kafka as rooted in history, but in a history that will fully manifest only in the future. In this, Kafka shows a strong resemblance to the novel's Enrique Ossorio, who in 1850 attempted to write about Argentina in 1979.

Piglia's references to Kafka in his narrative become a way for him to show the history of the Argentine Republic as participating in the horror of the twentieth century and an acknowledgment of his own novel as a participant in world literature.

KAFKA IN AMAZONIA

Few narrative worlds seem further from Kafka's than those of the novels by the Peruvian Mario Vargas Llosa. Vargas Llosa has described his own work as basically realist,[36] and, therefore, far from Kafka's nonrealist narrative. Unlike Borges, who took Kafka as one of his starting points as a writer, or Piglia, who saw in Kafka an example to follow when writing about the horrors of Argentine history and (then) present, to my knowledge Vargas Llosa has never mentioned Kafka as a direct influence. It is true he admires Kafka as one of the greatest of writers—in particular singling out *The Metamorphosis*, together with Thomas Mann's *Death in Venice* and Leo Tolstoy's *The Death of Ivan Illich*, as one "of the masterworks of the genre" (*"Death in Venice"*).[37] Furthermore, in his novel *Conversación en La Catedral* (*Conversation in the Cathedral*) (1969), Vargas Llosa has Santiago Zavala, a character loosely inspired in his own experiences as a university student and journalist, confess to his surprised left-wing collegemates: "I am only saying *The Making of a Hero* bored me and that I liked *The Castle*" (91).[38] (The novel, written during the time Vargas Llosa was aligned with the Left, states the author's real-life preference for so-called decadent modernist literature over the putatively progressive socialist realism promoted by communist parties). However, the references to Kafka in Vargas Llosa's works, both fictional and critical, are relatively few.[39] In fact, the quotation praising *The Metamorphosis* comes from Vargas Llosa's *"La muerte en Venecia: El llamado del abismo"* (*"Death in Venice*: The Call of the Abyss"), originally published in *La verdad de las mentiras* (1990), a collection of essays on the modern novel that does not include one on Kafka. But even if Vargas Llosa has been more clearly influenced by Faulkner and Flaubert, Kafka's *The Metamorphosis* serves as a constant point of reference in his 1987 novel *El hablador* (*The Storyteller*).

Framed by two chapters set in Firenze (the novel uses the Italian-Tuscan name for Florence), at its core *The Storyteller* tells of Saúl Zuratas, better known as "Mascarita" because of the masklike birthmark that covers his face. The son of an immigrant Jewish father and a Peruvian *criolla* mother, Saúl abandons a potentially brilliant career as an anthropologist to live with the Matsigenkas (in the novel *Machiguengas*) in Amazonia and become a storyteller. Told in alternating chapters—one narrated by an unnamed writer who exactly resembles Vargas Llosa,[40] the other by an indigenous storyteller, or "talker," the literal meaning of *hablador*, ultimately identified with Zuratas—the novel has been mostly read as a critical return to *indigenista* topics and styles,[41] or as the encounter between writing and orality.[42] However, here we consider the meaning of the presence of Kafka in Vargas Llosa's text.

Underlying Vargas Llosa's use of Kafka's story is the fact that, as Roy Chandler Caldwell Jr. notes, "The eponymous storyteller of Mario Vargas Llosa's novel *El Hablador* (1987) undergoes a transformation nearly as radical as Gregor in Kafka's as *Die Verwwandlung*" (50). *The Storyteller* presents Zuratas's *transformation*, Kafka's original title in German, from Jew and Peruvian to Matsigenka, and from anthropologist and intellectual to storyteller. Vargas Llosa, therefore, reads *The Metamorphosis* as an allegory of change, of personal transformation, rather than following its actual plot of human to insect therianthropy. In this sense, Vargas Llosa reads Kafka as a creator of "universal" stories that can be translated—in all meanings of the word—into Peru and used to express not only Zuratas's transformation but also the tensions implicit in all acculturation.

Zuratas's metamorphosis is also presented as a story of conversion like that of his namesake Saul of Tarsus:

> With hindsight, knowing what happened to him later—I have thought about this a lot—I can say that Saúl experienced a conversion. In a cultural sense and perhaps in a religious one also. It is the only concrete case I have had occasion to observe from close at hand that has seemed to give meaning to, to make real, what the priests at the school where I studied tried to convey to us during catechism through phrases such as "receiving grace," "being touched by grace," "falling into the snares of grace." From his first contact with the Amazon jungle, Mascarita was caught in a spiritual trap that made a different person of him. Not just because he lost all interest in law and began working for a degree in ethnology, or because of the new direction his reading took, leaving precisely one surviving literary character, Gregor Samsa, but because from that moment on he began to be preoccupied, obsessed, by two concerns which in the years to come would be his only subjects of conversation: the plight of Amazonian cultures and the death throes of the forests that sheltered them. (18–19)[43]

Perhaps, paradoxically, Vargas Llosa is also connecting Saúl Zuratas and the New Testament Saul. Both Sauls represent in the novel a tradition of conversion in a way, allegorized by Kafka in his novella; moreover, a transformation from a Jewish identity to a non-Jewish one. Cultural conversion, like religious conversion, is presented as bypassing rational processes.

Zuratas's transformation leads him to abandon all cultural and personal markers with one exception: Kafka's *The Metamorphosis*. Of course, underlying the emotional connection between Zuratas and Gregor Samsa is their shared "monstrosity." As we all know, *The Metamorphosis* begins with one of the most famous first lines in all literature: "As Gregor Samsa awoke one morning from uneasy dreams, he found himself transformed into a gigantic insect" (19). Even though Zuratas's birthmark is not part of any transformation, since he was born with it, the sense of monstrosity experienced by Gregor is something with which the anthropology student can identify.

The novel details several moments when he is discriminated against due to his appearance. As the "Vargas Llosa" narrator comments: "Walking through the streets with Saúl showed how painful a life he must have led at the hands of insolent, nasty people. They would turn around or block his path as he passed, to get a better look at him, staring wide-eyed and making no effort to conceal the amazement or disgust that his face aroused in them, and it was not a rare thing for someone, children mostly, to come out with some insulting remark" (13).[44] The novel gives a concrete example of Zuratas being treated like "some kind of gigantic insect": a drunkard tries to stop him and "Vargas Llosa" from entering a billiard parlor. He says, "You're not coming in here, monster." He was suddenly furious. "With a face like that, you should keep off the streets. You scare people" (14).[45] It is not surprising that Zuratas would identify with a character who was mistreated by his society, even if, unlike Gregor's case, his father supports and loves him.

The importance of Gregor Samsa for Zuratas was already intimated in the novel by the fact that his parrot—a token of Amazonia that also foreshadows the novel's disclosure of Zuratas's fate by the bird's identification with the spoken word—was named after Kafka's character. Although it strikes the reader as unsurprising that Zuratas would identify with the protagonist of *The Metamorphosis*, his relationship with Kafka's novella resembles that of a devout Jew with the Torah: "With the exception of Kafka, and *The Metamorphosis* in particular, which he had read countless times and virtually knew by heart, all his reading was now in the field of anthropology"

(17).[46] But he would soon abandon anthropology; by the end, only *The Metamorphosis*, which he has internalized like one of the book people in Ray Bradbury's *Fahrenheit 451*, remains.

A Jew among Peruvians, a Peruvian among Jews, discriminated against for his deformity, he finds tolerance only among the Matsigenka. However, if he were born among them, he would have been killed: the novel notes that, like the Spartans, they practice infanticide to rid themselves of children with birth defects, even if they tolerate all adult individuals.[47] As Kristal notes, "Vargas Llosa has crafted a character so marginal that even the fragile, helpless, and isolated Machiguenga community would have excluded him" (*Temptation of the Word* 161). Therefore, the appeal of *The Metamorphosis* for Zuratas resides in its presentation of a character who, by becoming some kind of insect, becomes the ultimate marginal, the absolute Other, to his family and to all of humanity. Zuratas could read Kafka's novella as an allegory of his situation of being "marginal among marginals, a man whose destiny would always bear the stigma of ugliness" (Vargas Llosa, *The Storyteller* 243).[48]

However, at the same time, one sees in Zuratas a quasi-religious relationship with *The Metamorphosis*, an echo of the "ethnic" Kafka whose work is rooted in the experiences of Bohemian Jews. Zuratas may not be a reader of the Torah or a devout Jew (in fact, since his mother is a *criolla* Peruvian, he may not technically be a Jew at all), but *The Metamorphosis* is, in *The Storyteller*, a marker of Jewishness in that it allegorizes not only a personal experience but a collective one, one that the otherwise deculturated Zuratas is not willing to give up.

In addition to these references, one of the stories told by the storyteller, who at the end of the novel is implicitly identified with Zuratas, is a retelling of *The Metamorphosis* translated in a manner that, at least according to the logic of the novel, the Matsigenka could understand:

> I was people. I had a family. I was asleep. Then I woke up. I'd barely opened my eyes when I understood. Alas, poor Tasurinchi! I'd changed into an insect, that's what. A buzz-buzz bug, perhaps. A Gregor-Tasurinchi. I was lying on my back. The world had grown bigger, it seemed to me. I was aware of everything. Those hairy, ringed legs were my legs. Those transparent mud-colored wings, which creaked when I moved and hurt me so much,

had once been my arms. The stench that surrounded me: was that my odor? I saw the world differently: I could see the underside and the top, the back and the front, at the same time. Because now, being an insect, I had several eyes. What's happened to you, Gregor-Tasurinchi? Did a bad witch eat a lock of your hair and change you? Did a little kamagarini devil get into you through your ass-eye and turn you into this? I was covered with shame at seeing myself the way I was. What would my family say? Because I had a family, like the other men who walk, it seemed. "What would they think, seeing me changed into a repulsive insect? All you can do with buzz-buzz bugs is squash them. Can you eat them? Can you cure evil with them? You can't even make filthy machikanari potions with them, perhaps. (203)[49]

This passage illustrates the many changes that Zuratas, as storyteller, makes to Kafka's story.[50] For instance, the storyteller modifies the original *Metamorphosis* stylistically, with its echoes of orality in its use of parataxis and its first-person narration. Furthermore, it clearly sets the story in Amazonia by referring to local flora and fauna, establishing that the unnamed insect is the buzz-buzz bug (cicada). But Zuratas also sets the story in the Matsigenka cultural world, as in the references to the possible uses for insects, noting that the buzz-buzz bug cannot be eaten, so indicating that in Amazonia, insects are often eaten, or noting that they are useless for magical potions, except those by the *machikanari* (evil wizards). Here Zuratas performs a translation—in its linguistic, cultural, and physical senses—of Kafka's novella. In fact, one can see Zuratas as exemplifying the change from "the idea of translator as mediator from a focus purely on mediating language to mediating cultures. In so doing, there is a recognition that meaning making is not simply a linguistic act, but rather that culture is a constituent element in the creation and reception of meanings" (Liddicoat 348). In his adaption of *The Metamorphosis*, as well as in all the stories told in the Amazonian chapters, Zuratas mediates between Western and Matsigenka cultures not only to the "listeners" within the text but also to the intended Western readers, who, through the "writing down" of his oral narration, get a clearer sense of the beliefs and worldview of this Amazonian group.

According the Schneils, an Evangelical anthropologist couple who give the "Vargas Llosa" narrator information about the Matsigenka: "They had been breathed out by the god Tasurinchi, creator of everything that existed, and did not have personal names. Their names were always temporary, related to a passing phenomenon and subject to change" (83). One can here remember that, according to Jacques Derrida, "one would then be tempted to say *first* that a proper name, in the proper sense, does not properly belong to the language; it does not belong there, *although and because* its call makes the language possible (what would a language be without the possibility of calling a proper name?)" (251). In a sense, the absolute otherness of the Matsigenka is evidenced by their having what, for Derrida, would be an "impossible" language, since they have no personal names. Thus, the most radical aspect of "Zuratas's" translation of *The Metamorphosis* is the reference to "Gregor-Tasurinchi," which reflects the proper name as being outside language and therefore untranslatable. While the reference to the protagonist of Zuratas's story as Tasurinchi marks the character as Matsigenka, the fact is that the name Gregor cannot be translated. "Zuratas" thus actually intervenes in Matsigenka society, introducing an element of individuation that their language had until then resisted. It is also possible to see in the continued presence of Gregor in the storyteller's discourse another instance of how Saúl Zuratas sees in Kafka's text and its protagonist a marker of identity, which he cannot abandon.

There are other metamorphoses in the novel, as well. The novel notes that the storyteller does much more than entertain the Matsigenka:

> The hablador, or habladores, must be something like the courier service of the community. Messengers who went from one settlement to another in the vast territory over which the Machiguengas were dispersed, relating to some what the others were doing, keeping them informed of the happenings, the fortunes and misfortunes of the brothers whom they saw very rarely or not at all. Their name defined them. They spoke. Their mouths were the connecting links of this society that the fight for survival had forced to split up. (92)[51]

The fact that Saúl Zuratas, a Peruvian Jew, has been able to transform himself into an *hablador*, that is, into a vital link in the cultural Matsigenka network, is itself a transformation comparable to that of Gregor Samsa.

As mentioned at the start of this section, the novel's dual narratives—
the alternating chapters by "Vargas Llosa" and "Zuratas," by the Western
novelist and the Matsigenka storyteller—are framed by two chapters set
in Firenze, presented as home of the canon and Western culture: he had
come to the city to "to read Dante and Machiavelli and look at Renaissance
paintings for a couple of months" (4).[52] In other words, it is clear that this
authorial figure, another textual iteration of "Vargas Llosa," is author of
both the "Vargas Llosa" and *hablador* chapters. As Lucille Kerr notes, "In
El hablador the modern literary author becomes identified with the traditional teller of tales. The one figure appears to mask and uncover the other,
to disfigure and define the other's face" (*Reclaiming the Author* 135). Thus,
another metamorphosis, in this case "Vargas Llosa's" from Western novelist to Matsigenka storyteller, is also implicit.

GUADALUPE NETTEL: THE BODY AS OTHER

While Zuratas's identification with Gregor is clearly rooted in their common "monstrosity," the future storyteller never evinces any sense of dissatisfaction with his own body. In fact, following what seem to be Matsigenka mores, he believes in maintaining a peaceful calm regardless of the
circumstances. In a note he sends "Vargas Llosa" after the latter attacks the
drunkard who insulted Zuratas, the anthropology student notes: "Anyone
who lets anger get the better of him distorts these lines [a magic symbol of
cosmic equilibrium], and when they're distorted they can no longer hold
up the earth" (14–15).[53] However, an intense awareness and dissatisfaction
with one's body is at the core of Mexican novelist Guadalupe Nettel's *El
cuerpo en que nací* (*The Body Where I Was Born*) (2011). This sense of the
body as deficient, if not quite monstrous, is already expressed in the first
sentence of the novel: "I was born with a white beauty mark, or what others
call a birthmark, covering the cornea of my right eye. That spot would
have been nothing had it not stretched across my iris and over the pupil
through which light must pass to reach the back of the brain" (7).[54] Rather
than being a constitutive part of who one is, the body in Nettel's novel, is
a problem that will be solved only by her acceptance of its flaws and virtues toward the end of the novel: "At last, after a long journey, I decided to

inhabit the body where I was born, in all its peculiarities. When all is said and done, it is the only thing that belongs to me and ties me to the world, and allows me to set myself apart" (174).[55] Obviously, this sense of reconciliation with the body is an option that was not available to Gregor Samsa. As critics have noted, this sense of the body as a problem, as Nettel puts it, of being born into the body, rather than the body being a constitutive part of who one is, is a dysmorphia. Robertson has noted that a similar dysmorphia characterized not only the protagonist of *The Metamorphosis*—per Robertson after the transformation, "Gregor is alienated from his own body" (51)—but also the text's author, Kafka himself.[56] Elizabeth Murcia argues that, "by identifying with Kafka's character, [Nettel's narrator] not only assumes a place in the world, but also identifies the postures others will have toward her" (Murcia 83).[57] Like *The Metamorphosis*, *The Body Where I Was Born* evinces a sense of alienation from society, social class, and especially family.

Before continuing to analyze Nettel's novel and her uses of Kafka's *The Metamorphosis*, it's worth noting that *The Body Where I Was Born* is a prime example of autofiction. As Manuel Alberca notes about this (sub)genre:

> Although autofiction is a narrative that presents itself as a novel, or without generic classification (but never as an autobiography or memoirs), it is characterized by having the appearance of an autobiography that is ratified by the identity in name of author, narrator, and character. It is precisely this crossing of genres that determines a narrative space composed of contradictory profiles, because it equally transgresses or at least contravenes the principle that establishes a distance between author and character that informs the novelistic pact, as well as, the principle of veracity that characterizes the autobiographical pact. (10–11)[58]

Thus, although *The Body Where I Was Born* is in English subtitled *A Novel*, this affirmation of the text's genre is absent from the Spanish original. Although it is generally considered a novel in reviews and interview, the only paratextual information that shapes the reader's expectations is that it is included in Anagrama's prestigious series *Narrativas hispánicas*. However, while most of the books included in this series are fiction, including

Bolaño's *The Savage Detectives*, it also includes autobiographical texts, such as the three volumes of Alfredo Bryce Echenique's memoirs. That said, the protagonist and first-person narrator is presented explicitly as Guadalupe Nettel, or better said, *a* Guadalupe Nettel. In fact, the narrator's mother, when she heard that her daughter was writing the book, took it as an autobiography, that is, as a text that presented itself as referring to real events: "Mom's already told me about your autobiography." After that he let out a kind of chuckle, adding, "Even though she hasn't read it, she says she'll take you to court for defamation" (166).[59] While one could argue that the author's mother is confusing the "novelistic pact" with the "autobiographical pact," the "narrator's following comments in *The Body Where I Was Born* would seem to give some validity to these concerns: "For the first time in over a year and a half, I sat down at the computer to write with gusto, determined to make this 'famous novel' a reality. I would finish it even if I was sued or whatever else. It would be a short and simple account. I wouldn't tell anything I didn't believe to be true" (166).[60] In fact, in interview after interview, Nettel stresses that her novel is close to her lived experience:

> I lived all those painful events as if they were a drama; and remembering them; reflecting on them; putting them on paper; and creating literature about them; was an opportunity to put order in mi mind and create distance from them. It was also a way to laugh and make fun of myself, of my obsessions, and of my family. I don't know how they are going to take it, but it was healthy and pleasurable (qtd. in Palapa Quijas).[61]

Thus Valeria Luiselli is not necessarily mistaken when she describes *The Body Where I Was Born* "as transparently autobiographical; or, perhaps more precisely, a long autobiographical essay."[62]

The Body Where I Was Born arguably belongs in a subgenre of autofiction in which authors attempt to come to grips with their parents or parental figures. This subgenre would include such works as Héctor Abad Faciolince's *El olvido que seremos* (*Oblivion: A Novel*) (2006), Patricio Pron's *El espíritu de mis padres sigue subiendo en la lluvia* (*My Father's Ghost Is Climbing in the Rain*) (2013), Renato Cisneros's *La distancia que nos separa* (*The Distance between Us*) (2015), and José Carlos Yrigoyen's *Orgullosamente solos* (Proudly Alone) (2016), among other works. However, while those autofictions center on the father or grandfather—and on their respective narrator's relationship with these figures—*The Body Where I Was Born*, perhaps reflecting the author's gender, highlights the protagonist's strained relationship with her mother, even while presenting a problematic view of her father and especially of her grandmother. Despite the obvious differences, then, it is tempting to see Nettel's interest in Kafka as at least partly responding to the family dynamics he presents in many of his works, including *The Metamorphosis*, and that are explicitly expressed in his famous "Letter to My Father."[63]

Kafka and *The Metamorphosis* are mentioned on only a couple of occasions in Nettel's novel. However, the sense of a hideous difference from family, friends, classmates, and every other human being present in Kafka's narrative underlies the narrator's existence. On wearing an eye patch, the novel notes:

> There were no other children at my school like me, but I did have classmates with other kinds of abnormalities. I remember a dwarf, a redheaded girl with a cleft lip, a boy with leukemia who left us before elementary school was over, and a very sweet girl who was a paralytic. Together we shared the certainty that we were not the same as the others and that we knew this life better than the horde of innocents who in their brief existence had yet to face any kind of misfortune. (9)[64]

A more direct connection with Gregor Samsa is created when, in response to her bad posture and eye problems, her mother "came up with a nickname, a term of endearment, which she claimed perfectly matched my way of walking" (11) So, "'Cucaracha!' she yelled every two to three hours. 'Stand up straight!' Or, 'Cucaracha, it's time for your atropine drops!'" (11).[65] Not surprisingly, "Guadalupe Nettel" develops an identification with insects and in particular cockroaches (in Spanish, *cucaracha*). After her friend Ximena commits suicide, "Guadalupe Nettel" begins having visions:

> I saw earthworms, beetles, and cockroaches. In my visions, the last in particular showed me friendliness, even kindness. Unlike other insects,

cockroaches didn't look at me with aggressive or challenging eyes, but the opposite; they seemed to be there to keep the other critters from coming to bother me. That's why, whenever I found one in my room, instead of the usual nervousness, a mysterious calm would come over me. (66)[66]

The basic idea of The Metamorphosis—the transformation of individual into insect, in this case a cockroach, the ultimate other—is a key to the text's description of the dynamics between mother and daughter.[67]

As she approaches adolescence, her already-existing dissatisfaction with her body is given an explicitly Kafkaesque turn.[68] Since she already saw herself as a cockroach, it is not surprising that she says: "I identified fully with the main character in The Metamorphosis, since what happened to him was something similar to what had happened to me. One morning, I too woke up with a different life, a different body, not knowing what it was I had turned into. Nowhere in the story does it say exactly what kind of insect Gregor Samsa was, but I quickly gathered it was a cockroach. He had turned into one; I was one by maternal decree, if not by birth" (81–82).[69] More surprising is this: "Reading The Metamorphosis was confusing. From the first pages, I couldn't tell if it was a misfortune or blessing what had happened to the character—who, as if it all wasn't enough, never displayed any sort of enthusiasm or drama. Like him, I too inspired some disgust in my classmates" (82).[70] This passage points to the conclusion of the "novel" where, as we saw, the narrator accepts her body, with all its flaws: "When all is said and done, it is the only thing that belongs to me and ties me to the world, and allows me to set myself apart" (174).[71] In other words, otherness, even if monstrous or painful, is ultimately what allows us to be individuals.

However, as mentioned earlier, the deepest sense of distance the narrator feels is from her mother, her father, and their social circle. Contradicting the usual narrative in which liberal or even radical children complain about their conservative parents, the narrator is critical of her parents' "progressive" social and sexual mores. She complains about her parents' belief in not lying to their children: "including the way babies are made, the uselessness of religion, and Santa Clause, in whom we were never allowed to believe. Living under these conditions stuck us at the margin of our society" (16)[72] In fact, this "progressiveness" led to the breakup of her family. In the novel, it caused her parents' separation: "Sexual freedom ended up hurting my family when my parents adopted a practice very much in fashion in the seventies: the then-famous "open relationship" (28).[73] In fact, the narrator acknowledges her difference from her parents in mores and morality: "It is said that the extremely conservative turn taken by the generation to which I belong is due largely in part to the emergence of AIDS; I am convinced that our attitude is very much a reaction to the highly experimental way our parents confronted adulthood" (22).[74]

In addition to the sense of distance from her body, the identification of "Guadalupe Nettel," the narrator, with Gregor Samsa is rooted in this sense of separation, of difference, of otherness, of alienation, not only from her classmates and contemporaries but also, and especially, from her mother, her father, and their generation. Kafka's importance to the real-life Guadalupe Nettel might be evidenced by her Twitter profile picture: a drawing of an insect with a human face with one eye visible and the other covered by hair.

CONCLUSION

This chapter has looked at some of the uses made by several key Latin American authors of one of the most important members of the modern Western canon: Franz Kafka. As we have seen, these authors—whose works were written from 1941 to 2011—provide a sample of how Latin American authors have found in Kafka a guide to interpreting and describing world, national, and personal realities. For Borges, Kafka provides a way to deal with such abstract topics as human isolation from the cosmos, and perhaps more urgently, the political dangers experienced by the world during the 1930s and 1940s. Piglia, on his part, found in the Czech master a way to connect the Argentine Dirty War with the horrors of European Nazism and, therefore, world history. Vargas Llosa uses *The Metamorphosis* to explore the fraught relationship between Hispanic and Indigenous Peru and the difficulties implicit in moving between cultures. Finally, Nettel finds in Kafka's best-known work a framework for understanding her sense of physical and personal alienation from her mother, family, and society in general.

None of the writers studied here betrays any sense of Kafka's foreignness or, for that matter, of their own foreignness. In fact, in the most widespread academic interpretation of the Czech master's work, Gilles Deleuze and Félix Guattari stress the distance between Kafka as a Bohemian and Jewish writer from the German-language mainstream:

> A minor literature doesn't come from a minor language; it is rather that which a minority constructs within a major language. But the first characteristic of minor literature in any case is that in it language is affected with a high coefficient of deterritorialization. In this sense, Kafka marks the impasse that bars access to writing for the Jews of Prague and turns their literature into something impossible—the impossibility of not writing, the impossibility of writing in German, the impossibility of writing otherwise. (16)

One must remember that Borges wrote his stories and most of his essays before Deleuze and Guattari proposed their interpretation of Kafka (in 1975); however, Piglia, Vargas Llosa—despite his antipathy toward most literary and critical theory—and Nettel could have read *Kafka: Toward a Minor Literature*.[75] While none of these authors refers to this interpretation of Kafka, each is writing within a larger Spanish-speaking world that could appear to be characterized by a dominant Peninsular literary language and tradition. In fact, the relationship between "the Matsigenka storyteller" and the "Western author" in *The Storyteller* might be seen as representing the relationship of minor and major writers. Notably, though, it is ultimately Vargas Llosa who is responsible for both narratives. He is therefore both "innovative" minor writer and major master.

There are some problems with the application of Deleuze and Guattari's concept of minority to Spanish-language Latin American literature. In particular during the 1980s, after the commercial and critical explosion of the Boom, which had in Vargas Llosa one of its protagonists, it was easy to see the difference between minor and major languages disappearing, at least in the case of the larger Hispanic countries and their authors. For instance, Nettel, the youngest of the authors studied here, "has not hesitated to pay homage to the movements that preceded her, recognizing especially the influence of Boom authors and their works in her own development as a writer" (Hecht 51). Moreover, many of the main contemporary Spanish writers—such as Javier Cercas or Enrique Vila-Matas—see in the "major" writers of Latin America, such as Borges, Vargas Llosa, García Márquez, and even the younger Piglia, masters from whom they developed and, on occasion, against whom they wrote. In fact, Cercas and Vila-Matas have been described by no less a figure than Bolaño as "first born of the Boom" ("Bolaño a la vuelta de la esquina").[76]

Be that as it may, Kafka, as all major Western writers—from the Greeks to Shakespeare and Cervantes to Zola and Flaubert to the great modernists and beyond—is part of the writerly arsenal that Latin American authors have felt free to use. Without necessarily renouncing their local cultural and literary traditions, for most Latin American writers, the Western canon, including Kafka, belongs to them.

5

Gabo's Canon

Gabriel García Márquez and the World Canon

ON DECEMBER 10, 1982, Gabriel García Márquez, known as "Gabo," entered the grand ballroom of the Konserthus, where, a few moments later, he would receive from King Carl Gustav XVI of Sweden the medal and parchment that designated him winner of the Nobel Prize in Literature. Surely, the highest consecration a writer can achieve, winning the Nobel was a moment of the greatest pomp and circumstance. Male awardees were dressed in white tie and tails, and women in the most elegant of evening gowns. But García Márquez had walked into the grand ballroom wearing a *liqui liqui*: an all-white long-sleeved shirt and pants, that according to biographer Gerald Martin, was "the closest thing when all is said and done to a recognizably Latin American lower-class uniform—with, oh horror, black boots" (434). In the grand scheme of things, including the grand scheme of García Márquez's life, his wearing a *liqui liqui* is a relatively minor event—after all, we remember the prize and his speech, "The Solitude of Latin America," rather than the clothes he wore. But his shunning of the tuxedo and donning of the *liqui liqui* was a conscious decision: "He had been talking about his *liquiliqui* since the day he heard the news. Sometimes he declared that it was to honour his grandfather the Colonel, sometimes, less modestly, that it was to honour his own most famous creation, Colonel Aureliano Buendía" (Martin 434). Martin even associates this local garb with Nicaragua's Augusto Sandino and, less believably, Cuba's José Martí (434).[1]

However, there was something appropriate—or something that could be interpreted as appropriate—about García Márquez donning a *liqui liqui* during the central ceremony of "our one global literary honor" (Deresiewicz). After all, according to the Nobel Prize Committee, García Márquez had been granted the award "for his novels and short stories, in which the fantastic and the realistic are combined in a richly composed world of imagination, reflecting a continent's life and conflicts" ("The Nobel Prize in Literature" 1982). By emphasizing the combination of "the fantastic and the realistic," this brief statement can be seen as a description of magical realism, the style that helped make *Cien años de soledad* (*One Hundred Years of Solitude*) (1967) a worldwide best seller and critical success. But, it also implies that in García Márquez's writing his "continent," that is, Latin America, was for the first time "reflected" in literature. This irruption of new literature and, by implication the region of the world it reflected, into the Eurocentric world republic of letters was represented, even allegorized, by García Márquez's intrusion in his *liqui liqui*—and black boots!—into an event characterized by a residual aristocratic etiquette at its most elaborate.

Philip Swanson has described the impact of *One Hundred Years of Solitude* as leading to García Márquez becoming "the voice of Colombian, Latin American, and even 'Third World' identity alongside with his identification with a new type of globally influential tropical, exotic, fantastic literature" (1). Not surprisingly, magical realism, this new type of "tropical literature," was imitated throughout the Global South and the Global North's South. As no less an authority than Homi Bhabha, whose theories of hybridity have long been used to understand the narrative of the Global South, argued in 1990, "'Magical Realism' after the Latin American Boom becomes the literary language of the emergent post-colonial world" (7). While Bhabha misreads the Boom—of the most celebrated members of the group, including Mario Vargas Llosa, Julio Cortázar, and Carlos Fuentes, only García Márquez can be considered a "magical realist"—he is correct when it comes to the impact of *One Hundred Years of Solitude* throughout the Global South. In fact, by the time García Márquez entered the grand ballroom of the Konserthus in his *liqui liqui*, this new "literary language" had been embraced by such major authors as future Nobel Prize winner Toni Morrison, whose magical realist masterwork *Song of Solomon* had come out in 1977, and the India-born British writer Salman Rushdie had published his Booker Prize–winning *Midnight's Children* (1981), a novel that would later also win both the twenty-five-year and forty-year "Booker of Bookers."

We can assume that many of these critics and writers would have sub-scribed to the Peruvian sociologist Aníbal Quijano's comment about García Márquez:

> For what by mode, if not the aesthetic-mythic, can an account be given of this simultaneity of all historical times in the same time? . . . Paradoxically, this strange way of revealing the untransferable identity of a history proves to be a kind of rationality, which makes the specificity of that universe intelligible. That is, in my opinion, what García Márquez does in *One Hundred Years of Solitude*. And that, without a doubt, is worth a Nobel Prize. (211)[2]

It may, then, surprise many of those who saw García Márquez in his *liqui liqui* as the representative of non-Western narrative, perhaps even non-Western ways of thinking, that his narrative was rooted on the creative appropriation of the canonical modernists of the first half of the twentieth century, in particular, Franz Kafka, James Joyce, Virginia Woolf, and William Faulkner. In other words, it is precisely the Western canon underlying García Márquez's innovations. This genealogy was also insinuated during the Nobel Prize ceremony: the music García Márquez selected to be played when he approached the King Carl Gustav XVI was not a *vallenato*, the music of the Colombian Caribbean, or a *cumbia*, the best-known Afro-Colombian rhythm, but Béla Bartók's *Intermezzo*, a modernist classic.

MAGICAL REALISM AS THE LITERATURE OF
THE GLOBAL SOUTH

As the Nobel Committee implied, and as García Márquez himself acknowledged in "The Solitude of Latin America," his innovative use of magical
realism, "in which the fantastic and realistic are combined," particularly
in *One Hundred Years of Solitude*, justified his winning of the Nobel Prize.
Even if he did not use the term *magical realism*, it is clear that, at least in
his speech, he saw it as a style capable of "reflecting a continent's life and
conflicts." There, he states on the relationship between his writing and the
reality depicted:

> A reality not of paper, but one that lives within us and determines each
> instant of our countless daily deaths, and that nourishes a source of insa-
> tiable creativity, full of sorrow and beauty, of which this roving and nos-
> talgic Colombian is but one cipher more, singled out by fortune. Poets
> and beggars, musicians and prophets, warriors and scoundrels, all crea-
> tures of that unbridled reality, we have had to ask but little of imagina-
> tion, for our crucial problem has been a lack of conventional means to
> render our lives believable.[3]

For García Márquez, earlier Latin American writers, no matter how gifted
or well known, had all failed in representing their cultures and societies,
because they used what he calls "conventional means" in their narrative.
As for the Nobel Prize committee, magical realism is, for García Márquez,
the means to render Colombian and Latin American "lives believable" not
only to local but, given the context of the speech, also to foreign readers.

As we have seen, major writers from throughout the Global South saw
themselves reflected in *One Hundred Years of Solitude*, in its depiction of
the "simultaneity of all historical times in the same time," to use Quijano's
phrase, as well as in its direct representation of a "Third World" reality.
Rushdie, for one, has noted the experience of recognizing his local reality
as he read García Márquez's masterpiece:

> I knew García Márquez's colonels and generals, or at least their Indian
> and Pakistani counterparts; his bishops were my mullahs; his market

streets were my bazaars. His world was mine, translated into Spanish. It's little wonder I fell in love with it—not for its magic (although, as a writer reared on the fabulous "wonder tales" of the East, that was appealing, too) but for its realism. ("Salman Rushdie on Gabriel García Márquez")

The Mozambican writer Mia Couto commented: "My sources have been fundamentally Latin American . . . Africa is full of Macondos, of towns like that, like Gabo's" ("Entrevista a Mia Couto, escritor y poeta mozam-biqueño").[4] For both Rushdie and Couto, Macondo, the town depicted in *One Hundred Years of Solitude,* was not an exotic and distant location, but a version of the worlds in which they had been raised.[5] Obviously, those who embraced the more "magical" side of magical realism, such as the Haitian American writer Edwidge Danticat, also found in the Colombian master a role model for their writing: "I am often surprised when people talk about the total implausibility of the events in García Márquez's fic-tion. Having been born and lived in a deeply spiritual and extraordinarily resourceful part of the Caribbean, a lot of what might seem magical to others often seems quite plausible to me" ("Gabriel García Márquez: An Appreciation"). For these writers, and for legions across the Global South, García Márquez's work was the first time their world was reflected in high literature. Similarly, for many critics throughout Europe and North Amer-ica, Latin America, and by extension the Global South, first became identifi-able as a distinct region in the world republic of letters in García Márquez's most characteristic works.

MAGIC, REALISM, AND COMBINED AND UNEVEN DEVELOPMENT

In the statements by Rushdie, Couto, and Danticat, there are two divergent arguments on the importance of magical realism as the literary and cultural logic of the Global South. On the one hand, for Rushdie and Couto, mag-ical realism is a technique used to reflect a social reality that has somehow resisted accurate representation by more traditional realist or, even, mod-ernist literary styles and techniques. As Couto noted, "All African writers have a debt with Latin American magical realism because in some way it motivated and authorized us to break with the European model" ("Entrevista a Mia Couto").[6] Obviously, this is not only the case of African writers. Rushdie is more explicit: "The trouble with the term 'magic realism' . . . is that when people say or hear it they are really hearing or saying only half of it, 'magic,' without paying attention to the other half, 'realism'" ("Salman Rushdie on Gabriel García Márquez"). We have already seen how Rushdie identified the colonels of *One Hundred Years of Solitude* with Pakistani and Indian counterparts; and Couto saw in García Márquez's Macondo a model for the representation of African village life. However, while Rushdie and Couto value García Márquez's magical realism for its ability to represent a reality that seems to exceed the bourgeois social and ideological parameters underlying realism, they do not necessarily imply a break with natural laws as characteristic of either Indian or African lives. For them, the magic is a literary device. However, others see in the depiction of magic the actual realist key of the style, because for them, as Danticat implies, the reality of the Caribbean and perhaps the Global South, exceeds that of Europe and North America.

While not stressing the supernatural, Julia Álvarez's *Yo!* has the eponymous character comment on Dominican society as intrinsically different from that of North America: "It's all one big story down here, anyway. The aunts all know that their husbands have mistresses but they act like they don't know. The president is blind but he pretends he can see. Stuff like that. It's like one of those Latin American novels that everyone thinks is magical realism in the States, but it's the way things really are down here" (197). In fact, García Márquez occasionally stressed the exceptionality of Latin America, often in more extreme terms than his Noble speech.[7] In an interview by Claudia Dreifus, the Nobel Prize winner agreed with Danticat: "The Latin American environment is marvelous. Particularly the Caribbean" ("Playboy Interview" 112). He proved this by telling the story of "a man in Aracataca who had the facility of deworming cows . . . by standing in front of the beasts" as an example of Latin America's marvelous reality (112).

Needless to say, these are mostly banal reasons and can ultimately be used as excuses for an uncritical celebration, or, for that matter, denigration, of the Global South. It's no accident that in 2013, García Márquez's native country took as its tourist slogan: "Colombia, realismo mágico."[8] Furthermore, by establishing an essential distinction between Global South and

Global North, the economic, social, and cultural logics that underlay the global system as a whole can easily be obscured. Finally, one can add that the corollary to the exceptionality of the South is the "normality" of the North, as if fascist or populistic politics, irrationality, and "magical" thinking were not the stuff of daily life in the United States and Europe. As Ignacio López-Calvo has accurately noted, "Ultimately, the postcolonial affirmation of non-Western thought as a form of resistance to hegemonic cultural impositions becomes simplified into a nostalgia for underdevelopment, superstition, and magic" (xxviii).

Given the above, it is no surprise that magical realism has never been hegemonic in Spanish-language Latin American letters. As we have noted, the other major Boom writers mostly composed works that cannot be classified as magical realist, such as Fuentes's *La muerte de Artemio Cruz* (*The Death of Artemio Cruz* 1962), Cortázar's *Rayuela* (*Hopscotch* 1963), or Vargas Llosa's *La ciudad y los perros* (*The Time of the Hero* 1963). And for the majority of contemporary Spanish-language Latin American writers, magical realism is anathema. Later magical realists, like Isabel Allende, Laura Esquivel, and even the more political Manuel Scorza, are often seen as authors of commercial literature rather than models for up-and-coming writers.[9]

LATIN AMERICAN LITERATURE AND GARCÍA MÁRQUEZ

One of the surprising aspects of García Márquez's Nobel Prize speech is that, of the three previous Latin American winners of the award, García Márquez refers only to Pablo Neruda (who won in 1971), describing him as "one of the outstanding poets of our time."[10] He did not mention the other two previous Latin American Nobel Prize in Literature winners at the time—the Chilean poet Gabriela Mistral (1945) and Guatemalan (proto-)magical realist Miguel Ángel Asturias (1967). Instead, García Márquez refers to Thomas Mann, even if he sounds somewhat critical of the "dreams of uniting a chaste north to a passionate south."[11] More importantly, he reminds his audience: "My master William Faulkner said, 'I decline to accept the end of man.'"[12]

The aesthetic distance between García Márquez and Mistral, a *postmodernista* poet whose apparent stress on maternal topics in her verse has led to simplified readings of her work,[13] and the personal distance between the Colombian and Guatemalan novelists,[14] might explain their absence from "The Solitude of Latin America." However, this lack of interest in earlier Latin American literature is a trait found throughout García Márquez's nonfiction writing. In fact, in his memoir *Vivir para contarla* (*Living to Tell the Tale* 2002), there are few references to novelists from the region, fewer to those of Spain, and none to authors from Brazil or Portugal.[15] An example of García Márquez's lack of interest in the narrative of the region is found near the beginning of his memoirs, where García Márquez returns with his mother to Aracataca, the town where he was born, and on which he would later model Macondo, where they run into the longtime local doctor. Informed that the young García Márquez wanted to become a novelist, the doctor asks: "Have you read *Doña Bárbara*?" The future novelist replied that he had read that novel and "almost everything else by Rómulo Gallegos," but he hid from the doctor the fact that because of "my fever of 104 degrees for the sagas of Mississippi, I was beginning to see the seams in our native novel" (32).[16] He describes the Venezuelan Gallegos, one of the best-known Spanish American novelists and then-perennial Nobel Prize candidate, as deficient in the craft of the novel.[17] Moreover, the inability to hide "the seams," something that any professional tailor or novelist should be able to do, is not a flaw he ascribes only to Gallegos; it is supposedly found in the "native"—in the Spanish original, *vernácula* (*Vivir para contarla* 35)—novel.

The meaning of the word *vernácula* in Spanish is quite close to that the first meaning of its English cognate. According to *Merriam-Webster's Dictionary*, *vernacular* is "a language or dialect native to a region or country rather than a literary, cultured, or foreign language," that is, "a nonstandard language or dialect of a place, region, or country," or "the normal spoken form of a language." Given this, one wonders whether by rejecting Gallegos's narrative and, more generally, the vernacular novel, García Márquez also rejects the Venezuelan and Colombian novel, the South American novel, and even the contemporary Spanish-language novel. When writing about his friends in the Barranquilla group of writers—Álvaro Cepeda, Germán Vargas, Alfonso Fuenmayor, and their mentor, the Catalan dramatist Ramon Vinyes—he describes them as "early admirers of Jorge Luis Borges, Julio Cortázar, Felisberto Hernández" (122).[18] However, during the time he is describing, the late 1940s and early 1950s, these Southern Cone writers were almost exclusively short-story writers: Borges never wrote novels; Cortázar would publish his first novel, *Los Premios* (*The Winners*), only in 1960; and Hernández had published his first novel in 1942, but García Márquez describes him as "the extraordinary Uruguayan storyteller" (387).[19] Curiously, the only Spanish-language novel García Márquez mentions is Arturo Barea's relatively little-known *La forja del rebelde* (*The Making of a Rebel*), "the first hopeful message from a remote Spain silenced by two wars" (122).[20] For the future Nobel Prize winner, with the exception of Borges, Cortázar, and Hernández, there were no literary gods or masters in the Spanish-speaking world. But immediately after García Márquez noted the influence of these Southern Cone short-story writers on the Barranquilla group, he adds that they were also admirers of "the English and North American novelists who were well translated by Victoria Ocampo's crew" (122).[21] If, on the one hand, he was critical of the Spanish-language novel, then on the other, he was an admirer of the Anglophone novel (in translation).

As the references to his Barranquilla group evidence, García Márquez's rejection of earlier Latin American narrative was characteristic of his generation, not an idiosyncratic gesture. Thus, the other (future) Nobel Prize winner of the Boom group, Mario Vargas Llosa, characterized the novel of Gallegos and other contemporaries as "primitive": "This tendency, initiated by the Peruvian Clorinda Matto de Turner, was given new impetus by the novel of the Mexican Revolution, and it achieved its highest expression with such writers as Mariano Azuela, Alcides Arguedas, Eustasio Rivera, Ricardo Güiraldes, Rómulo Gallegos, and Ciro Alegría . . . From a literary point of view, the primitive novel confused creation with information, art with artifice" (266). In contrast to García Márquez's identification with the Global South, Vargas Llosa has often been seen as a representative of Latin American Eurocentrism, but the embrace of the European and North American modernist novel is characteristic of most of the region's major writers of the 1960s.

GABO'S CANON

While García Márquez mentioned Thomas Mann in his speech "The Solitude of Latin America," the German author is not a major influence on his work.[22] However, the other novelist he named, Faulkner, was always at the core of his canon. In fact, in *Living to Tell the Tale*, there are several telling instances of the influence of Faulkner on his work. For example, when he recalls the Caribbean environments surrounding Aracataca, his native town, García Márquez notes: "Later, when I began to read Faulkner, the small towns in his novels seemed like ours, too. And it was not surprising, for they had been built under the messianic inspiration of the United Fruit Company and in the same provisional style of a temporary camp" (19–20).[23] If Couto saw Macondo in Africa, then García Márquez saw Yoknapatawpha in the Colombian Caribbean.

But the true importance of Faulkner's influence on García Márquez is literary, even if his original interest in the North American novelist was perhaps rooted in the social, racial, and material or physical analogies he found between the US South and Colombia, especially its Caribbean coast. According to *Living to Tell the Tale*, impacted by his visit to Aracataca, the young García Márquez decided to write his family story. However, before doing so, he began to reread Faulkner and Joyce: "Then I became aware that my adventure in reading *Ulysses* at the age of twenty, and later *The Sound and the Fury*, were premature audacities without a future, and I decided to reread them with a less biased eye. In effect, much of what had seemed pedantic or hermetic in Joyce and Faulkner was revealed to me then with a terrifying beauty and simplicity" (403).[24] Joyce is thus another of the central figures of the Modernist canon who influenced García Márquez deeply.

A third key modernist author also played a major role in García Márquez's literary development: Kafka. In fact, García Márquez's first story, "La tercera resignación" ("The Third Resignation") (1947), published when he was only eighteen, reads like a pastiche of Kafka. Despite this false start—or perhaps precisely because of it—Kafka was also a major influence on the mature García Márquez:

[It] determined a new direction for my life from its first line, which today is one of the great devices in world literature: "As Gregor Samsa awoke one morning from uneasy dreams he found himself transformed in his bed into a gigantic insect." These [and now he's again referring to Joyce and Faulkner in addition to Kafka] were mysterious books whose dangerous precipices were not only different from but often contrary to everything I had known until then. It was not necessary to demonstrate facts: it was enough for the author to have written something for it to be true, with no proof other than the power of his talent and the authority of his voice. (272)[25]

The device in question is magical realism, which here he describes as originating not only in his reading of Kafka but also in that of Joyce and Faulkner.

Virginia Woolf is a fourth major influence on the early García Márquez. Álvaro Cepeda, his fellow member of the Barranquilla group, introduced her work to the young Gabo, who on receiving a copy of the Spanish translation of *Mrs. Dalloway* proceeded to learn it by heart: "The recitations after meals ... were not poems of the Golden Age and Neruda's *Twenty Love Poems*, but paragraphs from *Mrs. Dalloway* and the ravings of its heartbreaking character, Septimus Warren Smith" (*Living to Tell the Tale* 339).[26] His passion for Woolf's masterpiece was such that he took the byline of Septimus for his early journalistic work.

The final major modernist influence on García Márquez was that of Ernest Hemingway. In a well-known essay from 1981, "Mi Hemingway personal" ("My Personal Hemingway"), García Márquez reminisces about the time he saw Hemingway in Paris in 1957:

My two greatest masters were the two North American novelists who seemed to have the least in common. I had read everything they had published so far, but not as complementary reading, but the exact opposite: as two different and almost mutually exclusive forms of conceiving of literature. One of them was William Faulkner ... The other was the ephemeral man who just said adios to me from the other side of the street, and had left me with the impression that something had happened in my life, and it had happened forever. (237)[27]

Given the few mentions made of Hemingway in *Living to Tell the Tale*, it would seem Hemingway was a minor influence during García Márquez's formative years, even if toward the end of his memoirs, when the Colombian novelist is trying to make a living selling books in the isolated town of Manaure, "The unexpected reading of Hemingway's *The Old Man and the*

Sea, which came as a surprise in the magazine *Life en Español*, completed my recovery from my sorrows" (459).[28] However, in 1950, as "Septimus," García Márquez had described Hemingway as "much lesser than Dos Passos, Steinbeck, and, of course, the most extraordinary and vital creator of the modern world, William Faulkner" ("Al otro lado del río entre los árboles" 289).[29] But when looking back at his career in 1981, just as he was about to receive the Nobel Prize, he described Hemingway with much greater enthusiasm.

It is tempting to also find social and cultural underpinnings, in addition to those purely technical or literary, for García Márquez's interest in these modernist authors. If García Márquez found in Faulkner a description of a world that in its inequality, racial hierarchization, premodern institutions, and even physical description, reminded him of the Colombian Caribbean, he could very well have found similar affinities between Colombia and the Ireland described by Joyce. As Vincent Cheng notes, "Joyce wrote insistently from the perspective of the colonial subject of an oppressive empire" (i). While Colombia had long been independent, it was still on the cultural, political, and economic periphery of the West. One could even describe the country's cultural and political subordination to the United States as neocolonial, a fact, evidenced culturally by the Anglophone tenor of Gabo's and the Barranquilla gang's canon, with the exception of Kafka.[30] Moreover, it is tempting to see not only Kafka, the privileged example of a "minor literature" for Deleuze and Guattari, but also Faulkner, as a (US) Southerner, and Joyce, as an Irish author, as exemplars of minor literature, defined as "that which a minority constructs within a major language" (Deleuze and Guattari 16). Something similar could be said about García Márquez, as a representative of Caribbean culture and language, writing in a country that has long prided itself in the purity of its Spanish, or regarding the contrast between his Caribbean Spanish and that of Bogotá, as well as that of Madrid.[31] One can also see in Woolf's writing an example of *écriture feminine*, which, though obviously different from the previous cases, also diverges from the writing of the male, urban, and white mainstream. Finally, it is significant that of all of Hemingway's novels, the one that had an early impact on García Márquez was set in Cuba, *The Old Man and the Sea*. However, with the partial exception of Faulkner, in García Márquez's *Living to Tell the Tale*, as well as in his early journalism, these modernist novelists are presented as important exclusively for their technical literary innovations rather than for the social and cultural contexts of their works.

In fact, in one of his early essays, "¿Problemas de la novela?," García Márquez notes:

> The novel, undoubtedly and fortunately influenced by Joyce, Faulkner or Virginia Woolf has not yet been written in Colombia. I say fortunately, because I don't believe that Colombians can now be an exception to the flow of influences. In her Prologue to *Orlando*, Virginia Woolf confesses her influences. Faulkner himself could not deny the influence that Joyce has had on him. . . . Franz Kafka and Proust roam free over the literature of the modern world. If we Colombians were to make the right decision, we would need to irremediably join this current. ("¿Problemas de la novela?" 269)[32]

Although, Proust is absent from *Living to Tell the Tale*, like all the authors presented by García Márquez as necessary influences, he is modern and a modernist. In fact, these modernist authors are presented as models for a new Colombian narrative to which the young García Márquez is clearly aching to contribute.

Not surprisingly, other members of the Boom share this concern with the modernization of the region's narrative. According to Vargas Llosa:

> Having discovered around this time the author of the saga of Yoknapatawpha County, which from the first novel of his that I read—*The Wild Palms*—left me so bedazzled that I still haven't recovered. He was the first writer whom I studied with paper and pencil in hand, taking notes so as not to get lost in his genealogical labyrinths and shifts of time and points of view, and also trying to unearth the secrets the baroque construction that each one of his stories was based on. (*A Fish in the Water* 280)[33]

As for García Márquez, the Peruvian novelist found in Faulkner an alternative to what, for them, was a staid, obsolete, and "primitive" Spanish-language Latin American narrative.

CONCLUSION: THE MAGICAL REALIST IMPERATIVE, TEMPORAL ACCELERATORS, AND THE REPUBLIC OF LETTERS

The success of *One Hundred Years of Solitude* led to the development of what Silvia Molloy has called "the magical realist imperative," that is, the expectation in the Global North that Latin American fiction conform to the narrative parameters established by García Márquez's masterpiece. As Molloy notes:

> With its exotic connotations, its potential for stereotypical casting, its "poetic" alienation into the realm of the "magical," that is the very far-away, the very other, magic realism has become, for the United States, a mode of Latin American representation, not a mode of Latin American production. As such—as representation, not as production—it is used to measure Latin American literary quality. It is used to both effect and confirm First World "discoveries" of undetected Latin American talent: readerly expectation (abetted by canny publishing strategies) explains, for example, the huge success of Isabel Allende outside Latin America, a phenomenon akin to the reception of Jerry Lewis in France. (375)

Molloy, who throughout the essay primarily targets US and, to a lesser degree, European academia for its flattening of the region's literature and complete marginalization of its intellectual production, also notes how magical realism has become the measuring stick by which "readerly expectations," in particular those of potential book buyers, determine the value of the region's narrative. The belligerence of later Spanish-language Latin American authors, such as Roberto Bolaño, toward magical realism can be seen as a reaction against this "magical realist imperative."[34]

But as Molloy insinuates, this magical realist imperative is not limited to Latin America; it is also applicable to the narrative of Global South as a whole.[35] As we have seen, writers from India, African countries, Latinx communities in the United States, and even African American authors have found in magical realism not only a mode for reflecting their realities, even an identity marker of their writing, but also, and equally important, the means to be understood by the critical and publishing establishment of the Europe and North America. López-Calvo notes: "In part thanks to magical realism, literary texts from culturally 'peripheral' regions of the world, from 'minor' languages and literatures, have finally been incorporated to the 'world of letters'" ("On Magical Realism as an International Phenomenon" xxvii).

It is possible, therefore, to see García Márquez as fulfilling in the late twentieth and early twenty-first centuries a role similar to that played by Faulkner and his narrative from the 1950s to the 1980s. As Pascale Casanova notes:

> Following his international consecration, Faulkner's work played the role of a "temporal accelerator" for a wide range of novelists of different periods, in countries structurally comparable, in economic and cultural terms, to the American South. All of them openly announced their use (at least in a technical sense) of this Faulknerian accelerator; among them were Juan Benet in 1950s Spain, Gabriel García Márquez in Colombia and Mario Vargas Llosa in Peru in the 1950s and 1960s, Kateb Yacine in 1960s Algeria, António Lobo-Antunes in 1970s Portugal, Édouard Glissant in the French Antilles of the 1980s, and so on. (77–78)

It is worth remembering that, while García Márquez mentioned three authors in his Nobel Prize speech, he designates only Faulkner as "my master." As we have seen, modernism, including Faulkner, was for García Márquez the measuring stick, the canon, by which he evaluated narrative. We must also keep in mind that critics and publishers from the capitals of the world republic of letters had also judged the works of writer from the Global South and other peripheries with a Faulknerian yardstick. According to Casanova, "The literary Greenwich meridian makes it possible to evaluate and recognize the quality of a work or, to the contrary, dismiss a work as an anachronism or to label it as 'provincial'" (90). However, following García Márquez's international consecration, one can speak about magical realism as a new temporal accelerator, even if one that primarily applies to the literature of the Global South and the South within the Global North. Paradoxically, the magical realist imperative is but another name for the canons, in the sense of standards of judgment, that make it possible for a work from the Global South not to seem provincial or anachronistic in Paris or—*pace* Casanova—New York, London, or Frankfurt.

One of the provincial capitals of this world republic of letters is surely Iowa City, designated by UNESCO a "City of Literature." In the introduction to one of the most disseminated manifestos rejecting magical realism by Spanish-language Latin American authors, "Presentación del país McOndo" (Introduction to McOndo Country, 1996), the Chileans Alberto Fuguet and Sergio Gómez describe the experience of three unnamed writers from the region at the International Writer's Workshop at the University of Iowa:

> Such is the Latin fever that the editor of a prestigious literary magazine hears that there are three Latin American writers loose on campus, only a few blocks away. The gentleman introduces himself to them and sets up a weekly literary lunch in the cafeteria by the river. His idea is to publish a special issue of his prestigious Magazine dedicated to this Latin explosion. (9)[36]

However, "the editor reads the Hispanic texts and two are discarded due to their disregard for the sacred code of magical realism. The editor stops any discussion by arguing that those texts 'could have been written in any country of the First World'" (10).[37] This unnamed editor is obviously upholding her republic's magical realist imperative.

The magical realist imperative that originated in the publication of García Márquez's *One Hundred Years of Solitude* and then its English translation that inspired writers throughout the Global South has also exerted its influence on the world literary canon. Not only is García Márquez included in the section "Contemporary World Literature" of the *Norton Anthology of World Literature*; several of his "disciples" are also to be found in this prestigious volume: Rushdie, Morrison, Mo Yan, Ben Okri, Leslie Marmon Silko, and Bessie Head. Moreover, of the only two post-Boom Latin American authors included in the anthology, one is García Márquez's follower Allende. The other is Bolaño, the latest Latin American author to have set up camp in the Western canon (in its meaning as list of books).

Given that the majority of contemporary authors from the Global South selected for the *Norton Anthology* are magical realists, the book serves as proof of the continued relevance of magical realism as the main narrative mode in world literature. However, the inclusion of Bolaño, who represents the rejection of magical realism by contemporary Spanish-language Latin American authors, is evidence of what may be a growing divide between the region's narrative and the rest of the Global South. Without denying the genius of García Márquez—and most critics of magical realism are still admirers of his works—the worldwide success of Bolaño could signal a growing opening to other modes of narrative production. Perhaps the magical realist temporal accelerator established when García Márquez wore his a *liqui liqui* is giving way to more pluralistic views on world literature.

6

Roberto Bolaño on/ in the Canon

ROBERTO BOLAÑO IS the great iconoclast of recent Latin American letters. In one of the reviews that best represents the rapturous response to the 2007 translation into English of the Chilean author's masterwork *Los detectives salvajes* (*The Savage Detectives* 1998), the Mexican critic Ilan Stavans, among the best-known mediators of the region's literature in US cultural circles, went out of his way to emphasize Bolaño's antiestablishment, if not subversive, bona fides. In a relatively brief text, he calls him "flamboyant, stylistically distinctive, counter-establishment voice," and "*escritor maldito*, the accursed writer, the ultimate pariah" ("Willing Outcast"). It's not surprising that earlier in the review, Stavans informs readers that "he also viciously attacked figures such as Isabel Allende and Octavio Paz." Yet one must note that criticizing Allende, as the author of best sellers, or Paz, for his embrace of liberal politics or his closeness to Mexico's ruling governments in the last decades of the twentieth century, has been a widespread sport among Spanish-speaking and Latin Americanist intelligentsia.

However, unmentioned by Stavans is that in Bolaño's interviews and essays, one finds disparaging opinions about much more generally admired authors, such as Diamela Eltit, a Chilean avant-gardist, or even, on occasion, no less a figure than Gabriel García Márquez.[1]

Bolaño's antiestablishmentarianism wasn't limited to his words or his fiction; it also supposedly characterized periods of his life. As Ignacio López-Calvo notes, many of the countercultural behaviors and actions associated with him, such as his supposed use of heroin or his visit with Roque Dalton, the Salvadoran writer murdered by his allegedly leftist comrades, respond to the "fact that Bolaño enjoyed creating his own myth by playing with fake identities and autobiographical traps that may trick his readers, critics, and biographers" ("On Roberto Bolaño" 22). That said, there is much in his life that gives credence to the image of the *poète maudite*. An autodidact—he did not graduate from high school—he was a founding member of the infrarealists, who, in López-Calvo's words, were "a marginal poetic movement that inspired many of the episodes in *Los detectives salvajes*. This bohemian group of provocateurs boycotted literary events by Octavio Paz, Carlos Monsiváis, and other iconic figures of the Mexican cultural establishment" (22). Their impact, more on the psychology of poets than on their literary production, is clearly expressed by Carmen Boullosa in her conversation with Bolaño:

> I liked the ceremonial nature of poetry readings and receptions, those absurd events full of rituals that I more or less adhered to, and you were the disrupters of these gatherings. Before my first poetry reading in Gandhi bookstore, way back in 1974, I prayed to God—not that I really believed in God, but I needed someone to call upon—and begged: Please, don't let the Infrarealists come. I was terrified to read in public, but the anxiety that arose from my shyness was nothing compared to the panic I felt at the thought that I'd be ridiculed: halfway through the reading, the Infras might burst in and call me an idiot.[2]

The shenanigans described in *The Savage Detectives*, such as when the visceral realists—the name given in the novel to the real-life infrarealists—plan to kidnap Octavio Paz, or their encounters with pimps and other criminals, are ultimately given verisimilitude by the reputation garnered by Bolaño and his confrères in Mexico. Bolaño, who was born in Chile, left Mexico for Spain in 1977, where he "lived the hard life of an economic migrant" (Birns and De Castro, 1), until he made a splash with the publication of his first major novels—*La literatura nazi en América* (*Nazi Literature in the Americas*) and *Estrella distante* (*Distant Star*) in 1996, and particularly the great success of *The Savage Detectives* in 1998. In life and in work, it seems that Bolaño rejected any and all establishments and still achieved success to boot.[3]

Given the above, it is perhaps not surprising that Bolaño's narrative has often been seen as subverting mainstream literary practices and norms. In fact, Benjamin Loy points out it is generally "characterized by a postmodern temporal perspective" (155), or even as "indelibly tinctured by the postmodern United States" (Birns, "Black Dawn" 186). It is a narrative that calls into question literature's traditional categories of center and periphery, canon, and author, among others (Loy 155, 158). For some, the proliferation of studies that make use of poststructuralist, postmodern, and post-everything theory to analyze his works is evidence of this rejection of categories and hierarchies that structure traditional views of literature.

But did Bolaño's antiestablishmentarianism extend to the canon?

BOLAÑO AND BLOOM

In most writing on Bolaño and the canon, generally based on his fiction, the Chilean writer is a disturber, if not debunker, of canonical considerations. Celina Manzoni, in a relatively early study of the topic, claims that "without any compunction [he] commits a mass expulsion from the Spanish-language literary canon" (351).[4] Héctor Hoyos argues that "Bolaño is an event that both exposes and unsettles canon formation itself" ("Roberto Bolaño, Solar Anus of World Literature"). Oswaldo Zavala consistently presents Bolaño as "overturning the verticalities imposed by the Western canon, but, at the same time, subjecting the modern Spanish American literary tradition to that same destabilizing impulse" (60).[5] Benjamin Loy concludes, "To Bolaño world literature cannot be written from the categories of the (academic) *canon* and the modern *original*" (164). Loy, who like Zavala, Hoyos, and many others, sees Bolaño as developing ideas and practices pioneered by Jorge Luis Borges, notes that against the Eurocentric canon and a world literature that privileges "unidirectional currents flowing from the center to the periphery, Borges and Bolaño propose a system of thought organized as network" (162). Given this lack of "compunction," it is not surprising that for some Bolaño is opposed to Bloom and other traditional views on the canon as a list of connected European and North American masterworks that impact contemporary writing.

Thus, Manzoni concludes—after noting that a passage in *Amulet* in which a character discerns the future canonicity of Vallejo, Borges, Kafka, Vachel Lindsay, Huidobro, and Alice Sheldon is a parodic intervention, "a canonical prophecy in which one hears the echo of the controversial reflection of . . . Harold Bloom" (335)—"it is closer to the absurd of Jorge Luis Borges's Chinese encyclopedia than to the scientific pretension of Bloom" (336).[6] Loy sees Bolaño as foreign to "Bloomian anxiety of influence" (163). Dunia Gras titles an article "Bolaño vs. Bloom: Una revisión del canon," though without ever referring to Bloom in the text. Despite this putative opposition, Bloom is absent in most of these essays. Only Manzoni includes in her bibliography a work by Bloom—*The Western Canon*—even though it is not explicitly quoted in her article, only serving as a supposed foil for Bolaño.

Contrasted with the absolute absence of any reference to Derrida, de Man, and most other poststructuralist thinkers,[7] it is a surprise that, as we have seen earlier in this study, Bolaño's favorite critic was precisely that bulwark of mainstream literary culture, Harold Bloom. For instance, in his interview with Eliseo Álvarez, he states: "For me, Harold Bloom is an example of a notable critic, although I am generally in disagreement with him and even enraged by him, but I like to read him." ("Positions Are Positions" 89).[8] In fact, Bloom himself noted that he maintained (an unfortunately unpublished) correspondence with Bolaño in which the Chilean author supposedly claimed to have been influenced by the scholar from New York.[9]

Moreover, Bloom even makes a brief and somewhat mysterious appearance in Bolaño's *2666* as part of a diagram, a variant of the semiotic rectangle, that, in addition to including the names of Vladimir Smirnov, a victim of the Stalinist repression, and the Stalinist Mikhail Suslov, as the two poles of the horizontal axis, has two vertical axes, with the first pole having Argentine philosopher of science and social democrat Mario Bunge opposed to Harold Bloom, and the second, the neoliberal thinker Jean François Revel facing neoconservative Allan Bloom.[10] However, of these names, only Harold Bloom is more than a one-off reference in his work. With this diagram, "Bolaño is linking his work to European, Western intellectual debates and dialogues, in which his work further participates" (Birns and De Castro 11). And among these debates are those regarding the canon.

Despite Bolaño's admiration for Bloom, his actual textual engagements with the latter's ideas are few. One of these is in a brief essay—perhaps recollection is the more accurate term—on Borges's *Obra poética*. In this text, dated between May 1999 and July 2001, Bolaño refers to Bloom's claim that "Pablo Neruda, more than any other poet . . . carries on Whitman's legacy" (199) ("el continuador por excelencia de la poesía de Whitman es Pablo Neruda" [186]). Bolaño adds:

> I think that Bloom is wrong, as he so often is, even as on many other subjects he's probably our continent's best literary critic. It's true that all American poets must—for better or for worse, sooner or later—face up to Whitman. Unfailingly, Neruda does so as the obedient son. Vallejo does so as the disobedient or prodigal son. Borges—and this is the source of his originality and his cool head—does so as a nephew, and not even a very close one, a nephew whose curiosity vacillates between the chilly interest of the entomologist and the stoical ardor of the lover. Nothing more alien to him than the quest to shock or to stir admiration. No one more indifferent to the vast masses of America on the march, although somewhere he wrote that what happens to one man happens to all men. ("The Book that Survives" 200)[11]

As was the case with Christopher Domínguez Michael,[12] Bolaño stresses the mistakes made by Bloom when reading Latin American literature—in this case the poetry of Neruda, Vallejo, and Borges—while at the same time acknowledging his admiration for the North American critic.[13] However, underlying his evaluation of these three authors, who, it must be noted, are almost unanimously seen as among the very greatest Spanish-language Latin American poets of the twentieth century, is a version of Bloom's most characteristic ideas. After all, *The Western Canon*'s chapter "Borges, Neruda, and Pessoa: Hispanic-Portuguese Whitman," makes the point that "it could be argued that Whitman's most vital influence has been upon Hispanic America: Borges, Neruda, Vallejo, and Paz" (476).[14]

What is original about Bolaño's take on these three poets—Borges, Neruda, and Vallejo—is that he actually shuffles their traditional descriptions and standings. Vallejo is among the most original of all modern poets; his *Trilce* (1922) is, as Michelle Clayton notes, "intransigently avant-garde" (16), whereas Borges is the most traditional of the three, especially his later work, as his blindness led him to favor conventional forms.[15] However, for Bolaño, it is Borges who deviates further from the standards of modern poetry as exemplified by Whitman while also being the most faithful to what is important about the US poet, perhaps to what makes the latter ultimately the standard of modernity: "And yet Borges's poetry is the most Whitmanian of all: Whitman's themes are always present in his verse, as are their counterarguments and rebuttals, the reverse and the obverse of history, the heads and tails of the amalgam that is America and whose success or failure is yet to be decided. But that isn't all he is, which is no small feat" (200).[16] Originality is the product of the assimilation of the tradition.

Beyond being an obvious borrowing from Piglia, and more indirectly, from Shklovsky,[17] what should also be evident is that the description of Borges as a nephew who both continues and deviates from the predecessor is nothing but a retelling of Bloom's belief that "great writing is always rewriting or revisionism and is founded upon a reading that clears space for the self, or that so works as to reopen old works to our fresh sufferings" (11).[18] For Bolaño, being a nephew, even more than a dutiful or even a rebellious son, is precisely the best way to be a "strong poet," as a nephew inherits family traits free from the Oedipal struggle that characterizes the relationship between father and son and therefore has greater potential to achieve a personal voice. Underlying Bolaño's innovation in reading the history of poetry—his image of the nephew and, presumably, also the niece, as truer continuance of a "father" poet than "his" children—is precisely a revision and correction of Harold Bloom (via Piglia and Shklovsky), one that, it must be noted, places Borges at the core of the region's poetic tradition.

ON CANONS AND THE CANON

While a brief perusal of Bolaño's criticism reveals a perhaps exaggerated leniency toward his contemporaries and especially friends—only he has been able to find "compassion" in Jaime Bayly's novels, written unapologetically and uncritically from the perspective of an upper-class *limeño*, even if gay[19]—his "canon," that is the authors he considers of importance and about whom he writes, is very conventional. Even as he recalibrates their canonical standing, Borges, Vallejo, and Neruda are all universally seen as among the region's master poets. His statements celebrating Nicanor Parra, whom Bolaño considered "the best living poet in the Spanish language" ("Fragments of a return" 72),[20] are part of a campaign in favor of a poet who was already part of the Chilean and Hispanophone canon.[21]

Thus, despite his extreme erudition, Bolaño's canon was, as he acknowledges in his interview with Boullosa, conventional:

> As to my idea of a canon, I don't know, it's like everyone else's—I'm almost embarrassed to tell you, it's so obvious: Francisco de Aldana, Jorge Manrique, Cervantes, the chroniclers of the Indies, Sor Juana Inés de la Cruz, Fray Servando Teresa de Mier, Pedro Henríquez Ureña, Rubén Darío, Alfonso Reyes, Borges, just to name a few and without going beyond the realm of the Spanish language. ("Roberto Bolaño by Carmen Boullosa")[22]

While the names mentioned here reflect the Mexican context of his beginnings as a reader and writer (the chroniclers of the Indies, Sor Juana, Fray Servando, Reyes, Henríquez Ureña) as well as his passion for poetry (only Cervantes, Fray Servando, and Henríquez Ureña are not primarily poets), none of them is completely outside the norm, as Bolaño admits. Pressed by Boullosa, Bolaño adds some non-Hispanic names: Pascal, de Sade, Fourier, Poe, "American literature of the 1880s, especially Twain and Melville, and the poetry of Whitman."[23] There is also Philip Dick, who is mentioned in other moments of the conversation. It is true that Fourier and Dick could seem to be outliers. Fourier is mostly a utopian social thinker, and Dick a science-fiction writer, generally outside the realm of high literature. However, in Dick's case, Bolaño may have simply been ahead of the curve: the author of *The Man in the High Castle* (1962) was included in the prestigious Library of America in 2008. Despite these and other wrinkles, this canon backs up the statement with which Bolaño concludes this part of the conversation: "Basically, I'm interested in Western literature, and I'm fairly familiar with all of it."[24]

Bolaño's testamentary speech "Sevilla me mata" ("Sevilla Kills Me") sheds light on his view of the region's literature, noting that "Borges is or should be at the center of our canon" (337).[25] Again, there is nothing original in this choice of Borges as the major writer of the Spanish-language Latin American tradition.[26] However, what is new about Bolaño is that he takes Borges's narrative and critical writings as a kind of starting point for his own work, not only in his fiction but also in his essays. As Zavala notes, "Bolaño's work must be read as the reappropriation and exhaustion of Borges's legacy within a continental modernity" (30–31).[27]

This Borgesian impact is explicit in the essay in which Bolaño deals with the "Western canon": "La traducción es un yunque" ("Translation Is an Anvil."). Its first paragraph notes the tensions and contradictions between specific linguistic canons and that of the West:

> What is it that makes an author, so beloved by those of us who speak Spanish, a figure of the second or third rank, if not an absolute unknown, among those who speak other languages? The case of Quevedo, as Borges reminds us, is perhaps the most flagrant. Why isn't Quevedo a living poet, by which I mean a poet worthy of being reread and reinterpreted and imitated in spheres outside of Spanish literature? Which leads directly to another question: Why do we ourselves consider Quevedo to be our greatest poet? Or why are Quevedo and Góngora our two greatest poets? (239)[28]

As we saw in an earlier chapter, Borges's answers call into question the validity of the "Western canon," even if he does not use that term. After all, Borges insists on Quevedo's greatness but notes that the worldwide popularity of an author depends on the presence of symbols—such as the white whale for Melville, or Cervantes's thin knight errant and obese squire—rather than necessarily on a work's intrinsic quality. Even if contradicted by his belief in the possibility of a translation equaling or even surpassing the achievements of the original—which would make it conceivable that the greatness of Quevedo could ultimately be rendered in other languages—Borges will evolve toward a personal, relativistic, sense of the classic and, therefore, the canon.

Bolaño's arguments take a different direction, even if still developing Borges's belief in absolute translatability. After noting that Sterne and Dickens owed much to Cervantes and that they read *Don Quixote* in English, Bolaño concludes:

> The wonderful thing—and yet also the natural thing, in this case—is that those translations of *Don Quixote*, good or not, were able to convey what, in the case of Quevedo or Góngora, wasn't conveyable and probably never will be: the quality that distinguishes an absolute masterpiece from an ordinary masterpiece, or, if such a thing exists, the quality that distinguishes a living literature, a literature that belongs to all mankind, from a literature that's only the heritage of a certain tribe or a part of a certain tribe. (240)[29]

To differentiate Quevedo from Cervantes, when it comes to their positions within the Spanish-language canon and that of the West as a totality, Bolaño distinguishes between "ordinary masterpieces," represented by Quevedo's works such as *El buscón*, and "absolute masterpieces," exemplified by *Don Quixote*.

For Bolaño, *Don Quixote* is an example of how, in the case of absolute masterpieces, their intrinsic quality is such that they are able to survive any and all translation. The fact that Sterne and Dickens read, learned from, and made use of *Don Quixote*, regardless of the actual quality of the translations available, is proof that Cervantes's novel is part of the Western and world canon, even if here Bolaño does not use that term as he does elsewhere. If for Borges, "No problem is as consubstantial to literature and its modest mystery as the one posed by translation" ("the Homeric Versions" 69),[30] in that, in a proto-deconstructive manner, it raises questions about originality and value; for Bolaño, translation becomes the core process by which value and originality are affirmed, and, in consequence, the Western canon is constituted:

How to recognize a work of art? How to separate it, even if just for a moment, from its critical apparatus, its exegetes, its tireless plagiarizers, its belittlers, its final lonely fate? Easy. Let it be translated. Let its translator be far from brilliant. Rip pages from it at random. Leave it lying in an attic. If after all of this a kid comes along and reads it, and after reading makes it his own, and is faithful to it (or unfaithful, whichever) and reinterprets it and accompanies it on its voyage to the edge, and both are enriched and the kid adds an ounce of value to its original value, then we have something before us, a machine or a book, capable of speaking to all human beings. (240)[31]

While Cervantes's novel has been able to visit all linguistic and cultural ports, Quevedo's works are stuck in those of the Spanish-speaking world. Thus, unlike Borges, who ends his discussions of the classics by noting (in "Sobre las clásicos") that their designation as such is ultimately arbitrary, Bolaño concludes by noting the necessary validity of classics and canon. It is a work's eminent translatability that proves it is an absolute masterpiece worthy of inclusion in the Western canon. Quevedo is not in the Western canon because his untranslatability proves his work is not worthy of inclusion, even if Spanish readers consider him (together with Góngora) as absolute masters. However, while Bolaño provides an answer as to why Quevedo is excluded from the Western canon, he does not really deal with another question posited at the start of the article: "Why do we ourselves consider Quevedo to be our greatest poet? Or why are Quevedo and Góngora our two greatest poets?" (239).[32]

Bolaño further discussed the question of what constitutes a masterpiece, more exactly, a classic, in his slightly earlier "Jonathan Swift": "Why does an author become a classic? Certainly not because he writes well; if that were the case, the world of literature would be overpopulated with classics" (179).[33] In other words, the status of classic is not the exclusive result of the literary "quality," at least as defined as writing well. The classic here seems analogous to the "absolute masterpiece," exemplified for Bolaño by *Don Quixote* and by Borges's works.

Perhaps even more so than the absence of contemporary "French theory," except as object of ridicule in his fiction,[34] the lack of any explicit reference to T. S. Eliot as a critic is one of the biggest surprises in Bolaño's writings.[35] However, in "Jonathan Swift" one finds a view of the relationship between a classic and the canon that reminds one of the ideas present in "Tradition and the Individual Talent"—even if the Anglo-British poet does not use either term as understood by the Chilean author:[36]

> A classic, as it is most commonly defined, is a writer or work that not only permits multiple readings but ventures into new territory and in some way enriches (that is, illuminates) the tree of literature and smooths the path for those who follow. A classic is the writer or work able to decode and reorder the canon. It is usually not a book that's considered required reading, at least from a small-minded perspective. And then "there are those classics whose main virtue, whose elegance and validity, is symbolized by the time bomb: a bomb that not only hurtles perilously through its age but is capable of flinging itself into the future. (179)[37]

Here Bolaño is repeating in the lingo of the late twentieth and early twenty-first centuries—*canon, decode, tree*—the idea already expressed by Eliot: "The existing monuments form an ideal order among themselves, which is modified by the introduction of the new (the really new) work of art among them" (526). Classics are precisely those works that "modify" this "ideal order." However, Bolaño adds a greater sense of dynamism to Eliot's model by noting the possibility of works capable of restructuring the canon in the future. *Don Quixote* is an easy example: seen as a work of entertainment during Cervantes's lifetime, it became a source of the modern novel afterward. In a shorter time frame, Borges published his stories in the 1940s but achieved world influence only in the 1960s.

OCTAVIO PAZ AND PABLO NERUDA

Bolaño's fiction, populated by poets and writers, can be read as a kind of commentary on Mexican, Latin American, and Hispanic letters: "*The Savage Detectives* is a novel about poets. In fact, it is an oral history about poets" (Birns and De Castro 13).[38] In relation to the surrealist connotations of "visceral realism" in *The Savage Detectives* and their real-life counterpart "infra-realism," Ricardo Gutiérrez-Mouat argues: "The rebellious connotation is important in Bolaño's adoption of the term, but in the Mexico of the 1970s, when surrealist politics had ceased to be relevant, the revolt was directed against the two great 'empires' of Latin American poetry in the 1970s, those of Octavio Paz and Pablo Neruda" (20).[39]

Regarding Paz, his reputation in Mexico was not only that of the country's premier poet, especially after the publication of *Libertad bajo palabra* in 1949,[40] but also that of the greatest critical interpreter of his country, in particular thanks to his foundational essay *El laberinto de la soledad* (*The Labyrinth of Solitude* 1950). It is thus not surprising that a group such as the "infrarealists" would rebel against a figure—writer, thinker, and even cultural arbiter—who occupied the central position in the Mexican cultural field. This rebellion, as we have seen, is thematized in Bolaño's novel.

The first mention of Paz in *The Savage Detectives* is in a diary entry by Juan García Madero, a would-be "visceral realist," near the beginning of the novel. (*The Savage Detectives* is composed of a number of different "textual" sources: diary entries and interviews). Unlike the real visceral realists, Ulises Lima and Arturo Belano (an alter ego for Bolaño who appears throughout his works), García Madero is a poet interested in form. While taking a workshop, García Madero asks the puzzled instructor about periphrasis, pentapody, nicharchean, and tetrastich, then adds: "The only Mexican poet who knows things like that by heart is Octavio Paz (our great enemy), the others are clueless, or at least that was what Ulises Lima told me minutes after I joined the visceral realists" (4).[41] Although Paz is here presented as "the enemy," in reality, this passage is indirectly praising the Mexican Nobel Prize winner. Deprecating the "visceral realists" and, through Belano, his younger self, Bolaño presents Paz as the only professional poet in Mexico.

This animosity toward Paz leads one of the "witnesses" who helps narrate the story, Luis Sebastián Rosado, an upper-class poet who becomes the lover of Luscious Skin, among the most marginal of the already-marginal "visceral realists," to imagine a "terrorist act," when informed that the group of poets had "something big in the works": "I saw the visceral realists getting ready to kidnap Octavio Paz, I saw them breaking into his house (poor Marie-José, all that broken china), I saw them emerging with Octavio Paz gagged and bound, carried shoulder-high or slung like a rug, I even saw them vanishing into the slums of Netzahualcóyotl in a dilapidated black Cadillac with Octavio Paz bouncing around in the trunk, but I recovered quickly" (155).[42] The kidnapping, however, never takes place, though it is reflective of the hatred the visceral realists claimed to feel toward Paz.

This animosity is buried toward the end of the novel. In another testimony in the novel, this one by Clara Cabeza, Paz's secretary, Paz goes to Parque Hundido, described as "a jungle swarming with thieves, rapists, drunks, and disreputable women" (474).[43] Paz visits Parque Hundido three times, during which he walks in circles, while Ulises Lima, then a middle-aged man, also walks in circles, but in the opposite direction. Paz recognizes Lima as a member of visceral realists, "a group of radical leftist lunatics [that] planned to kidnap me" (478).[44] During the third of these mysterious encounters, Cabeza approaches Lima, who identifies as "the visceral realist poet, none other than the second to last visceral realist poet left in Mexico" (490).[45] The depth of Paz's knowledge not only of poetic form but also of the history of Mexican poetry is evidenced by his response to Lima, as the latter joins him on the bench, Paz comments, "Visceral realist (as if the name was familiar to him), wasn't that Cesárea Tinajero's circle?" (490).[46] This is a scene of reconciliation:

> Thus the encounter is in the one sense the younger generation, now middle-aged, making up to the older generation for its earlier heedless and overweening rebellion. But it is also the older generation acknowledging the younger poets now fully in middle age, daunted, scathed, or disappeared—and acknowledging Ulises Lima, somebody so obscure that he would not be on any list of Mexican poets born since 1950 that Clara Cabeza could find. Don Octavio is making a gesture of preparation to them. The younger generation is repenting of its juvenile follies; but it is also the older generation saying, in effect, that they should have listened a bit more to the poets since 1950. The scene is all the more moving because Bolaño is so unsentimental a writer, so not prone to manipulate emotions. (Birns and De Castro 16)

While Cesárea Tinajero is presented as a mother figure, as the founder of the original "visceral realism" in the novel, and therefore part of Bolaño's attempt at creating an alternative and arguably feminist avant-garde trajectory for Mexican poetry, Paz's position in the actual history of poetry is ultimately reaffirmed throughout the novel. Moreover, although Tinajero's visceral realism is presented as a development of the real-life avant-garde *estridentismo*, both her and her movement are fictional. In the end, while the novel attempts to imagine alternate branches, fictional and real, in the tree of Mexican poetry, Paz remains a major figure. Instead of debunking the master, Bolaño ultimately vindicates him, even if with a touch of irony.

Neruda is also mentioned in *The Savage Detectives*. We already saw him named as one of the emperors of Mexican poetry together with Paz. In the novel, a young Belano cries when a Chilean theater director tells him, "Neruda was shit and that Nicanor Parra was the greatest poet in the Spanish language" (149).[47] (As we know, the mature Bolaño will become a great admirer of Parra). However, it is in the short story "Carnet de baile" ("Dance Card") that Bolaño develops his views on Neruda.

Published in 2001, in his short-story collection *Putas asesinas* (*Last Evenings on Earth*),[48] "Carnet de baile" ("Dance Card") is an apparently autobiographical narrative divided into sixty-nine entries reminiscent of Bible verses. While framed by the unnamed narrator's evolving relationship with Neruda's poetry, this story also describes a thinly fictionalized version of Bolaño's personal relationship with Chile and its culture, literature, and politics: in addition to retelling in greater detail "his" falling out with the theater director over Neruda's poetry, here identified as the Chilean filmmaker and writer "Alejandro Jodorovski" (usually spelled Jodorowsky), it includes versions of his often told visit to his native country in 1973 to "build socialism"; his jailing after Neruda's death, and his subsequent escape thanks to "detectives," who were his former schoolmates.

Limiting ourselves to the Neruda frame used by the story, "Dance Card" begins by acknowledging that the narrator's mother read Neruda's poetry to him as a child—"A single book, *Veinte poemas de amor y una canción desesperada* (*Twenty Love Poems and a Song of Despair*), Editorial Losada, Buenos Aires, 1961" (210).[49] This volume appears to be one few souvenirs the narrator, identified with Bolaño, inherited from his mother. (Bolaño's mother's name, María Victoria Ávalos Flores, is used in the story). But despite this sentimental beginning, the story narrates the narrator's growing disillusionment with Neruda's poetry. Later in life, his sister returns to Mexico from Spain and gives him his mother's copy of Neruda's poetry collection: "By that stage I didn't like Neruda anymore. Especially not *Veinte poemas de amor!*" (210).[50] The story thus details a history of reading Neruda, in particular, the latter's most popular poetry collection, which goes from childhood admiration to mature disdain. However, these brief comments on *Twenty Love Poems* take up about one page of the story, which continues to narrate "Bolaño's" relationship with Chile but returns time and again to Neruda.

Perhaps the key return of Neruda is in the following passage in which "Bolaño" narrates a series of hallucinations he once had. He first sees Hitler, but:

> 49. After two weeks, Hitler disappeared, and I was expecting him to be replaced by Stalin. But Stalin didn't show. 50. It was Neruda who next took up residence in my corridor. Not for two weeks, like Hitler, but three days—the shorter stay seemed to indicate that my depression was easing. 51. Neruda, however, made noises (Hitler had been as quiet as a block of drifting ice); he complained, murmuring incomprehensible words; his hands reached out as his lungs absorbed the air (the air of that cold European corridor) with relish. The pained gestures and beggarlike manner of the first night changed progressively, so that in the end the ghost seemed to have reconstituted himself as a grave and dignified courtier poet. 52. On the third and final night, as he was going past my door, he stopped and looked at me (Hitler had never done that) and, this is the strangest part, he tried to speak but could not, expressed his impotence with gestures and finally, before disappearing with the first light of dawn, smiled at me (as if to say that communication is impossible, but one should still make an attempt?). (217)[51]

"Bolaño's" vision is itself framed by brief stories of the torture of Chilean women militants, of the life of the little-known Belgian poet Sophie Podolski, all linked by their suicides, and of the homeless French poet Germain Nouveau. In "Dance Card," Bolaño characteristically links the poetic vocation with that of revolutionary politics, and political martyrdom with the sufferings of the artist. However, Neruda is not presented as a political or poetic martyr. Instead, the story espouses a liberal version of the horseshoe theory, or a definition of totalitarianism, in which the extreme Right, represented by Hitler, was to be followed by the equally expected figure of Stalin. However, in Bolaño's vision, in place of the communist leader, Hitler is followed by Neruda. As María Luisa Fischer notes, "Belano-Bolaño places the hallucinatory Neruda in the midst of the dilemma of the twentieth century, that of fascism and its fierce Stalinist counterpart, which is imbricated with that which is being experienced in the flesh by members of his generation."[52] After portraying in a pathetic and absurd light, the Abraham Lincoln brigades—"little old men climbing down from the buses, brandishing their fists" (238)[53]—Bolaño goes on to list by name writers he sees as victims (mostly) of the Left: "I think of Beltrán Morales, I think of Roberto Lira, I think of Mario Santiago, I think of Reinaldo Arenas. I think of poets who died under torture, who died of AIDS, or overdosed, all those who believed in a Latin American paradise and died in a Latin American hell. I think of their works, which may, perhaps, show the Left a way out of the pit of shame and futility" (218).[54] In this list Bolaño lumps together Morales (1945–1986), a Nicaraguan poet who sympathized with the Sandinista Revolution, suffered from mental problems, and died prematurely of a heart attack; Lira (1949–1981), a Chilean poet with schizophrenia who committed suicide in 1981; the infrarealist Mario Santiago Papasquiaro (*né* José Alfredo Zendejas Pineda, 1953–1998), an alcoholic and drug user who died after being run over by a car; and Arenas (1943–1990), the Cuban exile novelist who died of AIDS. In other words, these are, for him, the victims of Hitler and Neruda/Stalin, even if without exception they were not killed directly or indirectly by the Sandinistas Revolution, the Cuban government, or even the Chilean military dictatorship.

While it is difficult to imagine a more negative description than being a stand-in for Stalin, a gesture that finds some justification in Neruda's membership and support for the Communist Party during the Russian dictator's heyday, as well his political poetry, especially his "Ode to Stalin," "Dance Card" ends with an ambiguous vindication of the author of *Twenty Love Poems*, even if not necessarily that specific poetry collection:

66. Do we have to come back to Neruda as we do to the Cross, on bleeding knees, with punctured lungs and eyes full of tears? 67. When our names

no longer mean a thing, his will go on shining, his will go on soaring over an imaginary domain called Chilean Literature. 68. By then all poets will live in artistic communities called jails or asylums. 69. Our imaginary home, the home we share. (219)[55]

Is this a dystopian view of a future in which literature will have been banned? Is it the end product of the Hitler-Stalin duo represented in literature by Neruda? Whatever it is, Neruda's position in the canon is presented as unshakable. However, unlike the recuperation of Paz found in *The Savage Detectives*, which concludes in an ironic embrace of Paz by the visceral realists, and therefore Bolaño, that of Neruda is ultimately mired in contradiction: the Chilean Nobel Prize winner's unshakable canonicity is also a sign, perhaps even cause, of this unavoidable dystopia. Needless to say, the fact that Paz ended up as an anticommunist liberal while Neruda died a committed communist is also reflected in the different ways in which their works and figures are recuperated by Bolaño.

CONCLUSION

Like Borges and García Márquez, Bolaño's critical work consists of brief essays and reviews, even though the totality of his nonfiction work is substantial. *A la intemperie*, Bolaño's collected critical writings, is a book of 480 pages. However, the fragmentary and day-to-day nature of much of his criticism is one of the reasons it has been mostly marginalized from discussions of the Chilean novelist and has hindered any attempt at discerning in his work a coherent theory of the interrelationship between linguistic and cultural traditions and canons, and literature more generally. Moreover, Bolaño's passion for tweaking the cultural establishment, for the shocking *boutade*, as in his contradictory statements regarding the Boom masters, also makes it difficult to pinpoint his true opinions.[56]

That said, critics have correctly noted that Bolaño's "writing questions the cartographies formulated by the self-designated 'western center'" (Loy 158). However, it does so not by the disappearance of spatial frameworks or, for that matter, canonical considerations. For instance, Vopi's description of the Chilean novelist as "the last Latin American writer" ("el último escritor latinoamericano") ("Bolaño, epidemia" 191) is a sign of how his intellectual sources, the networks of writers from whom he learned and against whom he struggled, were primarily Latin American. However, he is also a Chilean writer, in particular in his novels *Distant Star* and *By Night in Chile*, even if his vision of what constitutes "Chileanness" is completely devoid of nationalist distortions—evidenced by his endorsement of Parra's poetic joke that "Chile's four great poets / are three: / Alonso de Ercilla and Rubén Darío" (qtd. in "Literature and Exile" 43).[57]

Likewise, one finds Bolaño resorting to the idea of a pan-American or hemispheric cultural identity, which had gained relevance during the antifascist and later anticommunist 1940s and 1950s, only to be dismissed during the revolutionary 1960s,[58] and was reinvented in the 1990s as a result of the impact of US mass and high culture. This sense of a Pan-American identity is seen in his description of himself as an "American" writer and of Twain and Melville as necessary sources for all such writers. Moreover, one can add that despite Volpi's claims that Bolaño "despised or envied" ("despreciaba o envidiaba") Spanish writers ("Bolaño, epidemia" 192), in his works there is a sense of a Hispanic identity, as the Peninsula and its culture are also spaces within which his characters, imagination, and intelligence moved; this is evidenced not only in his fiction, often set in Spain, but also in his essays on Spanish writers, such as his friends Enrique Vila-Matas and Javier Cercas in *Between Parentheses*, his critical Aleph.

Additionally, when looking at his fiction and essays there is a world cultural "cartography" that, as Loy and others noted, rejects conventional versions based on the model of center and periphery. For him, as for other thinkers of the 1990s and early twenty-first century, the world was flat.[59]

At the same time, his vision of the classic and the canon is fully compatible with more traditional hierarchies of literature as based on quality. If his master Borges—for whom issues of canon raised a number of paradoxes, such as the exclusion of Quevedo from the world canon—ended up embracing a relativistic notion of the classic as based on the decisions of the community of readers, as evidenced in his essay "Sobre los clásicos," Bolaño, throughout his writings, upholds a Western canon composed of "absolute masterpieces," even if his view of literature is more inclusive than that of the European and North American mainstream.

7

Indigenous Writers and the West

I, RIGOBERTA MENCHÚ: An Indian Woman in Guatemala (*Me llamo Rigoberta Menchú y así me nació la conciencia*) (1983), the mistitled English translation of the moving *testimonio* of the Quiché Maya indigenous activist and 1992 Nobel Peace Prize awardee Rigoberta Menchú Tum, has been the subject of enormous critical debate. For some, the inclusion of Menchú's *testimonio*, and *testimonio* in general, in the (university) classroom implied the democratization of the canon.[1] As Georg Gugelberger put it, "It is the genre that reflected homelessness and poverty and suddenly found an institutional home in the expanded canon" (11). Others, including right-wing pundit Dinesh D'Souza, claimed that the inclusion of *I, Rigoberta Menchú* in the curriculum implied the replacement of core Western classics by a work that does not represent "the zenith of Third World achievements but rather caters to the ideological proclivities of American activists" (74). These were, obviously, political discussions couched in aesthetic terms.

Subsequently, the debates went beyond questions of quality or even representation and democratization, but without losing their political substratum. While *I, Rigoberta Menchú* narrates in grueling detail the violence against Menchú's activist family by the Guatemalan military and paramilitary forces, as well as her personal and communal story of activism and personal growth, some key details of the text have been called into question. In fact, the anthropologist David Stoll claimed that Menchú's *testimonio* "is not reliable in certain important ways" (277) and therefore distorted the history of Guatemalan anti-indigenous violence and the resistance of the Quiché and the Maya in general.[2] Others, like Greg Grandin, have argued that beyond understandable mistakes or lapses, history has "confirmed Menchú's account of the causes of the Guatemalan repression" ("Rigoberta Menchú Vindicated"). There is no denying the importance of Menchú's activism—which includes the creation of *I, Rigoberta Menchú*—in bringing to the world's attention the genocide that the Guatemalan military had unleashed on its country's indigenous population and in bringing it to an end.[3] However, for the purposes of this admittedly brief and unavoidably superficial look at (two) key indigenous narratives, these important debates are of background importance.

Menchú's text (edited by Elizabeth Burgos-Debray) was arguably the main catalyst generating enthusiasm for *testimonio* among US and European critics during the 1980s and 1990s.[4] At the time, *I, Rigoberta Menchú* seemed to signal a major cultural shift in Spanish-language Latin American letters. Instead of the modernist narrative produced in the "lettered city" by writers such as Jorge Luis Borges or the Boom novelists (Gabriel García Márquez, Mario Vargas Llosa, Carlos Fuentes, and Julio Cortázar), *testimonio* promised for what seemed like the first time to bring to Latin American and world readers the voices of indigenous (and other) subaltern groups.

Testimonio as a genre has been notoriously difficult to define—it sometimes overlaps with literary genres, such as bildungsroman, autobiography, memoir, and autofiction, and with more journalistic ones, such as reportage and interview. For our purposes, however, we can delimit the genre to its most basic and characteristic format, represented by several of the best-known *testimonios*—such as *I, Rigoberta Menchú*, *Biografía de un cimarrón* (*Biography of a Runaway Slave*, Miguel Montejo and Miguel Barnet 1966), or *Si me permiten hablar* (*Let Me Speak! Testimony of Domitila, a Woman of the Bolivian Mines*, Domitila B. de Chungara and Moema Viezzer 1977)—while acknowledging that there are many texts considered *testimonios* that were produced differently.

For these particular texts, the definition provided by Ulises Zevallos is relevant. According to the Peruvian scholar, the *testimonio* is a genre in which "an unlettered narrator . . . tells her life, full of vicissitudes . . . to an interlocutor (promotor) . . . who transcribes it" ("un narrador iletrado . . . cuenta en primera persona su vida llena de vicisitudes . . . a un interlocutor (gestor) . . . que la transcribe") (211). Moreover, as we have seen, *testimonios* are sometimes considered representative not only of the narrator's experiences but also of those of the whole community. As Menchú famously noted in *I, Rigoberta Menchú*, she narrated "the story of all poor Guatemalans" (1) ("Mi situación personal engloba toda la realidad de un pueblo" [21]).[5] Even if mediated by an interlocutor or interviewer who ultimately edits the transcription and oversees the text's publication, the subaltern voices of *testimonios* were seen as disrupting the Eurocentrism of the world republic of letters and even the Western canon. Today, these debates—including the hopes and fears of proponents and opponents of *testimonio*—belong to the past. In fact, rather than becoming a dominant genre in the region's literature, *testimonio* has mostly faded, even as it has influenced the passion for the real of much later Spanish-language Latin American fiction, perhaps, including the rise of autofiction.[6]

The declension of the genre is partly due to the political evolution of the region and the world since 1983. *Testimonio* arguably represented the textual swan song of Central America's struggle for social change. The Nicaraguan Sandinista Revolution, the Civil War in El Salvador, and the genocide in Guatemala—and the mobilization against it—provided the context for the rapturous reception and, to a degree, the production of *I, Rigoberta Menchú* and other *testimonios*. With the demise of real socialism and the diminution of violent social tensions in the region, *testimonio* seemed to lose its reason for being, even if, instead of socialism or even true democracy, the end result of the social struggles of the 1980s and 1990s was the establishment of corrupt neoliberal pseudo-democracies throughout much of Central America.

But the decline of the testimonial genre is also the result of more posi-tive trends. It is true that at least since the seventeenth century, with Felipe Guamán Poma de Ayala, the author of the *Nueva crónica y buen gobierno* (New Chronicle and Good Government, 1615), there have been indigenous authors who mastered the craft of Western writing, but with the welcome fact that literacy has increased among the region's indigenous population, the need for interlocutors has mostly disappeared. In fact, we are living in the midst of a boom in literatures written by indigenous authors, often in autochthonous languages.[7] However, in the end, while *testimonio* helped expand the Latin American canon, as well as other canons, and helped pro-mote a greater receptivity to texts that challenged conventional notions of literariness, it did not lead to the full democratization of the literatures of the region or beyond.

In this last chapter, in addition to looking at *I, Rigoberta Menchú*, we also briefly analyze *Memorias de un soldado desconocido* (*When Rains Became Floods: A Child's Soldier's Story*) (2012), Lurgio Gavilán's book of memoirs. The text details Gavilán's incredible life that led him from peasant child in the Peruvian Andes to child combatant for the Shining Path, soldier, priest, husband, anthropologist, and professor at the Universidad Nacional San Cristóbal de Huamanga (Ayacucho) (though the narrative ends before he becomes an academic). *When Rains Became Floods* has been acclaimed by such disparate figures as John Beverley and Mario Vargas Llosa. Beverley declared it as "the most interesting work of literature to have come out of Latin America since *2666*" (*The Failure of Latin America* 108); Vargas Llosa describes it as "a human document that is read as if under a trance due to the terrible experience it communicates, its evident sincerity, and moral purity" ("El soldado desconocido").[8] Moreover, if *I, Rigoberta Menchú* was composed during the Central American revolutionary upheavals of the 1980s, and reacts against the brutality of the genocide against the Maya while expressing the lingering utopian aspirations of the times, *When Rains Became Floods* was written after the fall of socialism in 1989 and the defeat of the last, most violent of the region's revolutionary movements: the Shining Path (1992).[9] Without denying the cultural differences between the Maya Quiché and Andean cultural contexts, as well as the distinct historical and social evolution of Guatemala and Peru, the two texts represent some of the key changes that have taken place from the 1980s to the present in the region in general, and among indigenous intellectuals.

When Rains Became Floods is also the text in which the trajectory of the *testimonio* as a genre ends. After all, unlike *I, Rigoberta Menchú*, organized and edited by the anthropologist Elizabeth Burgos-Debray, who in legal terms was, at least at first, seen as the "author" of the text, in the case of *When Rains Became Floods*, which had its "rough draft" as a sort of *testimonio* assisted by Yerko Castro Neira, Gavilán's anthropology professor at the Colegio de México, the "narrator" subsequently took control of the text.[10] Thus, the evolution of the *testimonio* goes from narrations generated by illiterate interviewees in the first examples,[11] to those who are literate, such as Menchú, but unable to write a book at the time, to those who, like Gavilán, are able to take control of their own story and ultimately break free from the genre. In fact, since *When Rains Became Floods* was published, Gavilán has become one of the most important Peruvian—and Indigenous-Peruvian— authors, with a second autobiographical narrative, *Carta al teniente Shogun* (Letter to Lieutenant Shógun) (2019). His career is thus part of a movement in Latin American letters characterized by Indigenous authors who have mastered the art of literary writing and, in the case of Gavilán, other disciplines. In fact, Gavilán is an example of an indigenous author infiltrating the lettered city and helping change it.

MENCHÚ'S SECRETS

As critics have noted, a peculiarity of Menchú's *testimonio* is that, on the one hand, it presents an enormous amount of personal and cultural information, while on the other hand, it repeatedly stresses the need to keep secrets— that is, information that is acknowledged to exist but cannot be shared. Doris Sommer, who has studied this aspect of Menchú's text in detail, asks:

> How then are we to take Rigoberta's protestations of silence as she continues to talk? Are there really many secrets that she is not divulging, in which case her restraint would be true and real? Or is she performing a kind of rhetorical, fictional, seduction in which she lets the fringe of a hidden text show in order to tease us into thinking that the fabric must

be extraordinarily complicated and beautiful, even though there may not
be much more than fringe to show? (34)

As should be obvious, Sommer is here identifying in Menchú's text a
tension à la de Man between referential and figurative readings of these
"secrets."

But as Sommer also notes, the "secrets" are also connected directly to
Maya culture, its difference from, even opposition to, that of the West: "It
is the degree of our foreignness, our cultural difference that would make
her secrets incomprehensible to the outsider" (34). It is, therefore, worth
looking at some of the specific moments when Menchú withholds information from the reader and trying to discern what meaning—if any—these
instances of "secrecy" hold for our understanding of the relationship
between indigenous and Latin American, and ultimately, world cultures.

The first mention of a "secret" is from an epigraph from the *Popol Vuh*,
the eighteenth-century retelling in Western script of the Maya creation
myths and stories: "Learn to protect ourselves by keeping our secret" (7).[12]
Obviously, the text of *I, Rigoberta Menchú*—which means Burgos-Debray,
who is responsible for this and other epigraphs—[13] presents Menchú's
story as part of a history of cultural struggle that goes back to the conquest.
After all, who do the Maya need to protect themselves from but the Spaniards and their cultural and political descendants the Ladino (Hispanic)
Guatemalans?

But what is this secret about? A partial though somewhat enigmatic
answer appears on the same page, now in Menchú's words: "All this has
meant that we keep a lot of things to ourselves and the community doesn't
like us telling its secrets. This applies to all our customs" (7).[14] Most of the
cases provided by Menchú deal with Quiché religious syncretism. A key
example of these secrets is found after her discussion of the *nahual*—a
"protective spirit" "usually an animal" (18) ("como su sombra" "casi siempre es un animal el nahual" [39]), Menchú then notes:

We Indians have always hidden our identity and kept our secrets to ourselves. This is why we are discriminated against. We often find it hard to
talk about ourselves because we know we must hide so much in order to

preserve our Indian culture and prevent it from being taken away from
us. So I can only tell you very general things about the nahual. I can't tell
you what my nahual is because that is one of our secrets. (20)[15]

Since according to the passage, anti-indigenous bias has as its root the Maya
refusal to abandon their distinct identity and customs, assimilation would
lead to less difficult, even less dangerous, lives for the Quiché. However,
for Menchú, the preservation of Maya Quiché culture is worth paying the
price of experiencing discrimination.

In other passages, Menchú's secrets seem to indicate the preservation
of a distinct and mostly forgotten historical experience:

> It's also when they remind them that our ancestors were dishonoured
> by the white man, by colonization. But they don't tell them the way that
> it's written down in books, because the majority of Indians can't read
> or write, and don't even know that they have their own texts. No, they
> learn it through oral recommendations, the way it has been handed down
> through the generations. They are told that the Spaniards dishonoured
> our ancestors' finest sons, and the most humble of them. And it is to hon-
> our these humble people that we must keep our secrets. (13)[16]

What she is describing here is not the destruction of a generation of
Maya during the conquest, or the brutality of colonization, and not even
the destruction of Maya (pre-Columbian) culture, but rather a mysterious "dishonoring." (This may be a mistranslation, as in the Spanish original, Menchú literally refers to "rape": "nuestros antepasados fueron violados por medio de los blancos y la colonia" ["our ancestors were raped by
means of the whites and the colony"] (34). Given the unidiomatic Spanish
Menchú uses in this passage, it is not clear whether she is referring to the
rape of Maya women, one of the abuses committed by the conquistadors,
or to what the translator vaguely calls "dishonoring." Moreover, Menchú
writes about *hijos*, sons, being raped. But does this "rape" refer to cultural
humiliation or exploitation, as the reference to the colony might imply?
Despite these obscurities, what matters is that Menchú is pointing to a historical tradition distinct from that of other Guatemalans. Even if Menchú

is not responsible for the epigraphs from the *Popol Vuh*, the view of history present in the text is compatible with one that sees the conquest as a breaking point in history. Rather than one national community, Menchú's text implies a Maya Quiché community and traditions that are distinct from, even opposed to, those that characterize the rest of Guatemala. Moreover, this distinctiveness, even antagonism, goes back to the conquest. After all, if the conquest is seen as the beginning of most Hispanic American societies, even while the brutality of the conquistadors is acknowledged, what is founded here is Maya Quiché resistance rather than the national community. The memory of this "dishonoring" is a secret that must be kept and passed on; and by doing so, it becomes the basis for cultural resistance.

Zevallos has complained about the privileging of *I, Rigoberta Menchú* in the study of *testimonio*:

> When studying the relationship between *lettered* individuals and the subaltern, *I, Rigoberta Menchú* is always taken as the object of study, leading to conclusions that are not applicable to many Latin American *testimonios*. On the one hand, *I, Rigoberta Menchú* is the result of interviews that took place during a short period of time (eight days) and in the native language (Spanish) and location (Paris) of Elizabeth Burgos, the interviewer. On the other hand, the cultural, economic, and social differences existing between Elizabeth Burgos and Rigoberta Menchú lead the interviewee to keep the secrets of her indigenous culture when speaking with the interviewer. (213)[17]

However, even if the cultural and social distance between Burgos—at the time married to Régis Debray, a major figure in French political and intellectual life—and Menchú was much greater than is the norm between the interviewer and interviewee, it is an extreme case of the difference that always exists between interlocutor and narrator, rather than a contradiction. After all, the reason behind *testimonio* as a genre is the limited access to literacy and mastery of letters of whole social groups.

David Damrosch has noted that despite the cultural distinctiveness of the world described and defended by Menchú, there is one element that is clearly Western. Damrosch points out: "Burgos chose epigraphs for each chapter, taken chiefly from three sources: statements by Menchú herself;

passages from Asturias's novels depicting native culture; and quotations from the *Popol Vuh*, the classic Mayan story of creation and early history. This is, however, a text that Menchú herself never mentions and seems never to have seen" (244). Thus, Burgos's framing of Menchú's narrative ultimately contradicts the Quiché activist's life: she apparently has not read, or simply does not mention, the *Popol Vuh* (or, for that matter, Asturias's novels or stories). Instead, "The sacred text that she does refer to, frequently, is the Bible—naturally enough, as she was raised as a devout Christian, and like her father she became a catechist, instructing children in Catholic doctrine and leading Bible study groups in her village" (244). The Bible, through the lens of liberation theology, is the one Western canonical book that Menchú is clearly familiar with, and it informs much of her text and life. Moreover, her life as an activist led her to establish contacts with other Guatemalans, as well as international figures, including Burgos-Debray, arguably contradicting the call for separation one finds in *I, Rigoberta Menchú*.

WHEN RAINS BECAME FLOODS

While a thorough analysis of Lurgio Gavilán's important text and its political context is beyond the scope of this chapter, *When Rains Became Floods* is representative of some of the cultural shifts between 1983, when *I, Rigoberta Menchú* was composed, and 2012, when Gavilán's autobiographical text was published. In a curious coincidence, Gavilán's narrative begins in 1983, the year when Gavilán, only twelve years old, decides to join the Shining Path insurgency to be close to his brother, a guerrilla fighter: "There was nothing to do but to climb the Shining Path's ark or join the village militias (rondas campesinas)" (4).[18] Despite the violence that characterized both the Shining Path and the military, according to Gavilán, *When Rains Became Floods* "is not a history of violence, but rather a series of stories about ordinary life, devoid of theatrics and party politics"(2).[19] He does, however, present, in a characteristic laconic manner, representative moments of violence. Among these: he participates in the hanging of a young militant, punished for having fallen in love with a policeman; once in the army base, he becomes cognizant of numerous crimes, including mass murders and disappearances.

The book avoids any in-depth discussion of the self-proclaimed Maoist ideas of the Shining Path or, for that matter, the ideological justification for the violence of the military reaction. Gavilán, however, compares the Shining Path to "good rain . . . [that] gave us hope for life, for social justice" that became a destructive "flood" (4).[20] As this example illustrates, despite the overall austerity of his writing, Gavilán has a great ability to find images that make the reader understand his experiences and their social and political context. For instance, when describing the hunger and poverty experienced by him and other Shining Path militants, he notes: "Even as destitute as we were, we continued to believe in our Chairman Gonzalo [Abimael Guzmán, the leader of the Shining Path], who might appear in a helicopter at any moment and do away with the soldiers" (33).[21] In this manner Gavilán succinctly indicates the quasi-religious cult of personality that characterized the Shining Path. As Arturo Arias has noted specifically regarding *I, Rigoberta Menchú*, "The testimonio of the 1980s also implied the logic of collective political action" (87). It can be seen, in fact, as the last gasp of the revolutionary hopes that began in the 1959 with the triumph of the Cuban Revolution. Rather than faith in "collective political action," *When Rains Became Floods* evinces a quasi-magical cult of personality among the Shining Path. Moreover, as we know, the Shining Path is shown to be unworthy of leading any "collective political action" and is rightfully defeated. Political hope is ultimately absent from *When Rains Became Floods*.

In fact, we might see the omission of any discussion of the ideological components of the Shining Path or the military repression—or for that matter, most acts of violence in which Gavilán, as militia member and soldier must have been involved—as the equivalent of Menchú's secrets, but I would argue otherwise. After all, Menchú's secrets are predicated on cultural difference, resistance, and the impossibility (or undesirability) of intercultural communication. Even though Gavilán's lacunae and laconism can be secrets, they can also imply a common cultural knowledge shared by narrator and reader, and between author and reader. Gavilán assumes that the Peruvian reader is, to greater or lesser degree, cognizant about Quechua culture, even if not a Quechua speaker or without a home in the Andes. Even more obviously, Gavilán is aware that his readers are knowledgeable of the key traits of the Shining Path and the brutal history of insurrection and repression in the Peruvian Andes during the 1980s. The presence of cultural connections, no matter how weak, are what makes it possible for *When Rains Became Floods* to work as a post-*testimonio*.

Perhaps the best example of this expected shared commonality—though not identity—between narrator and reader is in the actual literary references Gavilán makes in his narrative. For instance, he mentions Vargas Llosa, though curiously not any of his fiction, but the report on the massacre of journalists in 1983 written by a commission the novelist headed.[22] He also mentions other authors generally included in the Peruvian canon, such as José María Arguedas, the greatest of the novelists who depicted Indigenous life. First in a mistranslated passage, Gavilán notes: "Peru is a multicultural and diverse nation with many bloods, as Arguedas insisted, an amalgam of cultures with a discriminatory idiosyncrasy. When have we ever been one Peru, a united country?" (2, translation adjusted).[23] Another allusion to Arguedas is found in the narration of Gavilán's return to Ayacucho in 2007 that concludes the story: "Brave bulls were being pulled along by ropes tied to their horns, just as the recruits had been pulled along from 1950 to 1960 'to serve the nation' or as Misitu was dragged into the ring for the Yawar fiesta" (90).[24] This is a reference to Arguedas's novel *Yawar Fiesta* (1941), which describes an Andean bullfight with a bull named Misitu. Another major Peruvian *indigenista* novelist, Ciro Alegría, is mentioned in the original Spanish text (but omitted from the English translation), in reference to the hunger Gavilán experiences while a Shining Path fighter: "I dreamed of great quantities of food: potato, yucca, rice, like the times when I ate sitting beside my mother. But when I woke up, all I could hear was my stomach growling. And we looked at one another like those squalid dogs in Ciro Alegría's story, but the party was there, always watching" (31, translation adjusted 31).[25] (Gavilán is referring to Alegría's 1939 novel *Los perros hambrientos* [The Hungry Dogs]). The poet César Vallejo is mentioned, together with St. Francis of Assisi (one of Gavilán's several lives was as a member of the Franciscans): "I am left with the words of Saint Francis of Assisi: 'Brothers, let us begin, we have done little or nothing,' or with the universal poet César Vallejo's judgment: 'sadly, humans . . . brothers there is much to be done'" (3).[26] Little known outside Peru, Alejandro Romualdo's poem—"Canto coral a Túpac Amaru, que es libertad" (Coral

Song to Túpac Amaru, who is freedom)—about the great indigenous leader who led a mass-scale revolt in the late eighteenth century, is referenced as one of the texts the young Gavilán learned at the military camp school (42–43). Finally, although he is not primarily a creative writer, José Carlos Mariátegui is also quoted when Gavilán cavils the purpose of his narrative: "What could it possibly be good for? Now I simply prefer— as José Carlos Mariátegui said—that the work speak for itself" (1).[27] While these references include authors outside the Western canon—though obviously, Saint Francis, Vargas Llosa, and Vallejo are canonical in different ways—they are all names a Peruvian reader would easily identify. In fact, one could argue that Gavilán is trying to create within his text a unified Peru that includes former Shining Path members, the military, and readers.

Orin Starn, who wrote the introduction for the English-language edition of *When Rains Became Floods*, notes about Gavilán: "He lists Franz Kafka and José Saramago among his literary inspirations" (xxi). Perhaps unsurprisingly, one finds in his articles, such as "Reflexiones del soldado desconocido" ("Reflections of the Unknown Soldier") references to Kafka, as well as in this case Bourdieu and Foucault.[28] As befits an aware writer and trained anthropologist, the Western canon is one of his cultural resources.

However, one also finds throughout *When Rains Became Floods* Indigenous cultural intertexts. Scattered throughout are the lyrics of songs—Shining Path chants, soldier songs, Franciscan hymns, military ones—some translated from Quechua, some originally in Spanish, most clearly imprinted by Andean culture. In this, and in other aspects, one finds in *When Rains Became Floods* parallels with Arguedas's writings, an author Gavilán obviously knows well, though the similarities also reflect both author's deep engagement with Quechua and, more generally, Andean orality. What Rama says about Arguedas, even if within a more modest scope, is applicable to Gavilán; like his great predecessor, when including songs, "He wanted the reader to hear the song as he heard it" (*Writing across Cultures* 172; "Quiere que el lector oiga, como él [el narrador], la canción" [*Transculturación narrativa* 283]). Probably following in the footsteps of Arguedas, Quechua oral genres are incorporated into fabric of his text.

We also find the deep imprint of Quechua language in Gavilán's prose. John Beverley describes the book as "beautifully written in Spanish (Gavilán learned Spanish during his period in the army camps), but a Spanish modified—suavizado or softened, we might say—by Quechua. (The great Peruvian novelist José María Arguedas, who was also partly from a Quechua-speaking background, achieved a similar effect in his writing)" (116–17). The North American scholar also notes that "the text would not be as it is without the deep experience of Quechua culture and language, of peasant and subproletarian life" (121). If by incorporating references to Peruvian classics—Vallejo, Arguedas, Romualdo, Mariátegui—Gavilán is implicitly writing within a national culture, his Spanish "softened" by Quechua, then his transcription of Andean song and his naturalized description of indigenous practices, foods, and urban and rural environments move this national culture toward that of the Andes.

The second edition of *Memorias de un soldado desconocido* includes a new epilogue titled "Los cabitos" ("The Little Corporals") that presents the testimonios of other *senderista* children who were taken up by the army and lived in the military camp under the protection of its officers. According to Beverley, in this section "Gavilán has himself become an intellectual mediator through whom 'stories'—otherwise completely unregistered—of the subaltern can appear" (121). In other words, Gavilán has gone from subject interviewed to interlocutor, to *gestor*.

Another reading, however, is possible of the epilogue and Gavilán's inclusion of other *testimonios,* so to speak. Gavilán begins by noting: "Ever since I began writing the manuscript I thought of them. We were children and teenagers who had been captured or rescued from the files of the Shining Path, we lived in the barracks, and we were called the 'little corporals': pioneers—together with the soldiers and officials—in the fight for the pacification of the Peruvian state, despite our youth" (*Memorias de un soldado desconocido.*)[29] Rather than the cultural distance between, say, the cosmopolitan Burgos-Debray, a member of the French cultural and political elite, and the Indigenous Menchú, we have a sense of commonality between Gavilán and the other "corporals." In fact, one could very well see in this need to bring in other voices, to compare and contrast one's life story, an echo of the testimonio's original goals: "*Testimonio* was never meant to be autobiography or a sworn testimony in the juridical sense, but rather a collective, communal account of a person's life. This is what

Menchú implies when she says, 'This is my testimony. I didn't learn it from a book and I didn't learn it alone . . . My personal experience is the reality of a whole people'" (Arias 87). In fact, this sense of a collective identity is characteristic not only of *testimonio* but particularly of Indigenous *testimonio*. Thus, Gavilán's consideration of other stories and their incorporation into his stories, rather than characterizing him as an interlocutor presents him as seeking to complement and correct his story by including those of his fellow *cabitos*. Even if these stories are not as extraordinary as his personal story—few life stories are—the epilogue represents the assumption of a collective voice in his text. The epilogue can thus be seen as qualifying the individualistic thrust that some have identified in Gavilán's text. For instance, Zevallos has noted "the insistence on the individual's decision-making explains Vargas Llosa's interest [in *When Rains Became Floods*]. The Peruvian writer [Vargas Llosa] has been the great proponent of neoliberalism and promotes the value of the self-made individual as the solution to social problems" (233).[30]

The original ending of this *post*-testimonio, in which a grown-up Gavilán returns to Ayacucho in 2007, also problematizes the celebration of neoliberalism that characterizes Vargas Llosa and much of Peru's politics and culture:

> I roamed these places in 1983. People were talkative and kind back then. Now they seem indifferent. They look you up and down as if you are an enemy, some strange creature. They don't trust anyone. They are as poor as they were then. Economically, nothing has changed for them. They still plant their root vegetables, their peas, and their corn. If the Peruvian Communist Party's promises had come true— that everyone would be equal, that no one would be rich or poor, that we would all have the same opportunities without egotism or man's exploitation of man, or if the state was interested in the peasants, in their agriculture, in educating their children as they always say in the presidential campaigns— surely these men would no longer be scraping through these fields just to survive, as I have scraped through my life in order to tell this story. (97)[31]

As Zevallos notes, "Neither of the parties [Shining Path and government] has fulfilled its promises. Little has changed and scarcity continues in the provinces. The only thing that has changed is the attitude of the people" (234).[32] This ending also belies the promises of *the other path* of neoliberalism. After more than twenty years of neoliberal policies, poverty continues to be the same. However, it is subjectively worse, since the solidarity that characterized Andean life before the uprising of the Shining Path is gone, destroyed by the distrust generated by the violence, as well as by the now hegemonic individualistic ethos.

Writing about this passage, Beverley has noted: "In the same way as the peasants (from whom he is descended), Gavilán says he "scratches" on/ in the episodes of his own life ("he arañado en mi vida") to produce his story. And the writing of that story—an auto-graphia—is also an act of scratching, inscribing a surface with a pen or tool or a finger stroke" (119). Regarding the original end of *When Rains Became Floods*, Beverley argues that "Gavilán . . . suggests in this final scene of his memoir a kind of writing in the soil, akin to the labor of plowing and cultivating." (119). Beverley deduces from Gavilán's text: "The emphasis on being unknown, *desconocido*, in the Spanish-language title of Gavilán's book, has the effect of marking the narrator as a subaltern voice that appears at the margin of literature and high culture, and that as such is almost unintelligible" (119).

But a different interpretation of Gavilán's work is possible. By presenting his writing as part of a cultural continuity with Indigenous agricultural practices, Gavilán is asserting that intellectual pursuits are consistent with his Andean background. Therefore, Gavilán is an example of what Sara Castro-Klarén has designated as the bicultural colonial subject, one who has mastered both Western and Andean cultures: "The bi-cultural colonial subject is a capable subject precisely because he can move from one side to the other, keep them apart, bring them together, cross over, set them side by side in dialogue, struggle for complementarity and reciprocity, or simply keep them at a distance depending on the play of the given moment" (156). While Castro-Klarén lists the mestizo historian Inca Garcilaso de la Vega (sixteenth century), the Indigenous historian Felipe Guamán Poma (seventeenth century), the scholar and activist José Carlos Mariátegui (early twentieth century), and the novelist José María Arguedas (twentieth century) as exemplars of this bicultural subject, we can also add Lurgio Gavilán to this extraordinary list.

While it would be a mistake to see any ethical or intellectual evolution—
or, for that matter, opposition, between Menchú and Gavilán, it is clear
that there is a growth of intellectual possibility and ambition, even as the
options for political and ideological change have been significantly narrowed.
Despite everything, Gavilán's work signals the development of Peruvian
culture in an ever more multicultural direction, as his "secrets," if we can
call them that, are ultimately known by the majority of his readers. While
I, Rigoberta Menchú was ultimately a successful political intervention, helping to bring about peace in Guatemala, no matter how limited, Gavilán's
text at best presents an intervention in the realm of culture and memory.
Politically, it is limited to stating his dissatisfaction with the world as it is.
Nevertheless, in his biculturality, in his mastery of both Andean indigenous and Western cultures, Gavilán's text reactivates the promise found in
all these authors from the Andes, and beyond, of going beyond the limita-
tions of Western rationality and its canon.

EPILOGUE

WRITING AFTER THE eclipse of the Pink Tide in the region, John Beverley notes about Latin America's position that "precisely in its failure carries the possibility of another form of modernity that points beyond the logic and current ubiquity of market capitalism" (139). For the US American scholar, the failure of Latin American countries to become modern neoliberal capitalist states opens the door to the development of civilizational alternatives. Be that as it may, throughout this book I have looked at how Spanish-language Latin American authors have related to "Western civilization," as befits their craft, as represented in the Western literary canon. After all, if Latin America is truly a distinct civilization somehow opposed to that of the West and the US—whether, as Samuel Huntington believed, due to its intrinsic barbarity that poses a "challenge" to US culture and institutions, or according to Beverley, based on its potential anticapitalism—it would be evidenced in the practice and theory of major Spanish American authors. However, from Borges, to García Márquez, to Bolaño, to Piglia, to Vargas Llosa, to Gavilán, and perhaps to Menchú (with her use of progressive Catholicism), Western culture is a resource they used to create their works. The fact is that Latin American culture has grown and developed in a permanent dialogue with that of Europe and, more recently, its North American offspring.

This doesn't imply the denial of local difference—another book could have been written celebrating Borges's use of the gauchesque, García

Márquez as a Caribbean writer, and so on. Neither does it imply a denial of the need to create a more inclusive culture within Spanish America, as evidenced textually in Gavilán's work. Nor does it deny that languages and cultures remain hierarchically stratified. On this inequality, note, for example, the percentages of book published in the US that are translations compared to those in Spain, Mexico, or Argentina.[1] Latin American authors may be able to use the classics of Western culture as resources, but it is less likely that US or French authors will make use of the Latin American classics.

Instead, underlying the relationship between Latin America and the West is this, as filmmaker Bong Joon-Ho notes: "We all live in the same country now: of capitalism." This is a country originally Western but now universal. Therefore, the urgent response to the apocalyptic political, social, and environmental problems capitalism has raised must be developed not only by "Latin America" but also by what used to be called the exploited and oppressed of the world as a whole.

NOTES

INTRODUCTION

1. "Creo que nuestra tradición es toda la cultura occidental, y creo también que tenemos derecho a esta tradición, mayor que el que pueden tener los habitantes de una u otra nación occidental" (Borges "El escritor argentino y la tradición" 272).

2. "Todavía no se ha escrito en Colombia la novela que esté indudable y afortunadamente influida por Joyce, por Faulkner o por Virginia Woolf. Y he dicho 'afortunadamente', porque no creo que podríamos los colombianos ser, por el momento, una excepción al juego de las influencias" (García Márquez, "¿Problemas de la novela?" 213).

3. "En fin, me interesa y creo que conozco un poco toda la literatura occidental" (Bolaño, "Carmen Boullosa entrevista a Roberto Bolaño" 110).

4. Mariano Siskind makes a related point in *Cosmopolitan Desires: Global Modernity and World Literature in Latin America* (2014): "I believe . . . that one should read the differential affirmation of a cosmopolitan and disruptive aesthetic identity not in terms of a particularistic cultural politics but as a strategic literary practice that forces its way into the realm of universality, denouncing both the hegemonic structures of Eurocentric forms of exclusion and nationalistic patterns of self-marginalization" (6).

5. "Debemos pensar que nuestro patrimonio es el universo; ensayar todos los temas, y no podemos concretarnos a lo argentino para ser argentinos: porque o ser argentino es una fatalidad y en ese caso lo seremos de cualquier modo, o ser argentino es

una mera afectación, una máscara"
(Borges, "El escritor argentino y la
tradición" 273–74).

6. Borges wrote several reviews on
    Tagore. The best known is his 1937
    review "Rabindranath Tagore, *Col-
    lected Poems and Plays*," included in
    Selected Non-Fiction (180–81).

7. For instance, the noted historian
    Greg Grandin argues: "After Barack
    Obama's 2012 re-election, many con-
    servatives came to realize that nei-
    ther appeals to cultural wedge is-
    sues nor promises of immigration
    reform would necessarily help the
    Republican Party when it came to
    Latino voters. Latino voters are not
    loyal to Democrats because of the
    promise of immigration reform, the
    National Review's Heather MacDon-
    ald wrote, but because they value 'a
    more generous safety net, strong
    government intervention in the
    economy, and progressive taxation'"
    (281). Grandin is correct that most
    Latinx voters choose Democratic
    candidates, but there is significant,
    recalcitrant support for Republi-
    cans, even for Trump, whose poli-
    cies and discourse are anti-Latino.
    According to a *Washington Post* ar-
    ticle, in 2020 Trump improved his
    numbers among Hispanic voters,
    not only in Florida, where he re-
    ceived 47 percent of the vote, but
    also in Texas, where he improved
    from 34 percent to 41 percent of the
    vote ("How Independents, Latino
    Voters, and Catholics Shifted from
    2016 and Swung States for Biden and
    Trump," *Washingtonpost.com* 12 Nov.
    2020, Alcantara et al.).

CHAPTER 1

1. The translated title is different from
    the original. In English, a standard
    is "a musical composition (such as
    a song) that has become a part of
    the standard repertoire" (accord-
    ing to *Merriam-Webster Dictionary*).
    According to Gioia, "most [stan-
    dards] had been composed before I
    was born . . . Some of the tunes came
    from Broadway . . . Others made
    their debut in movies . . . A few . . .
    originated far away from jazz's land
    of origin . . . And, of course, many
    were written by jazz musicians them-
    selves" (xiv). Even though the vast
    majority of these songs belong to
    the pre-rock era, they all "serve as
    sources of inspiration for great jazz
    performances" (xiv). It is precisely
    those great performances that argu-
    ably constitute a true jazz canon. In
    other words," Although George Ger-
    shwin's "Summertime" is one of
    Gioia's standards, it is not part of the
    jazz canon, but Billie Holiday's ver-
    sion (1936), Louis Armstrong's and
    Ella Fitzgerald's collaboration (1957),
    or Miles Davis's instrumental rendi-
    tion (1966) are potential candidates
    for inclusion. (All are among Gioia's
    "Recommended Versions" [413]). It
    is the performance rather than the
    "standard" played that truly matters.

2. While a standard can be a measuring
    stick—and so a canon, in its original
    Greek meaning—in jazz, standards

are simply those songs frequently played by musicians. That said, the popularity of a song among musicians often corresponds to its quality. There are exceptions to the association of standards with works of quality, though. For instance, the novelty song "Tiger Rag" was a standard during the early years of jazz. Gioia writes about the song's fall from grace in modern jazz: "For later leading-edge jazz performers—whether beboppers or hard-boppers, cool players or soul jazz exponents, free or fusion advocates—'Tiger Rag' has held little appeal" (436).

3. "Catálogo de autores u obras de un género de la literatura o el pensamiento tenidos por modélicos" (Catalog of authors or works considered as models in a genre of literature or thought). While widely used in literary studies, the word *canon* in the Bloomian sense of a catalog of masterworks is less well known outside this field.

4. The *Diccionario de la lengua española* defines *clásico*: "Dicho de un autor o de una obra: Que se tiene por modelo digno de imitación en cualquier arte o ciencia" ("Said of an author or work: Is held as a model worthy of imitation in any art or science"; the same definition was already present in the 1992 edition).

5. According to Josep Massot, in his interview with Anagrama founder Jorge Herralde: "Few publishing houses like Anagrama validate unknown authors with the trust found in its brand" ("Pocas editoriales como Anagrama validan a autores desconocidos por la confianza que da el sello) ("Anagrama, 40 años creando prestigio"). Notably, the Spanish subtitle of Bloom's work changes the title's meaning. By describing, the "Western canon" as "the Books and School of the Ages," Bloom is stressing the pedagogical function of the canon as a unitary, even timeless, concept, even as he characteristically privileges Shakespeare as "book and School." According to Bloom, "Dante's *Divine Comedy*, according to Stefan George, was 'the book and School of the ages,' though that was more true for poets than for anyone else and is properly assigned to Shakespeare's plays" (7). The Spanish subtitle "la escuela y los libros de todas las épocas," in a clearly non-Bloomian way, accepts plurality by referring to "books from all periods" rather than the original "The Books and School of the Ages."

6. Sánchez Prado remembers that "Bloom's work was published in their 'Argumentos' series, devoted to the essay and to contemporary critical thinking—genres that in Spanish are not always as starkly divided as in English. *El canon occidental* shared a catalog with Gilles Deleuze's *Crítica y clínica*, Pierre Bourdieu's *Las reglas del arte*, and Edward W. Said's *Cultura e imperialismo*. In Latin America and Spain, these works were published and read side by side, in a critical continuum. Bourdieu, Deleuze, Said, and Bloom were authors that I absorbed simultaneously, with great dedication and with little sense of contradiction" ("On Cosmopolitanism and the Love of Literature").

7. A clear example of how even in the midst of a theoretical discussion earlier meanings of canon are still used is the following by Antonio Cornejo Polar in a 1997 essay: "Critical texts written in English generally use a bibliography of works in the same language and dispense or do not quote the [texts] laboriously composed in Latin America during many years. Moreover, their extreme preference for the narrow postmodern theoretical canon is a compulsion that can lead to ridiculous heights" ("Los textos críticos en inglés suelen utilizar bibliografía en el mismo idioma y prescindir, o no citar, lo que trabajosamente se hizo en América Latina durante largos años. Por lo demás su extrema preferencia por el estrecho canon teórico posmoderno es una compulsión que puede llegar hasta el ridículo") ("Mestizaje e hibridez" 343). Here *canon* is not used in a positive sense of models to be followed, and the word simply refers to "body of related works."

8. "La idea de canon es confrontable con términos próximos en relación opositiva o sinonímica, entre ellos algunos tales como tradición, clásico, margen y centro. Estas consideraciones equivalen a ala intención de no ceñir la discusión al que podría denominarse el efecto Bloom derivado de su hiperbólico título *El canon occidental*" (Cella, 8).

9. In 2002, the *OED* inserted its entry for canon as "A body of literary works traditionally regarded as the most important, significant, and worthy of study; those works of esp. Western literature considered to be established as being of the highest quality and most enduring value; the classics (now frequently in *the canon*)."

10. A lucid history of the evolution of the concept of the canon—from antiquity to the twentieth-century United States—is found in Jan Gorak's *The Making of the Modern Canon* (1–88).

11. Redfield notes on the extremely influential first group of "Yale critics" that "the department was dominated by its iconic New Critics—the first "Yale Critics"—almost all of whom were political conservatives and devout Christians. (The chair of the English department was singled out for praise by William F. Buckley in the book with which he made his name as a young conservative firebrand in 1951, *God and Man at Yale*)" (104). This new criticism was the dominant critical school before the rise of deconstruction.

12. The actual word *canon* is used only twice in A. Bloom's book. Writing about Aristotle's *Ethics*, A. Bloom argues: "And shame, a quality of the noble and a great enemy of reason, is mentioned only in order to be banished from the canon" (279). Here, of course, *canon* means "a body of principles, rules, standards, or norms." The canon, in the sense of a catalog of great books, makes a brief apparition in A. Bloom's text: "If one only reads Great Books, one can never know what a great, as opposed to an ordinary, book is; there is no way of determining who is to decide what a Great Book or what the canon is" (344). Here A. Bloom

is, avant la lettre, contradicting H. Bloom. For the latter: "If we were literally immortal, or even if our span were doubled to seven score of years, say, we could give up all argument about canons. But we have an interval only, and then our place knows us no more, and stuffing that interval with bad writing, in the name of whatever social justice, does not seem to me to be the responsibility of the literary critic" (32). Notably, the chapter titled "Books" in *The Closing of the American Mind* is a defense of the (unnamed) canon and of the great books, even if these go mostly unlisted: "I have begun to wonder whether the experience of the greatest texts from early childhood is not a prerequisite for a concern throughout life for them and for lesser but important literature" (62). Consistent with the book's key arguments, A. Bloom decries the decline in popular tastes. According to him, young people don't read Tolstoy or Dickens, but "there is always a girl who mentions Ayn Rand's *The Fountainhead*, a book, though hardly literature, which with its sub-Nietzschean assertiveness, excites somewhat eccentric youngsters to a new way of life. A few students mention recent books that struck them and supported their own self-interpretation, like *The Catcher in the Rye*" (62–63). About the latter's popularity among young people, Allan Bloom notes: "It is an uneducated response. Teachers should take advantage of the need expressed in it to show such students that better writers can help them more" (63).

13. Allan Bloom used the word *canon* only once to mean a catalog of great books. E. D. Hirsch also uses *canon* once, but as part of an analogy to the books of the Bible: "Horace Kallen, that enthusiast for cultural pluralism, proposes that the following make up its canon: 'It's book of Genesis would of course be "The Declaration of Independence"'" (100). Among the texts included by Hirsch are George Washington's "Letter to the Jewish Congregation," "articles from *The Federalist*," Abraham Lincoln's "House Divided Speech," and "The Truman Doctrine" (101). For Hirsch, this "canon" is political, not literary, even if he concludes: "Cultural revision is one of our best traditions" (101).

14. Harold Bloom is explicit in his disdain for right-wing defenses of the canon and left-wing critiques. Unlike other major literary critics of his generation, Bloom's politics were to the left of the mainstream. He was a critic of the Iraq War and among the first to identify the ever-rightward turn of the Republican Party as a move toward fascism: "No, 'Benito Bush' deserves, if we had a functioning civil law in the world, to be condemned for crimes against humanity" ("According to Harold Bloom, What We Are Seeing Is the Fall of America"). He was even more passionate in his condemnation of Donald Trump: "I would prefer not to speak about politics, but in my country we are living a kind apocalypse. We have a monster as a President, an antiChrist, a beast of evil" ("No quisiera hablar hoy de política pero en mi

país se está viviendo una especie de apocalipsis. Tenemos un monstruo como Presidente, un anticristo, una bestia del mal") (Para Harold Bloom, Donald Trump es "un monstruo, un anticristo, una bestia del mal").

15. Allan Bloom's *The Closing of the American Mind* was published in two separate Spanish translations in 1989. In Barcelona, as *El cierre de la mente moderna* (with *modern* replacing *American*) translated by Adolfo Martín for Plaza y Janés; and in Buenos Aires, with the completely different title *La decadencia de la cultura* (The Decadence of Culture), translated by Julio Sierra for Emecé.

16. I am privileging responses published in newspapers and magazines over more academic venues because what interests me here is the impact of *The Western Canon* on the cultural mainstream rather than on Spanish American and Spanish academics.

17. Other works by Bloom translated into Spanish include *Kabbalah and Criticism* in 1978; *The Breaking of the Vessels* in 1986, *Ruin the Sacred Truths: Poetry and Belief from the Bible to the Present* in 1991, and *The Book of J* in 1995. On the translations of Bloom into Spanish see Pulido (194–95).

18. "El capítulo consagrado a la literature hispano-portuguesa [*sic*] es un desastre. Asesorado por un especialista en Carpentier —el profesor Roberto González Echevarría— Bloom asegura que el novelista Cubano es el escritor latinoamericano más importante del siglo. Después despacha a Borges, Neruda y Pessoa como alumnos aplicados de Walt Whitman. Un crítico que ignora al Siglo

de Oro es obviamente incapaz de apreciar a Darío, García Lorca, Cernuda, Vallejo o Paz, para no hablar de la novela hispanoamericana, inexistente en *El canon occidental*" (Domínguez Michael 58).

19. Despite describing *The Western Canon* as "this excessive hit parade of letters" ("este desmesurado hit parade de la palabra") and claiming that "it brought few new interpretative ideas" ("trajo escasas novedades de interpretación"), Villoro's "El rey duerme: Crónica hacia *Hamlet*" chronicles the seminar on Shakespeare he attended while the Mexican novelist was a visiting professor at Yale. Bloom's seminar coincided with the publication of *The Western Canon* early in 1994. The Colombian novelist Juan Gabriel Vásquez refers to Bloom's "marvelous small book" *The Anxiety of Influence* ("librito maravilloso") in his reading of his predecessor Gabriel García Márquez ("Malentendidos alrededor de García Márquez").

20. "La literatura *light*, leve, ligera, fácil, una literatura que sin el menor rubor se propone ante todo (y casi exclusivamente) divertir" (Vargas Llosa, *La civilización del espectáculo*).

21. A more complete version of the quotation is: "No me siento heredero del boom de ninguna manera ... ¿quiénes son los herederos oficiales de García Márquez?, pues Isabel Allende, Laura Restrepo, Luis Sepúlveda y algún otro. A mí, García Márquez cada día me resulta más semejante a Santos Chocano o a Lugones" (Bolaño, "Entrevista con Roberto Bolaño").

22. "La ligereza de lo desechable y de lo efímero, las novelas del Crack oponen la multiplicidad de las voces y la creación de mundos autónomos" (Palou, "La feria del crack").

23. According to critic Burkhard Pohl, "While the Crack emphasizes the return to the totalizing aesthetic presuppositions of the generation of the 1950s and 1960s, the inventors of McOndo—as the texts collected in the anthology confirm, among them the contributions of the Mexicans David Toscana, Naief Yehya and Jordi Soler—defend a literature voluntarily youthful or at least opened towards daily life in the cultural field, a deliberate inscription in the cultural codes of the Anglo Saxon international mainstream" ("Mientras que el *Crack* subraya precisamente la vuelta a los presupuestos estéticos totalizantes de la generación de los 50 y 60, los inventores de *McOndo* —y lo confirman los textos reunidos en la antología susodicha, entre ellos las contribuciones de los mexicanos David Toscana, Naief Yehya y Jordi Soler— defienden una literatura voluntariamente juvenil o por lo menos abierta hacia lo cotidiano en el ámbito cultural; una deliberada inscripción en los códigos culturales del *mainstream* internacional anglosajón") ("Ruptura y continuidad" 60)."

24. As should be apparent, this transformation in Spanish-language literature corresponds closely to the transition from modern to postmodern cultural tendencies. Instead of the opposition between literature and mass culture, the latter becomes the paradigm by which the former can be understood. Timothy Robbins's comments on Fuguet can easily apply to many other writers: "What Fuguet expresses through his exploration of mass culture in the globalized milieu is the power of mass culture in a postmodern context to perpetuate the status quo through a feeling of false advocacy or through a feeling of apathy and lack of control. In essence, mass culture for these authors fills the void brought about by the destabilization of the various structures of power" (26). With some caveats, this embrace of mass culture and existing political structures can be applied even to the works of older writers, such as Vargas Llosa's precursor "autofiction" *Aunt Julia and the Scriptwriter* (1977). On the relationship of that work with later McOndo literature, see my *Spaces of Latin American Literature* 112–13.

25. For many, the 1989 inclusion of Isabel Allende in the Academia de la Lengua in Chile and her awarding of the prestigious Premio Nacional e Literatura in 2010, and Paulo Coelho's naming to the Academia Brasileira de Letras in 2002, exemplify this loss of standards.

26. "La escuela del Resentimiento es hija del igualitarismo autoritario del 68 y la importación del pensamiento logocida francés" (Domínguez Michael 57)

27. "El multiculturalismo, núcleo de la Escuela del Resentimiento no sólo es una versión postmoderna del zhadanovismo, sino la muy tardía victoria cultural, en las universidades,

de esa izquierda fracasada que fue (y es) la norteamericana" (Domínguez Michael 57).

28. "¿No es acaso el indigenismo, de Manuel Gamio al subcomandante Marcos, una versión lírica y rupestre del multiculturalismo?" (Domínguez Michael 58).

29. "La batalla de Bloom es, en clave mexicana, la que dieron Reyes, los Contemporáneos, Octavio Paz" (Domínguez Michael 58).

30. In a 2021 essay, Sánchez Prado notes that "one must acknowledge that Bloom's infamous term 'the School of Resentment' is still leveled these days in the Spanish-speaking world to police any desire to account for race, gender, class, or social justice in our literary and cultural fields, so the reactionary effects of his conservatism also made the trip" ("On Cosmopolitanism and the Love of Literature").

31. "Un medio literario donde su reinvendicación del genio resonaba de una manera particularmente fuerte" (Sánchez Prado, *El canon y sus formas* 103).

32. Without proposing anything like an equal relationship between Mexican and US cultural media, it is noteworthy that writers from the former have long had a presence in US, especially New York–based journals and newspapers. Carlos Fuentes was a frequent presence in US written and visual media, and Enrique Krauze, Carmen Boullosa, Álvaro Enrigue, and Valeria Luiselli routinely publish in US media. The latter three have lived in New York.

33. Neither John Guillory's *Cultural Capital* nor Jan Gorak's *The Making of the Modern Canon* have been translated into Spanish.

34. According to Vicky Unruh, given the centrality of book reviewing and literary commentary in Mariátegui's public activity, he can be considered "one of Latin America's first practicing literary critics" (45).

35. See Mariátegui's "Nacionalismo y vanguardismo: En la literatura y el arte," as well as his section on Vallejo in his *Seven Interpretive Essays on Peruvian Reality*.

36. "Eguren, en el Perú, no comprende ni conoce al pueblo. Ignora al indio, lejano de su historia y extraño a su enigma. Es demasiado occidental y extranjero espiritualmente para asimilar el orientalismo indígena" (Mariátegui, *7 ensayos* 302).

CHAPTER 2

1. In her "Response," Sor Juana notes paradoxically that while these authors are not properly examples she's followed, they have helped her intellectual development: "I confess as well that although it is true, as I have said, that I needed no examples, yet the many I have read, in both divine and human letters, have not failed to help me" (*Sor Juana Inés de la Cruz: Selected Works*, 186). ("Confieso también que con ser esto verdad

tal que, como he dicho, no necesitaba de ejemplares, con todo no me han dejado de ayudar los muchos que he leído, así en divinas como en humanas letras") (Sor Juana Inés de la Cruz, *Obra selecta II* 467).

2. Pascale Casanova describes the Western autonomous literary space as beginning with the Renaissance (and pre-Renaissance) Tuscan humanists, who transformed what would become Italian into a literary language (49), and were followed by humanists from France (49). Casanova adds: "To this initial Tuscan-French core were gradually added Spain and then England" (55).

3. Sor Juana probably knew Hypatia through indirect sources, since she was mentioned in several early Christian histories. Moreover, the stress on Hypatia's virginity and saintliness, despite her having been a pagan killed by a Christian mob, may have also made her figure useful in Sor Juana's self-defense. See Watts's *Hypatia: The Life and Legend of an Ancient Philosopher* (2017).

4. "*Primero sueño*, que así intituló y compuso la Madre Juana Inés de la Cruz, imitando a Góngora" (Sor Juana Inés de la Cruz, *Obra selecta: Tomo II* 70).

5. I study Sor Juana's connections with the Spanish cultural center in *The Spaces of Latin American Literature*.

6. As I indicated in *Mestizo Nations: Culture, Race, and Conformity in Latin American Literature*, mestizaje "while literally meaning miscegenation, can be understood as proposing the creation of a homogenous culture or race out of Amerindian,

African and European . . . elements" (xiii). For a full discussion of *mestizaje* and its role in Latin American literature and culture from colonial times to the present see *Mestizo Nations*.

7. "¿Pues no ves la impropiedad de que en Méjico se escribe y en Madrid se represente?" (*Sor Juana Inés de la Cruz: Obra Selecta Tomo I* 328).

8. "¿Pues es cosa nunca vista que se haga una cosa en una parte, porque en otra sirva?" (*Sor Juana Inés de la Cruz: Obra Selecta Tomo I* 328).

9. "No habrá cosa que desdiga, aunque las lleve a Madrid: que a especies intelectivas ni habrá distancias que estorben, ni mares que les impidan" (*Sor Juana Inés de la Cruz: Obra Selecta Tomo I* 328).

10. "No es exagerado afirmar que, mientras vivió, su fama alcanzó los límites del inmenso mundo hispánico y que esa fama perduró todavía muchos años, como puede comprobarse por las sucesivas ediciones . . . y en los poemas que le dedicaron sus contemporáneos, durante el periódo comprendido entre su muerte y el primer tercio del siglo xviii" (Glantz xiii).

11. "Sus obras van cayendo en el olvido, como las de Góngora, y, aunque solemos verla mencionada, es casi un lugar común advertir que ya no se le toma en cuenta como poeta sino como una docta, erudita, grande mujer" (Glantz xiii)

12. In addition to Gorriti and the Peruvian novelists Clorinda Matto de Turner, best known as author of *Aves sin nido* (*Torn from the Nest*, 1889), and Mercedes Cabello de Carbonera, Gorriti's published anthology of the

works presented in the anthology *Veladas literarias de Lima (1876–77)* (1892), includes male authors such as Ricardo Palma, already Peru's best-known nineteenth-century writer, and Carlos Salaverry, the Romantic poet.

13. Curiously, in the *Veladas literarias* anthology, there is only one reference to Stowe, made by Benicio Álamos González. According to this liberal Chilean politician, in a text that primarily stresses the importance of the education of women, "Statesmen and the sublime inspiration of Misses Beecher Stowe have been able to extinguish the cancer of slavery" ("Hombres de estado y la sublime inspiración de Misses Beecher Stowe, han podido extinguir el cancer de la esclavatura") (358–59). According to Briggs, "from its publication . . . Matto's *Aves sin nido*, would be compared to Harriet Beecher Stowe's *Uncle Tom's Cabin*" (150). In 1890, the Mexican critic Francisco Sosa Escalante argued, referring to a certain Piñeyro, who had written on *Uncle Tom's Cabin* as representing "a moral necessity": "What Piñeyro . . . says regarding Mrs. Beecher Stowe, we can say about Mrs. Matto. The latter desires the redemption of the Indian, the former struggled for that of the Black" ("Lo que el señor Piñeyro . . . dice respecto a Mrs. Beecher Stowe, podemos decir nosotros de la Sra. Matto. Ésta anhela la redención del indio; aquella pugnaba por la del negro") (199).

14. Celso Thomas Castilho provides a list of different editions of *Uncle Tom's Cabin* and performances of the play based on the novel in Spanish America (792n8).

15. There were only a few male authors, particularly among the major authors, who could be considered literary critics. For instance, if the writings of Manuel González Prada, Ricardo Palma, José Martí, and Domingo Faustino Sarmiento are "literary criticism," it is a very small fraction of their writing. As a (relatively) lengthy engagement with literary topics, Cabello's "La novela moderna" is thus an exception not only within women's writing but also within Spanish American writing of the time.

16. "Dos escuelas, opuestas la una a la otra, han sostenido . . . larga y furiosa lucha . . . la una lleva la enseña del Romanticismo, la otra del Naturalismo" (Cabello, "La novela moderna" 4373).

17. "El triunfo definitivo pertenece a al Naturalismo . . . Sus reglas, sus principios, sus doctrinas son acatadas y acogidas no sólo por los novelistas de la vieja Europa, sino también por la joven América" (Cabello "La novela moderna" 4373).

18. "Y así como el romanticismo se creó un mundo donde no se vislumbra la realidad de la vida humana, así el naturalismo creóse un hombre donde no se vislumbra la realidad de los sentimientos y afectos que agitan el alma humana" ("La novela moderna" Cabello 4373).

19. Cabello quotes Victor Hugo, who declares, "Walter Scott has drunk an unknown genre from the fountains of nature and truth" ("Walter Scott ha bebido en los manantiales de la

naturaleza y la verdad un género desconocido," "La novela moderna" 5055).

20. "Hoy nosotros con nuestro espíritu analítico y positivista, necesitamos la novela que engaste a Walter Scott en Emilio Zola. Antitéticos el uno del otro, pero simbólicos y magníficos" (Cabello, "La novela moderna" 5055).

21. "Y Walter Scott y Zola, simbolizando uno al ser moral y el otro al ser material, completarán el arte realista" (Cabello, "La novela moderna" 5055).

22. A slightly longer version of Cabello's text is: "Para que la escuela española en la que hay novelistas como el ilustre Leopoldo Alas, Picón, Palacio Valdés, Pereda, Ortega Munilla . . . será la que innove el Naturalismo, convirtiéndolo en el realismo psicológico y filosófico. A la cabeza de esa escuela está Emilia Pardo y Bazán" ("La novela moderna" 4015).

23. Benito Pérez Galdós is absent from this list, but Cabello mentions him earlier in the essay, presenting him in less favorable light as a *costumbrista* (4015).

24. "Una nueva constelación inmediata a las que reverberan con los inmortales nombres de Jorge Sand, Fernán Caballero, Gertrúdis Gómez de Avellaneda y Carolina Coronado" (Matto de Turner 184).

25. Carolyn Vellenga Berman notes that "Sand rejects the attempts to gain *civic* rights for women before gaining civil rights" (109). In other words, Sand believed it was necessary for women to have full economic rights to own and sell property and legal rights to be able to sign and enforce contracts—before they were given the vote.

26. Francesca Denegri has noted: "*Índole* (Nature) and *Aves sin nido* (*Torn from the Nest*), her two Andean novels, are structured around a series of small details in misti (Andean White) social and cultural life that provide an image of Peruvianess quite different from that found in the romantic and sentimental novels that circulated in the literary circles of Lima during the three decades before the publication of Matto's novels" ("*Índole* y *Aves sin nido*, sus dos novelas andinas, están estructuradas en torno a una serie de pequeños detalles de la vida social y cultural misti, que proporciona una imagen de la peruanidad. bastante distinta de la que se desprendía de las novelas románticas y sentimentales que circularon en los circulos literarios limeños en las tres décadas previas a la publicación de las novelas de Matto") (171). Moreover, Matto's novels were almost immediately compared to Stowe's *Uncle Tom's Cabin*. Matto's literary tastes writing show that she never fully left sentimentality behind.

27. However, there are other moments when Matto de Turner presents more conventional, male-centered lists of canonical authors. In a brief review of a forgotten Peruvian poet Teobaldo Corpancho, Matto mentions "Sosa, Rubén Darío, Nájera, Arízaga, Obligado, Mirón, Acosta, Prieto, Peza, or any other name that in our literary republic means poet

and poetry" ("Sosa, Rubén Darío, Nájera, Arízaga, Obligado, Mirón, Acosta, Prieto, Peza, u otro cualquier nombre que en nuestra república literaria, significa poeta y poesía") (*Leyendas y recortes* 138). This list of exclusively male authors includes Darío, one of the greatest Spanish-language poets, well-known poets like Mexicans Manuel Gutiérrez Nájera and Salvador Díaz Mirón, less well-known poets like the Mexicans Francisco Sosa, Guillermo Prieto, and Juan de Dios Peza, the Ecuadorian Rafael María Arízaga, the Argentine Rafael Obligado, and the Salvadoran Vicente Acosta.

28. In *El conde Tolstoi* (1896), Cabello makes clear the centrality of France even in the reception of Russian authors, such as Tolstoy, who had already been translated into Spanish, in 1884: "not a small part has been played in the resonance of the Russian novel, French enthusiasm, influenced by politics and, perhaps, certain literary rivalries born in Paris"("no escasa parte han llevado en la resonancia de las novelas rusas, los entusiasmos artísticos con miras políticas de Francia, y quizá ciertas literarias rivalidades, nacidas en París") (2). (Cabello is referring to the resistance to Zola and naturalism by other French writers).

29. "Fue, creo, Pedro Henríquez Ureña el primero que entre nosotros se preocupó de hacerles un hueco a los problemas del canon" (Rojo).

30. "Teníamos andado ya un siglo de vida republicana (Ayacucho se pelea en 1824 y Henríquez Ureña está publicando el ensayo al que me refiero en 1925)" (Rojo).

31. The full title of Nervo's biography and literary revalution is *Juana de Asbaje: Contribución al centenario de la independencia de México* (Juana de Asbaje: Contribution to the Centenary of the Independence of Mexico). The process of Spanish American Independence began in 1810, with the Argentine *Revolución de Mayo* and Hidalgo declaration of Mexico's Independence, and it ended in 1824 in Ayacucho). Despite Nervo's rediscovery of Sor Juana, Henríquez Ureña considered only nineteenth-century male authors when constructing his list of classics: "The literary history of Spanish America must be written around a few central names: [Andrés] Bello, [Domingo Faustino] Sarmiento, [Juan] Montalvo, [José] Martí, Rubén Darío, and [José Enrique] Rodó" ("La historia literaria de la América española debe escribirse alrededor de unos cuantos nombres centrales: Bello, Sarmiento, Montalvo, Martí, Darío, Rodó" (49).

32. I am working with the English translation (*Women*) that adds articles to the Spanish-language "original" *Recados para América*.

33. Mistral writes about Norah Borges, who, at least in the exposition in Madrid (1935) she reviews, included numerous portraits of children: "A woman without children is simply not possible, and in such an isolated case it could never be Norah, who found herself in a barren condition. She then sought them until she found them; better yet, she conceived them with a pencil, which called to them like a whistle, and thus, one finds them here, the

multitude of little ones" (70). ("Mujer sin hijos no puede haberla, no podia ser ella, Norah, quien se quedase en tal sequía. Se los buscó hasta encontrárselos: mejor aún: se los llamó con el lápiz, que también es silbo convocador y aquí está la parvada" ("Norah Borges, la Argentina").

34. The reason Mistral, as most Spanish American women writers mentioned in this brief chapter, is better described as "proto-feminist" is that her politics don't always coincide with the basic demands of, for instance, the suffragettes who were roughly her contemporaries. As Licia Fiol-Matta notes, "Mistral's writings on the subject of women's enfranchisement were articulated within separate-spheres discourse. She wrote that women had special aptitudes different from men's; she was cautious regarding the vote; she avoided the 'feminist' label; she believed that men were rational beings whereas women were 'affective'" (91). Similar ideas were espoused by earlier women writers, such as Cabello.

35. Despite the fact that Mistral does not refer to Sor Juana's poetry in *Women*, her diaries reveal that she was acquainted with the writings of the great baroque poet: "When reading, between the two Juanas I prefer the Uruguayan one [Juana de Ibarbourou]; when listening, to keep next to me, I prefer Juana of Mexico, the precious nun . . . How I love Sor Juana . . . How she was ahead of her time, with an anticipation that causes stupor, she experienced what so many men and some women live today: the fever of culture during their youth, afterwards, science's taste of rotten fruit in their mouth, and finally, search for that simple glass of clear water that is eternal Christian humility" ("Para leerlas, entre las dos Juanas me quedo con la uruguaya; para oírlas. para tenerlas al lado. me quedo con la Juana de México, con la preciosa monja" . . . Cómo la quiero yo a Sor Juana . . . Cómo ella se anticipó a su época, con anticipación tan enorme que da stupor, vivió en si misma lo que viven hoy muchos hombres y algunas mujeres: la fiebre de la cultura en la juventud, después el sabor de fruta caduca de la ciencia en la boca, y por último, la búsqueda contrita de aquel simple vaso de agua clara, que es la eterna humildad cristiana") (*Bendita mi lengua sea* 117). Needless to say, Mistral gives a very conservative reading of Sor Juana's life.

36. In her diaries, Mistral provides a more androcentric list of the Latin American contemporaries she believed were of importance: Juana Ibarbourou and Carlos Sabat Ercasty (Uruguay); Rafael Arévalo Martínez, described as a "great and deep poet" ("grande, profundo poeta") (Guatemala); Rafael Maya (Colombia); José María Eguren, Alberto Guillén, and Alberto Hidalgo (Peru); Teresa de la Parra (Venezuela); Jorge Manach (Cuba); Pablo Neruda, though Mistral is critical of his writing "futurisms that neither sell nor are read" ("futurismos que no se venden ni se leen") (Chile); Joaquín García Monge (Costa Rica); and Xavier Villaurrutia, Carlos Pellicer, Jaime Torres Bodet, and José Gorostiza (*Bendita mi lengua sea* 112–13)

37. In a letter to Victoria Ocampo, Mistral notes on Woolf's "A Room of Her Own," in a translation by Borges, that "the *Sur* collection came, and it struck me as magnificent, just magnificent, worthy of you. The first time that a feminist argument has really hit home for me is in this work by V[irginia] Woolf. I have a lot to tell you in this regard. Next time. I thank you, as a personal service, for having it translated and for having it sent to me" (*This America of Ours* 43) ("Vino la colección de *Sur*, que me ha parecido magnífica, así magnífica, Digna de usted. La primera vez que a mí me llega un alegato feminista es en la lectura de ese trabajo de V. Woolf. Habría mucho que decir a este respecto. Otro día. Le agradezco como un servicio personal, el que usted lo haya hecho traducir y me lo haya hecho llegar" (*Esta América nuestra* 57).

38. I am referring to John Guillory's comments on Thomas Gray's "Elegy in a Country Churchyard": "*Only death* can silence Milton in the imaginative narrative future . . . but the "mute, inglorious Milton" of the elegy is silenced by what constitutes *muteness*—not an inability to speak but an inability to read and write" (*Cultural Capital* 116).

39. Even Mariátegui, whose "Women and Politics" and "Feminist Demands," both from 1924, directly deal with the condition of women and seem to predict second-wave feminism, includes only Magda Portal in his discussion of Peruvian literature in *Seven Interpretative Essays*.

40. As we will see in "Gabo's Canon," Allende is often considered an epigone of García Márquez. However, there seems to be a process of revaluing her work. On this, see "Twentieth Century Women Writers and the Feminist Novel," by Maria Rosa Olivera-Williams, and "Magical Realism and the Marvelous Real in the Novel," by Amarallyl Chanady, both forthcoming in *The Oxford Handbook of the Latin American Novel*.

41. The complete list of Spanish American authors (and texts) included by Seigneurie and colleagues includes the *Popol Vuh*, Sor Juana, Jorge Isaacs, José Martí, Rubén Darío, Pablo Neruda, Miguel Ángel Asturias, Jorge Luis Borges, Julio Cortázar, Gabriel García Márquez, and Roberto Bolaño.

CHAPTER 3

1. The dates given in the text are those of first publication. "Pierre Menard, author of the *Quixote*" was included in *Ficciones* (1944); "The Immortal" and "Averroes's Search" in *The Aleph* (1949); "The Maker" in *Dreamtigers* (1960); and "Shakespeares's Memory" in *Shakespeare's Memory* (1983).

2. As an example of these less obvious intertextual connections, Rodríguez Monegal has argued, "'The Aleph' is a parodic reduction of *The Divine Comedy*" (*Jorge Luis Borges* 414).

3. Borges's inclusion in the canon is also evidenced in his influence on writers from all cultures, nations, and linguistic traditions. For instance, works as diverse as Philip Dick's *The Man in the High Castle* (1962), Ellery Queen/Theodore Sturgeon's *The Player on the Other Side* (1963), John Barth's stories in *Lost in the Funhouse* (1968), Thomas Pynchon's *Gravity's Rainbow* (1973), Umberto Eco's *The Name of the Rose* (1980), Milorad Pavić's *Dictionary of the Khazars: A Lexicon* (1984), and Luis Fernando Verissimo's *Borges and the Eternal Orangutans* (2000); to mention works across the high-popular literature divides and written in English, Italian, Serbo-Croatian, and Portuguese.

4. According to De Man, "His main characters are prototypes for the writer, and his worlds are prototypes for a highly stylized kind of poetry or fiction. For all their variety of tone and setting, the different stories all have a similar point of departure, a similar structure, a similar climax, and a similar outcome; the inner cogency that links these four moments together constitutes Borges's distinctive style, as well as his comment upon this style. His stories are about the style in which they are written" (125).

5. Even if Updike implicitly devalues the presence of Argentine culture and tradition in Borges's works, he is a perceptive reader of the relationship between the author of *Ficciones* and the European literary tradition. By noting the "strangeness" of European civilization, Updike notes Borges's difference from Europe.

Furthermore, the image of the librarian is intrinsically ambiguous, even if the context of the essay attempts to limit the library's texts to those of European provenance.

6. "Como Joyce, como Goethe, como Shakespeare, como Dante, como ningún otro escritor, Francisco de Quevedo es menos un hombre que una dilatada y compleja literatura" (670).

7. Bloom's first mention of Quevedo is in a reference to the difference established by Neruda between "Hispanic American" and Spanish vanguard poets of the 1920s and 1930s: "In an interview in 1966 with Robert Bly, Neruda distinguished the poetry of Hispanic America (his own and César Vallejo's) from that of the modern Spanish poets, so many of whom had been his friends: Lorca, Hernández, Alberti, Cernuda, Aleixandre, Machado. They had behind them, in the Spanish Golden Age, the great poets of the Baroque—Calderón, Quevedo, Góngora—who had named everything that mattered" (479). The second is in the following comparison between Neruda and Whitman, where the US scholar provides the following bizarre description of Neruda's "Heights of Macchu Picchu": "Both poets address multitudes, with Neruda's metaphors a blend of High Baroque Quevedo and magical realism or surrealism" (483).

8. The vagaries of taste, or, according to Bloom, changes in social mores, seem to have begun to leave Goethe behind, at least outside the German republic of letters. One reads in Bloom's *The Western Canon*: "Of all the strongest Western writers,

Goethe now seems the least available to our sensibility. I suspect that this distance has little to do with how badly his poetry translates into English. . . . A poet and wisdom writer who is his language's equivalent of Dante can transcend inadequate translation but not changes in life and literature that render his central attitudes so remote from us as to seem archaic. Goethe is no longer our ancestor, as he was Emerson's and Carlyle's" (203). Borges would agree. In "Sobre los clásicos," Borges writes about Goethe's masterwork: "For Austrians and Germans, *The Faust* is a work of genius; for others, one of the most famous ways to boredom" ("Para los alemanes y austríacos el *Fausto* es una obra genial; para otros, una de las más famosas formas del tedio" 773).

9. Included in *Otras inquisiciones*, first published in 1952, "Quevedo" had first seen the light of day as the *prólogo* to an anthology of the Spanish poet's *Prosa y verso* published by Emecé in 1948.

10. "Como la otra, la historia de la literatura abunda en enigmas. Ninguno de ellos me ha inquietado, y me inquieta, como la extraña gloria parcial que le ha tocado en suerte a Quevedo. En los censos de nombres universales el suyo no figura" (Borges "Quevedo" 660).

11. As early as 1956, Borges will have changed his mind regarding who the central writer was of the Spanish-language tradition. That year, in a brief aside in an also brief text that deals with the Spanish philosophers Miguel de Unamuno and José Ortega y Gasset, Borges notes: "Forty years of experience have taught me that, in general, *others* are right. On some occasion, I considered inexplicable that generation of men have venerated Cervantes rather than Quevedo; today I see no mystery in this preference" ("Cuarenta años de experiencia me han enseñado que, en general, los *otros* tienen razón. Alguna vez juzgué inexplicable que las generaciones de los hombres veneraran a Cervantes y no a Quevedo; hoy no veo nada miserioso en tal preferencia") ("Nota de un mal lector" 12).

12. "El modernismo es, y sigue siendo, el movimiento literario de las letras hispánicas" (Borges, "Darío" 125); "Auditivamente, no ha sido superado ni siquiera igualado" (125–26).

13. Casanova studies Darío precisely as a "central figure in the literary history of Latin America and Spain who, though he was not consecrated in Paris, rearranged the literary landscape of the Hispanic world by importing the latest editions of modernity from Paris" (96). For Casanova, Darío is precisely the example of a writer who belongs to the core of the Spanish-language canon but apparently because of a lack of "originality," he's presented as an "importer" not as an "innovator," so does not break into the world republic of letters.

14. "Un símbolo que se apodere de la imaginación de los hombres . . . Dante, los nueve círculos infernales y la rosa paradisíaca; Shakespeare, sus orbes de violencia y de música" ("Quevedo" 660).

15. Borges also identifies "symbols"

for Homer, Lucretius, Sophocles, Cervantes, Swift, Melville, Kafka, Góngora, Mallarmé, and Whitman ("Quevedo" 37, 660).

16. "No hay escritor de fama universal que no haya amonedado un símbolo; este, conviene recordar, no siempre es objetivo y externo . . . Whitman, como protagonista semidivino de *Leaves of Grass*. De Quevedo, en cambio, sólo perdura una imagen caricatural" ("Quevedo" 660). The reference to caricature ("imagen caricatural") alludes to the fact throughout the Spanish-speaking world the name of Quevedo has been used in the title of collections of tales and jokes, of which he was presented as protagonist.

17. "La grandeza de Quevedo es verbal" ("Quevedo" 661).

18. "Para gustar de Quevedo hay que ser (en acto o en potencia) un hombre de letras; inversamente, nadie que tenga vocación literaria puede no gustar de Quevedo" ("Quevedo" 660).

19. "La superstición de la inferioridad de las traducciones —amonedada en el consabido adagio italiano— procede de una distraída experiencia" (Borges, "Las versiones homéricas" 239).

20. The complete quotation is as follows: "A éste, al principio, lo pensé tan singular como el fénix de las alabanzas retóricas; a poco de frecuentarlo, creí reconocer su voz o sus hábitos, en textos de diversas literaturas y de diversas épocas" (Borges, "Kafka y sus precursores" 710).

21. "El *Discurso del método* de la historia de la construcción del canon" (Piglia "Vivencia literaria" 157).

22. "*La experiencia de los escritores . . .* que ilumina y valora las obras del pasado. La esencia de la noción de canon es el hecho de que la escritura del presente *transforma y modifica* la lectura del pasado y de la tradición. Es la experiencia literaria la que decide que algunos textos, algunos libros, sean rescatados del mar de las palabras escritas y puestas a funcionar como 'literatura'. (Y también la que decide por qué algunos libros que en algún momento fueron considerados gran literatura con el paso del tiempo se pierden y son olvidados" (Piglia 156).

23. "La literatura produce lectores y las grandes obras cambian el modo de leer. *Rayuela* de Cortázar, hizo leer de otro manera el *Adán Buenosayres* de Leopoldo Marechal y ayudó a sacarlo del olvido y ayudó a ubicarlo en el canon" (156).

24. "La literatura produce lectores y las grandes obras cambian el modo de leer" (Piglia, "Vivencia literaria" 156).

25. "La novela policial ha creado un tipo especial de lector. Eso suele olvidarse cuando se juzga la obra de Poe; porque si Poe creó el relato policial, creó después el tipo de lector de ficciones policiales" (Borges, "El cuento policial" 67).

26. Marechal and Fernández both belonged in Cortázar's personal canon. In 1981, in his introduction to Roberto Arlt's works, Cortázar remembers his early years as an apprentice writer in the 1940s: "As I finish rereading him [Arlt], I [feel] as if I had stepped out from a time machine that has returned to me the Buenos

Aires of the 1940; and I realize how many Argentine writers that then seemed to me to be at the level of Arlt, Güiraldes, Girondo, Borges, and Macedonio Fernández (afterward Leopoldo Marechal would join them, but that is another story), had faded from my memory like so many other cigarettes" ["Ahora que salgo de su relectura como de una máquina del tiempo que me hubiera devuelto a mi Buenos Aires de los años cuarenta, me doy cuenta de cómo muchos escritores argentinos que en ese entonces me parecían a la altura de Arlt, Güiraldes, Girondo, Borges y Macedonio Fernández (después vendría Leopoldo Marechal, pero ésa es otra historia) se me habían ido esfumando en la memoria como otros tantos cigarrillos" (n.p.).

27. "Si no me equivoco, las heterogéneas piezas que he enumerado se parecen a Kafka; si no me equivoco, no todas se parecen entre sí. Este último hecho es el más significativo. En cada uno de esos textos está la idiosincrasia de Kafka, en grado mayor o menor, pero si Kafka no hubiera escrito, no la percibiríamos; vale decir, no existiría" (Borges, "Kafka y sus precursores" 711).

28. "¿Cuál es la tradición argentina? Creo que podemos contestar fácilmente y que no hay problema en esta pregunta. Creo que nuestra tradición es toda la cultura occidental, y creo también que tenemos derecho a esta tradición, mayor que el que pueden tener los habitantes de una u otra nación occidental" (Borges "El escritor argentino y la tradición" 272).

29. A fuller version of the quotation: "Recuerdo aquí un ensayo de Thorstein Veblen . . . sobre la preeminencia de los judíos en la cultura occidental . . . dice que sobresalen en la cultura occidental porque actúan dentro de esa cultura y al mismo tiempo no se sienten atados a ella por una devoción especial' 'por eso—dice—a un judío siempre le será más fácil que a un occidental no judío innovar en la cultura occidental'" (Borges, "El escritor argentino y la tradición" 273).

30. "Creo que los argentinos, los sudamericanos en general, estamos en una situación análoga; podemos manejar todos los temas europeos, manejarlos sin supersticiones, con una irreverencia que puede tener, y ya tiene, consecuencias afortunadas" (Borges, "El escritor argentino y la tradición" 273).

31. Piglia, in one of his superb lectures on Borges presented on Argentine Public Television in 2013, noted that "The Argentine Writer and Tradition" is one of the few essays by Borges where his growing conservatism is present: "The only point . . . we can consider as linked to his political position is that he speaks about a Western tradition, an idea that was posited by the North Americans during the Cold War to oppose the Soviets . . . The West was counterposed to Soviet socialism. I think that when he speaks about the Western tradition, I think he's there participating in this issue, because he also participated, he wrote in the magazines of the Congress for Cultural Freedom. He was also active in the anticommunist struggle.

Because, to say it in fashionable terms, he was not an Eurocentrist. He always thought that the great literatures were Arab; always said that the best book ever written was *The Arabian Nights*. He was not someone ensconced in the tradition of the West. He was a writer always interested in literatures that could be called minor, literatures outside the tradition, outside the British novel. And within the Western tradition he always chose minor writers." "El único punto para empezar a pensar, que nosotros podíamos considerar ligado a su posición política, es que él habla de la tradición occidental, que era la idea que manejaban los norteamericanos en la Guerra Fría para oponerse a los rusos, a la cultura soviética. Occidente era lo que había que contraponer al socialismo soviético. Entonces cuando él dice la tradición occidental, me parece que ahí está interviniendo en esa cuestión, porque también intervenía, escribía en las Revistas del Congreso por la Libertad de la Cultura. Era también activo en su lucha anticomunista, porque él, para decirlo como se suele decir ahora que está de moda, no era eurocéntrico, él siempre pensó que las grandes literaturas eran árabes, siempre dijo que el mejor libro que se había escrito eran 'Las mil y una noches'; no era alguien que estaba incrustado en la tradición occidental, fue un escritor que siempre se abrió a las literaturas que uno podría considerar menores, literaturas que están afuera de la tradición, de la novela inglesa . . . Y dentro de las tradiciones occidentales siempre

eligió escritores menores" (Piglia, "Borges por Piglia, clase 4"). Borges was an anticommunist, a militant in the Cold War, and became a card-carrying member of the Congress for Cultural Freedom, but there may be problems of chronology in his narrative. After all, "The Argentine Writer and Tradition" was first given as a lecture in 1951; the Congress for Cultural Freedom was founded in 1950, and its main English-language magazine, *Encounter*, was founded in 1953, the same year its Spanish-language magazine *Cuadernos del Congreso por la Libertad de la Cultura* was first published.

32. In his "Nostalgia del latín," Borges writes: "America, that America called Spanish America, or South America" ("América, esa América que se llama Hispanoamérica o América del Sur") (222).

33. While criticizing nationalism, in one of these drafts included in Balderston's "Detalles circunstanciales," Borges notes: "Nationalism proposes the imitation of this imaginary or conjectural man. It invites us to be Argentine or Guatemalan" ("El nacionalismo nos propone la imitación de ese hombre imaginario o conjetural. Nos invita a ser argentinos, o guatemaltecos" [8]). Piglia is thus mistaken when he claims: "He then sees in the Irish tradition, which he admires enormously, like he admires enormously the Jewish tradition, something similar to what happens in South America; for the first time he's talking about South America in that conference; something I find very strange. It's Argentine literature, 'The Argentine Writer and

Tradition,' but it is also South America, I would say, the Río de la Plata; one has to locate South America as that, no" ("Entonces él ve en la tradición irlandesa a la que admira muchísimo, como admira muchísimo a la tradición judía, a la tradición digamos de lectura judía, algo parecido a lo que pasa en Sudamérica, dice por primera vez, está hablando de Sudamérica en la conferencia, que es muy raro. Es la literatura argentina, 'El escritor argentino y la tradición', pero también es Sudamérica, yo diría, el río de la Plata, habría que ubicar qué Sudamérica es esa no").

34. "La imagen de la literatura peruana como un inico sistema suficientemente integrado no resiste el peso de la evidencia contraria; esto es, la verificable existencia de varios sistemas y de su muy alto grado de autonomía" (Cornejo Polar, "Literatura peruana" 43).

35. Cornejo Polar makes explicit the underlying cultural, ethnic, and class oppositions he sees as characteristic of Peru's "contradictory totality": "Peruvian literature is not only testimony of what Basadre has called 'Peruvian life' . . . is this same life, that we now know is multiple, plural, and heterogeneous, made, paradoxically, out of dramatic, even bloody, oppositions and conflicts" ("la literatura nacional peruana no sólo es testimonio de lo que Basadre llamo 'la vida peruana' . . . es esa misma vida, que ahora sabemos múltiple, plural y heteroclita, hecha paradóicamente a fuerza de oposiciones y conflictos dramáticos e incluso sangrientos", "Literatura peruana" 50).

36. "Por eso repito que no debemos temer y que debemos pensar que nuestro patrimonio es el universo; ensayar todos los temas, y no podemos concretarnos a lo argentino para ser argentinos: porque o ser argentino es una fatalidad y en ese caso lo seremos de cualquier modo, o ser argentino es una mera afectación, una mascara" (Borges, "El escritor argentine y la tradición" 273–74).

37. "Clásico es aquel libro que una nación o un grupo de naciones o el largo tiempo han decidido leer como si en sus páginas todo fuera deliberado, fatal, profundo como el cosmos y capaz de interpretaciones sin término. Para los alemanes y austríacos el *Fausto* es una obra genial; para otros, una de las más famosas formas del tedio, como el segundo *Paraíso* de Milton o la obra de Rabelais. Libros como el de *Job*, la *Divina Comedia*, *Macbeth* (y, para mí, algunas de las sagas del Norte) prometen una larga inmortalidad, pero nada sabemos del porvenir, salvo que diferirá del presente. Una preferencia bien puede ser una superstición" (Borges, "Sobre los clásicos" 773). There is no English translation of this important text.

38. "Hacia el año treinta creía, bajo el influjo de Macedonio Fernández, que la belleza es privilegio de unos pocos autores; ahora sé que es común y que está acechándonos en las casuales páginas del mediocre o en un diálogo callejero. Así, mi desconocimiento de las letras malayas o húngaras es total, pero estoy seguro de que si el tiempo me deparara la ocasión de su estudio, encontraría en ellas todos los alimentos que

requiere el espíritu. Además de las barreras lingüísticas intervienen las políticas o geográficas. Burns es un clásico en Escocia; al sur del Tweed interesa menos que Dunbar o Stevenson. La gloria de un poeta depende, en suma, de la excitación o de la apatía de las generaciones de hombres anónimos que la ponen a aprueba, en la soledad de sus bibliotecas" (Borges, "Sobre los clásicos" 773).

39. "Las emociones que la literatura suscita son quizá eternas, pero los medios deben constantemente variar, siquiera de un modo levísimo, para no perder su virtud. Se gastan a medida que los reconoce el lector. De ahí el peligro de afirmar que existen obras clásicas y que lo serán para siempre" (Borges, "Sobre los clásicos" 773).

40. "Clásico no es un libro (lo repito) que necesariamente posee tales o cuales méritos; es un libro que las generaciones de los hombres, urgidas por diversas razones, leen con previo fervor y con una misteriosa lealtad" (Borges, "Sobre los clásicos" 773).

41. In his last finished essay, "Borges y Derrida: Boticarios," Emir Rodríguez Monegal notes that, "trained in the thinking of Borges since I was fifteen years old, many of the novelties attributed to Derrida seemed to me somewhat tautological. I couldn't understand why it took him so long to reach the luminous perspectives that Borges had inaugurated so many years ago. The celebrated 'deconstruction' impressed me with its technical rigor and the infinite seductiveness of its textual mirroring, but it seemed to me familiar: I had practiced it in Borges" ("Educado en el pensamiento de Borges desde los quince años, muchas de las novedades de Derrida me han parecido algo tautológicas. No podía entender cómo tardaba tanto en llegar a las luminosas perspectivas que Borges había abierto hacía ya tantos años. La famosa 'desconstrucción' me impresionaba por su rigor técnico y la infinita seducción de su espejeo textual pero me era familiar: lo había practicado en Borges" 6). Rodríguez Monegal links Borges's deconstructive "luminous perspectives" to the Argentine author's biography.

CHAPTER 4

1. José Carlos Mariátegui begins his pioneering 1929 review of *Portrait of the Artist as a Young Man* by noting: "The example of Joyce possesses the same sudden and urgent resonance as that of Proust or Pirandello" ("El caso Joyce se presenta con la misma repentina y urgente resonancia del caso Proust o del caso Pirandello") ("James Joyce" 177). That there were more Spanish Americans fluent in English and French than in German guaranteed a greater readership for these authors beyond their translations. However, the first translation of a work by Proust, *Por el camino de Swann*, by Pedro Salinas, was published in 1920, while Joyce's *Portrait*

of the Artist as a Young Man was
translated in 1926 by Dámaso Alonso.

2. "La metamorfosis de Franz Kafka, en
la falsa traducción de Borges publi-
cada por la editorial Losada de Buenos Aires" (García Márquez, *Vivir
para contarla* 298).

3. WorldCat gives the date of publication of Losada's *La metamorfosis* as
1943. Most critics who have studied
Borges's translation, including Sarah
Roger, date the publication to 1938.
Both Sorrentino and Pestaña con-
cur that the so-called translation
by Borges is actually a reprinting of
the earliest translation of Kafka (and
of *The Metamorphosis*) into Spanish originally published in 1925 in
José Ortega y Gasset's *Revista de
Occidente*.

4. Already in "Kafka and His Precursors," Borges proposes that the Czech
author is "as singular as the phoenix"
(106) ("singular como el fénix" 71).
Later texts are even more effusive.
Toward the end of his life, in 1983,
Borges stated: "Kafka has been one
of the greatest authors in all of literature. In my opinion, he's the greatest
of this century" ("Kafka ha sido uno
de los grandes autores de toda la literatura. Para mí es el primero de este
siglo") ("Un sueño eterno" 232).

5. A brief and superficial review of the
bibliography of the impact of these
other modernist writers in the region includes José Luis Venegas's
*Decolonizing Modernism: Joyce and
the Development of Spanish American
Fiction* (2010); the volume edited
by Brian Price, César Salgado, and
John Pedro Schwartz, *TransLatin
Joyce: Global Transmissions in*

Ibero-American Literature (2014);
Herbert E. Craig's *Marcel Proust
and Spanish America: From Critical
Response to Dialogue* (2002); and
Rubén Gallo's *Proust's Latin Americans* (2014). At the time of writing, I
am aware of no monograph studying
Kafka's influence on the literature of
the region. However, the anthology
*Kafka en dos orillas: Antología de la
recepción crítica español e hispanoamericana* (2013), edited by Elisa
Martínez Salazar and Julieta Yelin,
studies his reception in the Hispanic
world.

6. In his 1983 article on Kafka, Borges
notes: "I prefer his short stories and,
even though there is no reason for
me to choose or another story, I
would select that story about the
building of the wall" ("A mí me gus-
tan más sus relatos breves y aunque,
no hay ahora ninguna razón para que
elija a uno sobre otro, tomaría aquel
cuento sobre la construcción de la
muralla" ("Un sueño eterno" 232).

7. In the case of "The Lottery in Babylon," Efraín Kristal notes, "Toward
the opening of 'The Lottery in Babylon' Borges offers a formulation that
reads almost like a baroque version
of a Zeno paradox, involving the He-
brew alphabet: "The letter [Beth], in
the nights when the moon is full, con-
fers upon me power over men whose
mark is the letter Ghimel, but it sub-
ordinates me to those of the Aleph,
who must obey those of Ghimel in
moonless nights" (*Invisible Work* 127).

8. "Wakefield prefigura a Franz Kafka,
pero éste modifica, y afina, la lectura
de Wakefield. La deuda es mutua; un
gran escritor crea a sus precursores.

Los crea y de algún modo los justifica" (Borges, "Nathaniel Hawthorne" 678).

9. While Borges has a (brief) article from 1949 dedicated primarily to the question of allegory and modern narrative—"De las alegorías a las novelas" ("From Allegories to Novels")—it makes no reference to Kafka.

10. "Un error estético lo dañó: el deseo puritano de hacer de cada imaginación una fábula lo inducía a agregarles moralidades y a veces a falsearlas y a deformarlas" (Borges, "Nathaniel Hawthorne" 673).

11. "En el desorden aparente de nuestro misterioso mundo, cada hombre está ajustado a un sistema con tan exquisito rigor —y los sistemas entre sí, y todos a todo— que el individuo que se desvía un solo momento, corre el terrible albur de perder para siempre su lugar. Corre el albur de ser, como Wakefield, el Paria del Universo" (qtd. in Borges, "Nathaniel Hawthorne" 677).

12. "En esta breve y ominosa parábola —que data de 1835— ya estamos en el mundo de Herman Melville, en el mundo de Kafka. Un mundo de castigos enigmáticos y de culpas indescifrables" (Borges, "Nathaniel Hawthorne" 677). One can add that Borges's mention of Melville is clearly a reference to "Bartleby, the Scrivener," a story the Argentine author translated in 1944. In his prologue to his translation of "Bartleby," Borges notes, "I would observe that Kafka's work casts a curious ulterior light on 'Bartleby.' Melville's story defines a genre that, around

1919, Franz Kafka would reinvent and further explore: the fantasies of behavior and feelings or, as they are now wrongly called, psychological tales" ("Bartleby, the Scrivener" 246) ("Yo observaría que la obra de Kafka proyecta sobre *Bartleby* una curiosa luz ulterior. *Bartleby* define ya un género que hacia 1919 reinventaría y profundizaría Franz Kafka: el de las fantasías de la conducta y del sentimiento o, como ahora malamente se dice, psicológicas" ["Bartleby" 119]).

13. "Si Kafka hubiera escrito esa historia, Wakefield no hubiera conseguido, jamás, volver a su casa; Hawthorne le permite volver, pero su vuelta no es menos lamentable ni menos atroz que su larga ausencia" (Borges, "Nathaniel Hawthorne" 678).

14. Some, including Borges, have seen in the indecipherability of Kafka's stories an echo of the putative capriciousness of the Old Testament God: "You may say that there is nothing strange about that, since Kafka's world is Judaism, and Hawthorne's, the wrath and punishments of the Old Testament" ("Nathaniel Hawthorne" 56) ("Se dirá que ello nada tiene de singular, pues el orbe de Kafka es el judaísmo, y el de Hawthorne, las iras y los castigos del Viejo Testamento" ["Nathaniel Hawthorne" 677).

15. According to Borges, "Hawthorne was a man of continual and curious imagination; but he was refractory, so to speak, to reason. I am not saying he was stupid; I say that he thought in images, in intuitions, as women usually think, not with a

dialectical mechanism" ("Nathaniel Hawthorne" 51). ("Hawthorne era hombre de continua y curiosa imaginación; pero refractario, digámoslo así al pensamiento. No digo que era estúpido; digo que pensaba por imágenes, por intuiciones, como suelen pensar las mujeres, no por un mecanismo dialéctico" [673]. (It goes without saying that this is an unfortunately misogynistic moment in Borges's writings).

16. "Ahora la obra de Kafka es ante todo una alegoría del Estado, pero con el tiempo será una alegoría del universo" (qtd. in Roger 46).

17. "Yo he escrito también algunos cuentos en los cuales traté ambiciosa e inútilmente de ser Kafka. Hay uno, titulado 'La biblioteca de Babel' y algún otro, que fueron ejercicios en donde traté de ser Kafka. Esos cuentos interesaron pero yo me di cuenta de que no había cumplido mi propósito y que debía buscar otro camino" (Borges, "Un sueño eterno" 232).

18. The reference to Babel may be one to Kafka's "The Great Wall of China." There, Kafka writes: "First, then, it must be said that in those days things were achieved scarcely inferior to the construction of the Tower of Babel . . . I say this because during the early days of building a scholar wrote a book in which he drew the comparison in the most exhaustive way. In it he tried to prove that the Tower of Babel failed to reach its goal, not because of the reasons universally advanced . . . the tower failed and was bound to fail because of the weakness of the foundation . . . he maintained that the Great Wall alone would provide for the first time in the history

of mankind a secure foundation for a new Tower of Babel" (134).

19. "El universo (que otros llaman la Biblioteca) se compone de un número indefinido, y tal vez infinito, de galerías hexagonales, con vastos pozos de ventilación en el medio, cercados por barandas bajísimas" (Borges, "La biblioteca de Babel" 469).

20. "La Biblioteca es total y que sus anaqueles registran todas las posibles combinaciones de los veintitantos símbolos ortográficos (número, aunque vastísimo, no infinito) o sea todo lo que es dable expresar: en todos los idiomas" (Borges, "La biblioteca de Babel" 469).

21. "Había ciertos leones de piedra, había una letrina sagrada llamada Qaphqa, había unas grietas en un polvoriento acueducto que, según opinión general, daban a la Compañía; las personas malignas o benévolas depositaban delaciones en esos sitios" (Borges, "La lotería en Babilonia" 458). Federico Finchelstein has noted about this passage: "Here 'the Company' fills the empty spaces of meaning with an ideology that produces something new, magical and suggestive. But this gift presents a dimension of meaning located beyond reason. It is a gift of death. This is, in short, the oxymoronic moment of fascist totalitarianism. The reference to Kafka as a sacred latrine emphasizes this contradiction" (155).

22. "No se publica un libro sin alguna divergencia entre cada uno de lo ejemplares. Los escribas prestan juramento secreto de omitir, de interpolar, de variar. También se ejerce la mentira indirecta" (Borges, "La lotería en Babilonia" 460).

23. "La Compañía, con modestia divina, elude toda publicidad. Sus agentes, como es natural, son secretos . . . Ese funcionamiento silencioso, comparable al de Dios, provoca toda suerte de conjeturas. Alguna abominablemente insinúa que hace ya siglos que no existe la Compañía y que el sacro desorden de nuestras vidas es puramente hereditario, tradicional; otra la juzga eterna y enseña que perdurará hasta la última noche, cuando el último dios anonade el mundo. Otra declara que la Compañía es omnipotente, pero que sólo influye en cosas minúsculas: en el grito de un pájaro, en los matices de la herrumbre y del polvo, en los entresueños del alba. Otra, por boca de heresiarcas enmascarados, que no ha existido nunca y no existirá. Otra, no menos vil, razona que es indiferente afirmar o negar la realidad de la tenebrosa corporación, porque Babilonia no es otra cosa que un infinito juego de azares" (Borges, "La lotería en Babilonia" 460).

24. Sarlo notes: "'The Lottery in Babylon' (and also, although it is more openly metaphysical, 'The Library of Babel') could be read not only as philosophical but also as political-philosophical fictions" (78).

25. "Ese leve peligro (por cada treinta números favorables había un número aciago) despertó, como es natural, el interés del público" (Borges, "La lotería en Babilonia" 457).

26. "Otra inquietud cundía en los barrios bajos. Los miembros del colegio sacerdotal multiplicaban las puestas y gozaban de todas las vicisitudes del terror y de la esperanza; los pobres (con envidia razonable o inevitable) se sabían excluidos de ese vaivén, notoriamente delicioso. El justo anhelo de que todos, pobres y ricos, participasen por igual en la lotería, inspiró una indignada agitación, cuya memoria no han desdibujado los años. . . . Hubo disturbios, hubo efusiones lamentables de sangre; pero la gente babilónica impuso finalmente su voluntad, contra la oposición de los ricos. El pueblo consiguió con plenitud sus fines generosos. En primer término, logró que la Compañía aceptara la suma del poder público. (Esa unificación era necesaria, dada la vastedad y complejidad de las nuevas operaciones.) En segundo término, logró que la lotería fuera secreta, gratuita y general" (Borges, "La lotería en Babilonia" (457–58).

27. Roberto Lépori presents this story as the moment when Borges goes from being a liberal to a conservative, even a radical rightist in the vein of Lugones. According to Lépori, "The Lottery in Babylon" "can be read as an attack on democracy" ("un ataque a la democracia," 8). However, given Borges's personal opposition to fascism and Nazism, it is more appropriate to see in it the beginning of his disillusionment with democracy, which developed during the Peronist regime and reached its sad conclusion in the great writer's early, temporary support for Southern Cone dictatorships of the 1970s.

28. Piglia has referred to Kafka on numerous occasions in other texts. The most sustained critical encounter with Kafka is in his *El último lector*, which examines his correspondence with Felice Bauer. Toward

the end of his first television les-
son on Borges, Piglia concludes:
"Borges and Kafka are the writers
of the twentieth century" ("Borges
y Kafka son los escritores del siglo
veinte"). In his third class, he clari-
fies his evaluation of these writers:
"We know Kafka is the best of all"
("Sabemos que Kafka es el mejor
de todos").

29. "A Elías y Rubén, que me ayudaron
a conocer la verdad de la historia"
(Piglia, *Respiración artificial*, 11).

30. "En este juego infinito de descifra-
mientos, el de Emilio Renzi toma la
forma de un dilema: ¿cómo narrar el
presente? ¿cómo narrar la búsqueda
de Marcelo Maggi? ¿cuál es el lenguaje que narra la relación de la Argentina con su(s) historia(s)?" (Avelar 421).

31. "Si hay una historia empieza hace tres
años. En abril de 1976, cuando se publica mi primer libro, él me manda
una carta" (Piglia, *Respiración artificial* 15).

32. Daniel Balderston, in his introduction to his translation of the novel,
points out: "The two men to whom
the novel is dedicated are among
the thousands of the 'disappeared,'
and the action begins in April 1976,
just days after the military coup of
March 24, 1976" (2).

33. Although it is beyond the scope of
these comments, Piglia's linkage between European Fascism—in his
case Nazism—and the Southern
Cone dictatorships of the 1970s and,
more generally, Spanish American history, are precedent for, and
possible influence on, Roberto
Bolaño.

34. "La utopía atroz de un mundo convertido en una inmensa colonia peni-
tenciaria, de eso le habla Adolf, el
desertor insignificante y grotesco, a
Franz Kafka que lo sabe oír, en las
mesas del café Arcos, en Praga, a
fines de 1909. Y Kafka le cree. Piensa
que es posible que los proyectos im-
posibles y atroces de ese hombrecito
ridículo y famélico lleguen a cum-
plirse y que el mundo se transforme
en eso que las palabras estaban cons-
truyendo: El Castillo de la Orden y
la Cruz gamada, la máquina del mal
que graba su mensaje en la carne de
las víctimas. ¿No supo él oír la voz
abominable de la historia?" (Piglia,
Respiración artificial 208).

35. "La palabra *Ungeziefer*, dijo Tardewski, con que los nazis desig-
narían a los detenidos en los campos de concentración, es la misma
palabra que usa Kafka para designar
eso en que se ha convertido Gregorio Samsa una mañana, al despertar"
(Piglia, *Respiración artificial* 208).

36. In a 2017 conversation with Rubén
Gallo, after being asked about his
lifelong commitment to journalism, Vargas Llosa replied: "Perhaps that's why I am a realist writer
and not one of fantastic literature. I never attempt to create a
world that is totally independent
from the real world. In my novels
I have attempted to show a world
that has at least the appearance of
the real world" ("Quizá por eso soy
un escritor realista y no un escritor
fantástico. Yo nunca trato de crear
un mundo completamente soberano,
independiente del mundo real. En
mis novelas he querido mostrar un

mundo que tiene por lo menos la apariencia del mundo real") (*Conversación en Princeton*).

37. "Una de las obras maestras del género" (Vargas Llosa, "*La muerte en Venecia*" 19).

38. "Sólo digo que *Así se templó el acero* me aburrió y que me gustó *El castillo*" (Vargas Llosa, *Conversación en La Catedral* 124).

39. Vargas Llosa's most sustained reflection on Kafka is "La tumba de Kafka," a 2019 article detailing his visit to Prague, to his tomb, and to the Franz Kafka Muzeum. He dwells briefly, though with analytical care, on Kafka's works, in particular *The Metamorphosis*, in his *Cartas a un joven novelista* (*Letters to a Young Novelist*, 1997).

40. Although no name is given to the first-person narrator, his writerly career hews close to well-known facts of Vargas Llosa's life. For instance, like Vargas Llosa, he lives in Madrid and then Paris, is obviously successful, and had a TV program titled *La torre de Babel*.

41. Kristal notes: "*The Storyteller* can be read as a literary expression of Vargas Llosa's concerns about Peru's autochthonous cultures after he ceased to believe in Marxist solutions;" and, "*The Storyteller* is not an *indigenista* novel because it does not purport to document the complex historical, political, or anthropological reality of Peruvian Indians . . . But the novel does address the issue of *indigenismo* through the narrator, a man who had sympathized with *indigenismo* in his youth but who became disenchanted with it as he grew older" (*The Temptation of the Word* 158). William Rowe, after noting that the parts told by the "storyteller," "read like a bad indigenista novel" (61), adds: "What is clearly shown by this text, whose author is placed in Florence, symbol of the perfection of European high culture and center from which the marginalities look the same, is that Vargas Llosa cannot conceive of simultaneous and opposing sets of signs, that is, of a heterogeneous culture, but only of an alienated discourse as the sole way in which the Other can speak within the nation, leaving us the only option an eventual integration or disappearance of the Other into a single national discourse—an apologetics for acculturation" (61).

42. Critically, Jean Franco argues that "the novel is composed, on the one hand, by an autobiographical narrative by Mario Vargas Llosa and, on the other, by a pastiche of Matsigenka folklore and legends. The novel is a narrative of the search for the Other that pretends to be the voice of the Other" ("La novela se compone por una parte, de una narración autobiográfica contada por Mario Vargas Llosa y por otra, de un pastiche del folclore y la leyenda Machinguenga. La novela es un relato de una búsqueda del Otro a la vez que pretende ser la voz del Otro") ("¿La historia de quién? La piratería postmoderna?" 34). As the article's title notes, this makes the novel an example of "postmodern piracy."

43. "Visto con la perspectiva del tiempo, sabiendo lo que le ocurrió después

—he pensado mucho en esto— puedo decir que Saúl experimentó una conversión. En un sentido cultural y acaso también religioso. Es la única experiencia concreta que me ha tocado observar de cerca que parecía dar sentido, materializar, eso que los religiosos del colegio donde estudié querían decirnos en las clases de catecismo con expresiones como «recibir la gracia», «ser tocado por la gracia», «caer en las celadas de la gracia». Desde el primer contacto que tuvo con la Amazonía, Mascarita fue atrapado en una emboscada espiritual que hizo de él una persona distinta. No sólo porque se desinteresó del Derecho y se matriculó en Etnología y por la nueva orientación de sus lecturas, en las que, salvo Gregorio Samsa, no sobrevivió personaje literario alguno, sino porque, desde entonces, comenzó a preocuparse, a obsesionarse, con dos asuntos que en los años siguientes serían su único tema de conversación: el estado de las culturas amazónicas y la agonía de los bosques que las hospedaban" (Vargas Llosa, *El hablador* 21–22).

44. "Andando por la calle con Saúl se descubría lo molesta que tenía que ser su vida, por la insolencia y la maldad de la gente. Se volvían o se plantaban a su paso, para mirarlo mejor, y abrían mucho los ojos, sin disimular el asombro o la repulsión que les inspiraba su cara, y no era raro que, los chiquillos sobre todo, le dijeran majadería" (Vargas Llosa, *El hablador* 16).

45. "—Tú no entras, monstruo. —Se había enfurecido súbitamente—. Con esa cara, no debías salir a la calle, asustas a la gente" (Vargas Llosa, *El hablador* 16).

46. "Con excepción de Kafka, y, sobre todo, *La metamorfosis*, que había releído innumerables veces y poco menos que memorizado, todas sus lecturas eran ahora antropológicas" (Vargas Llosa, *El hablador* 19).

47. "Suddenly he touched his enormous birthmark. 'I wouldn't have passed the test, pal. They'd have liquidated me', he whispered. 'They say the Spartans did the same thing, right? Those little monsters, those Gregor Samsas, were hurled down from the top of Mount Taygetus, right?'" (Vargas Llosa, *The Storyteller* 25). ("—Yo no hubiera pasado el examen, compadre. A mí me hubieran liquidado —susurró—. Dicen que los espartanos hacían lo mismo, ¿no? Que a los monstruitos, a los gregorios samsas, los despeñaban desde el monte Taigeto, ¿no?" [Vargas Llosa, *El hablador* 27]).

48. "Un marginal entre los marginales, un hombre cuyo destino estaría, siempre, acosado por un estigma de fealdad" (Vargas Llosa, *El hablador* 233).

49. "Yo era gente. Yo tenía familia. Yo estaba durmiendo. Y en eso me desperté. Apenas abrí los ojos comprendí ¡ay, Tasurinchi! Me había convertido en insecto, pues. Una chicharra–machacuy, tal vez. Tasurinchi–gregorio era. Estaba tendido de espaldas. El mundo se habría vuelto más grande, entonces. Me daba cuenta de todo. Esas patas velludas, anilladas, eran mis patas. Esas alas color barro, transparentes, que crujían con mis movimientos, doliéndome tanto, habrían sido antes

mis brazos. La pestilencia que me envolvía ¿mi olor? Veía este mundo de una manera distinta: su abajo y su arriba, su delante y su atrás veía al mismo tiempo. Porque ahora, siendo insecto, tenía varios ojos. ¿Qué te ha ocurrido, pues, Tasurinchi–gregorio? ¿Un brujo malo, comiéndose una mecha de tus pelos, te cambió? ¿Un diablillo kamagarini, entrándose en ti por el ojo de tu trasero, te volvió así? Sentí mucha vergüenza reconociéndome. ¿Qué diría mi familia? Porque yo tenía familia como los demás hombres que andan, parece. ¿Qué pensarían al verme convertido en un animalejo inmundo? Una chicharra–machacuy se aplasta nomás. ¿Sirve acaso para comer? ¿Para curar los daños sirve? Ni para preparar los bebedizos sucios del machikanari, tal vez" (Vargas Llosa, *El hablador* 196).

50. For a detailed analysis of the differences between Kafka's and Vargas Llosa's version of *The Metamorphosis*, see Chandler Caldwell.

51. "El hablador, o los habladores, debían de ser algo así como los correos de la comunidad. Personajes que se desplazaban de uno a otro caserío, por el amplio territorio en el que estaban aventados los machiguengas, refiriendo a unos lo que hacían los otros, informándoles recíprocamente sobre las ocurrencias, las aventuras y desventuras de esos hermanos a los que veían muy rara vez o nunca. El nombre los definía. Hablaban. Sus bocas eran los vínculos aglutinantes de esa sociedad a la que la lucha por la supervivencia había obligado a resquebrajarse" (Vargas Llosa, *El hablador* 91).

52. "El proyecto tan bien planeado y ejecutado hasta ahora —leer a Dante y Machiavelli y ver pintura renacentista durante un par de meses" (Vargas Llosa, *El hablador* 7).

53. "El que se deja ganar por la rabia tuerce esas líneas y ellas, torcidas, ya no pueden sostener la tierra" (Vargas Llosa, *El hablador* 17).

54. "Nací con un lunar blanco, o lo que otros llaman una mancha de nacimiento, sobre la córnea de mi ojo derecho. No habría tenido ninguna relevancia de no haber sido porque la mácula en cuestión estaba en pleno centro del iris, es decir justo sobre la pupila por la que debe entrar la luz hasta el fondo del cerebro" (Nettel, *El cuerpo en que nací*).

55. "Me decidí a habitar el cuerpo en el que había nacido, con todas sus particularidades. A fin de cuentas era lo único que me pertenecía y me vinculaba de forma tangible con el mundo, a la vez que me permitía distinguirme de él" (Nettel, *El cuerpo en que nací*).

56. After noting Kafka's participation in groups and activities that promoted physical well-being, Robertson argues: "In Kafka's case, however, this physical activity does not indicate an untroubled acceptance of his body. It is one side of a deep ambivalence. The other side finds expression in constant complaints in his diary about his thin, unhealthy body, which he fears is too long for his weak heart to be able to pump blood through it. Some alarming diary entries imagine a hideous punishment being inflicted on his body" (49).

57. "Al identificarse con el personaje de Kafka, no sólo asume un lugar en el mundo, sino que además asigna las posturas que los otros tendrán en relación con ella" (Murcia, 83).

58. "Aunque la autoficción es un relato que se presenta como novela, es decir como ficción, o sin determinación genérica (nunca como autobiografía o memorias), se caracteriza por tener una apariencia autobiográfica, ratificada por la identidad nominal de autor, narrador y personaje. Es precisamente este cruce de géneros lo que configura un espacio narrativo de perfiles contradictorios, pues transgrede o al menos contraviene por igual el principio de distanciamiento de autor y personaje que rige el pacto novelesco y el principio de veracidad del pacto autobiográfico" (Alberca 115–16).

59. "—Ya me contó mi mamá lo de tu autobiografía. —Y después de soltar una especie de carcajada añadió–: Aunque no la ha leído, dice que te llevará a corte por difamación" (Nettel, *El cuerpo en que nací*). This episode is based on the real-life concern expressed by Nettel's mother: "My mother was very fearful, even though she said she hadn't read it. But her friends made positive comments so she began to think it was not so ominous that her daughter write about her." ("Mi madre tenía mucho miedo, aunque dice que no lo leyó. No lo sé. Pero como sus amigos le hicieron buenos comentarios le fue pareciendo menos ominoso que su hija escribiera acerca de ella)" (Nettel, "Guadalupe Nettel").

60. "Por primera vez en un año y medio me senté a escribir con gusto en la computadora decidida a convertir en realidad esa 'famosa novela'. Voy a terminarla aunque me lleven a juicio o lo que sea. Será un relato sencillo y corto. No contaré nada en lo que no crea" (Nettel, *El cuerpo en que nací*).

61. "Viví todos estos sucesos dolorosos como un drama, y recordarlos, reflexionar, ponerlos en papel y hacer con ellos literatura fue una oportunidad de poner distancia y orden en mi cabeza, y también de reírme, de burlarme un poco de mí misma, de mis obsesiones y de mi familia. No sé cómo lo van a tomar ellos, pero fue sano y muy placentero" (Nettel qtd. in Palapa Quijas).

62. "El cuerpo en que nací es una novela transparentemente autobiográfica. O tal vez, más precisamente, un largo ensayo autobiográfico" (Luiselli).

63. Vargas Llosa, whose *La tía Julia y el escribidor* (*Aunt Julia and the Scriptwriter*) (1977) is perhaps the first Latin American autofiction, has written about Kafka's "Letter to My Father": "I got along very poorly with my father, of whom I was afraid, and I felt completely identified with that text from its first lines, especially when Kafka accuses his progenitor of having made him insecure, distrusting of everyone and of his own vocation" ("Me llevaba muy mal con mi padre, al que le tenía pánico, y me sentí totalmente identificado con ese texto desde las primeras líneas, sobre todo cuando Kafka acusa a su progenitor de haberlo vuelto inseguro, desconfiado de todos, de sí mismo y de su propia vocación") (Vargas Llosa, "La tumba de Kafka").

64. "Recuerdo a una nena muy dulce que era paralítica, un enano, una rubia de

labio leporino, un niño con leuce-
mia que nos abandonó antes de ter-
minar la primaria. Todos nosotros
compartíamos la certeza de que
no éramos iguales a los demás y de
que conocíamos mejor esta vida que
aquella horda de inocentes que, en
su corta existencia, aún no habían
enfrentado ninguna desgracia" (Nettel, *El cuerpo en que nací*).

65. "Tanto parecía llamarle la atención
esa tendencia mía al enconchamiento
que terminó encontrando un apodo
o «nombre de cariño» que, según
ella, correspondía perfectamente a
mi manera de caminar. —Cucaracha!
—gritaba cada dos o tres horas—, ¡en-
dereza la espalda! —Cucarachita, es
hora de ponerse la atropina" (Nettel,
El cuerpo en que nací).

66. "Veía ahora lombrices de tierra, es-
carabajos y cucarachas. Estas últimas
en particular mostraban en mis vi-
siones una actitud amable, incluso
benevolente hacia mi persona. A
diferencia de los demás insectos, las
cucarachas no me miraban con ojos
agresivos y desafiantes, al contrario,
parecían estar ahí para impedir que
otros animales vinieran a molestarme.
Por eso, cada vez que encontraba una
en mi cuarto, en vez del nerviosismo"
(Nettel, *El cuerpo en que nací*).

67. Nettel had already resorted to comparison with the cockroach in an earlier story, "Guerra en los basureros"
(War in the Trashcans) in her collection *El matrimonio de los peces rojos* (The Wedding of the Red Fish)
(2013). While the story aims to disgust, it also insinuates a peculiar
connection between the protagonist, an entomologist, and his subject of study: "Some, associated with

my discipline, have pointed out that
when I enter a laboratory or classroom, I always find comfort in the
corners of the room. Likewise, when
I walk down the street, I always feel
more secure walking near the walls.
Although I don't really know why
this is the case, I have concluded
that it's a habit connected with my
deepest nature" ("algunas personas
vinculadas a mi campo de investiga-
ción me han hecho notar que cuando
entro en un laboratorio o en las aulas
de clase, casi siempre prefiero aco-
modarme en las esquinas; del mismo
modo en que, cuando camino por
la calle, me muevo con mayor se-
guridad si estoy cerca de un muro.
Aunque no sabría explicar exactamente por qué, he llegado a pensar
que se trata de un hábito relacio-
nado con mi naturaleza profunda")
(43). In fact, when the protagonist
sees a cockroach for the first time,
there is a connection between the
young boy and his future object of
study: "I thought that insect looked
at me and in its eyes I recognized the
same surprise and distrust I felt for
it" ("Me pareció que aquel insecto
me miraba y en sus ojos reconocí la
misma sorpresa y desconfianza que
yo sentía por él" (50). The connections with Nettel appear in an interview: "Cockroaches crawl alongside
the house walls. I also walk close to
the walls, partly to protect myself
and partly to just go unnoticed" (qtd.
in Hecht 53).

68. "As the protagonist approaches
adolescence, a critical moment in
identitary formation, when vital
experiences, as well as the body,
experiment crucial transformations

that will definitely influence an individual's future, there is a feeling of strangeness that is intimately related with the marginal trait of the [Kafka's] character. Kafka becomes a point of reference for her understanding of her own reality" ("Conforme la protagonista se acerca a la adolescencia, en un momento crítico de la formación identitaria, cuando tanto las experiencias vitales como el cuerpo sufren transformaciones cruciales que repercutirán definitivamente en el futuro del individuo, se produce un sentimiento de extrañeza que se relaciona íntimamente con el carácter marginal del personaje. Kafka se vuelve para ella un punto de referencia para entender su propia realidad") (Murcia 82).

69. "Me identificaba por completo con el personaje de *La metamorfosis*, a quien le ocurrió algo semejante a mi historia. Yo también me había levantado una mañana con una vida distinta, un cuerpo distinto y sin saber bien a bien en qué me había convertido. En ningún lugar del relato se dice exactamente qué insecto era Gregorio Samsa, pero yo asumí muy rápido que se trataba de una cucaracha. Él se había convertido en una mientras que yo lo era por decreto materno, si no es que desde mi nacimiento" (Nettel, *El cuerpo en que nací*).

70. "Mi lectura de *La metamorfosis* fue de lo más confusa. Durante las primeras páginas, no conseguía saber si era una desgracia o una bendición lo que le había ocurrido al personaje que, por si fuera poco, nunca

demostraba ningún entusiasmo pero tampoco dramatismo. Como él, yo también causaba cierta repulsión entre mis compañeros" (Nettel, *El cuerpo en que nací*).

71. "Por fin, después de un largo periplo, me decidí a habitar el cuerpo en el que había nacido, con todas sus particularidades. A fin de cuentas era lo único que me pertenecía y me vinculaba de forma tangible con el mundo, a la vez que me permitía distinguirme de él" (Nettel, *El cuerpo en que nací*).

72. "Como la inutilidad de la religión, la existencia de Santa Claus, en quien nunca nos permitieron creer, o la forma en que los niños vienen al mundo" (Nettel, *El cuerpo en que nací*).

73. "La libertad sexual terminó por perjudicar a mi familia cuando mis padres adoptaron una práctica muy de moda durante los años setenta: la entonces famosa «apertura de pareja" (Nettel, *El cuerpo en que nací*).

74. "Se dice que el giro tan conservador que dio la generación a la que pertenezco se debe en gran medida a la aparición del sida, yo estoy segura de que nuestra actitud es en buena parte una reacción a la forma tan experimental en que nuestros padres encararon la vida adulta" (Nettel, *El cuerpo en que nací*).

75. Piglia has referred on more than one occasion to Deleuze. In fact, he includes a reference to *Kafka: Toward a Minor Literature*, and to Deleuze's *Foucault*, in his *Las tres vanguardias: Saer, Puig, Walsh*. However, Deleuze and Guattari are absent from *Crítica*

y ficción (1986), his first major critical work and the one nearest chronologically to *Respiración artificial* (1980).

76. "Los primogénitos del boom" (Bolaño, "Bolaño a la vuelta de la esquina").

CHAPTER 5

1. As far as I can tell, there are no photographs by Martí, a dapper nineteenth-century gentleman, or Sandino, wearing a *liqui liqui*.

2. "¿Y qué si no mítico puede ser ese tiempo de todos los tiempos? Paradojalmente, ese modo extraño de revelar la intransferible identidad de una historia, resulta ser una racionalidad, pues hace inteligible el universo, la especificidad de ese universo. Eso es, a mi juicio, lo que básicamente hizo o logró García Marquez en *Cien años de soledad*. Eso, sin duda, vale un Premio Nobel" (Quijano "Modernidad, identidad y utopía en América Latina" 62).

3. "Una realidad que no es la del papel, sino que vive con nosotros y determina cada instante de nuestras incontables muertes cotidianas, y que sustenta un manantial de creación insaciable, pleno de desdicha y de belleza, del cual este colombiano errante y nostálgico no es más que una cifra más señalada por la suerte. Poetas y mendigos, músicos y profetas, guerreros y malandrines, todas las criaturas de aquella realidad desaforada hemos tenido que pedirle muy poco a la imaginación, porque el desafío mayor para nosotros ha sido la insuficiencia de los recursos convencionales para hacer creíble nuestra vida" (García Márquez, "La soledad de Latinoamérica").

4. "Mis fuentes han sido fundamentalmente latinoamericanas. Y además, África está llena de Macondos, de pueblos así, como el de Gabo" (Couto, "Entrevista a Mia Couto, escritor y poeta mozambiqueño").

5. There are numerous other testimonies from Global South writers about the affinity between García Márquez's fictional world and local realities. This is from López-Calvo: "At a 2013 literature conference in Incheon, South Korea, I had an interesting conversation over breakfast with the writers Kole Omotoso, from Nigeria, and Syl Cheney Coker, from Sierra Leone. They coincided in their reaction to reading Gabriel García Márquez's *One Hundred Years of Solitude* (1967): 'What I read there was no different from everyday life in my home country,' both agreed" ("On Magical Realism as an International Phenomenon" xvi).

6. "Todos los escritores africanos tenemos una deuda con lo que se conoce como realismo mágico latinoamericano porque creo que de alguna forma nos alentó y nos autorizó a romper con el modelo europeo" (Couto, "Entrevista a Mia Couto").

7. García Márquez is presenting, in somewhat simplistic terms, a version of Alejo Carpentier's "the real marvelous." In Carpentier's celebrated prologue to *El reino de este*

mundo (*The Kingdom of This World* 1949), he wrote: "Because of the virginity of its landscape, because of its formation, because of its ontology, because of the Faustian presence of the Indian and the Black, because of the Revelation its recent discovery constituted, because of the fertile racial mixtures it favored, the Americas are far from having used up their wealth of mythologies" (198). Carpentier concludes: "But what is the history of the Americas but the chronicle of the real marvelous" (198). ("Y es que, por la virginidad del paisaje, por la formación, por la ontología, por la presencia fáustica del indio y del negro, por la revelación que constituyó su reciente descubrimiento, por los fecundos mestizajes que propició, América está muy lejos de haber agotado su caudal de mitologías.?" And: "¿Pero qué es la historia de América toda sino una crónica de lo real maravilloso?" [30, 31]). For a lucid reading of the history of magical realism from the early works of Asturias, Carpentier, and Arturo Uslar Pietri to García Márquez and its worldwide expansion, see Mariano Siskind's "The Global Life of Genres and the Material Travels of Magical Realism" in *Cosmopolitan Desires* (59–100).

8. According to the Colombian Ministry of Commerce, Industry, and Tourism in 2013, "'Colombia, Magical Realism' is the new slogan for the promotion of tourism from foreign countries, conceived with the purpose of creating interest in foreign tourists who procure 'different,' 'magical,' 'unique,' and 'surprising' experiences. It is constructed on the strategy of answering this interest and the answer is Colombia" ("Colombia, realismo mágico" es el nuevo eslogan para la promoción del turismo en el exterior, concebida para despertar el interés de los turistas extranjeros que procuran vivencias "diferentes", "mágicas", "únicas" y "sorprendentes", y construida sobre la estrategia de dar una respuesta, y la respuesta es Colombia) ("Colombia, realismo mágico" n.p.).

9. Feminist critics such as María Rosa Olivera-Williams have begun to reevaluate both Isabel Allende and Laura Esquivel (see Olivera-Williams, "Boom" 287–89, and her forthcoming "Twentieth-Century Women Writers").

10. "Uno de los poetas insignes de nuestro tiempo" (García Márquez, "La soledad de América Latina").

11. "Sueños de unión entre un norte casto y un sur apasionado" (García Márquez, "La soledad de América Latina").

12. "Mi maestro William Faulkner dijo en este lugar: 'me niego a admitir el fin del hombre'" (García Márquez, "La soledad de América Latina").

13. In his 1950 article "Otra vez el premio Nobel," García Márquez gives qualified praise to Gabriela Mistral while stating his preference for Neruda: "In Chile, Gabriela Mistral received the desired award. Her poetic work is of undeniable worth. However, it would be necessary to forget the existence of her great conational Pablo Neruda in order to affirm that

Mistral was the South American poet who truly deserved the Nobel Prize in Literature" ("Gabriela Mistral, en Chile, se hizo acreedora al codiciado premio. Su obra poética tiene un valor indudable. Pero sería necesario olvidar a otro gran compatriota suyo, Pablo Neruda, antes de afirmar que era la Mistral quien verdaderamente merecía, en Suramérica, el Premio Nobel de Literatura") (194). Regarding Mistral's use of traditional "feminine" topics, Licia Fiol-Matta argues: "Traditional interpretations of Mistral's 'maternal' figure, such as the desexualized mother, the stock matronly figure, and the avuncular figure, illustrate aspects of gender that apply to her. Although they all point to the question of her gender variance, the failure to take queer sexuality into account leaves the analysis short of interpretive power" (44).

14.　Gerald Martin refers to García Márquez's reaction: "The announcement that another father figure always rejected by García Márquez, Guatemalan writer Miguel Ángel Asturias, had been awarded the Nobel Prize for Literature, the first Latin American novelist ever to be so honoured. (A poet, the Chilean Gabriela Mistral, had won in 1945.) This was obviously interpreted all over the world as a symbolic acknowledgement of the ongoing Boom of the Latin American novel. Asturias and García Márquez, the two greatest 'magical realists' who seemed to have so much in common, would soon come to cordially detest one

another. Asturias, belatedly crowned, would fear the young pretender, and García Márquez, newly acclaimed, would seem bent on parricide" (323).

15.　Although García Márquez found little of value in Spanish American narrative, he was a fanatic of Spanish-language poetry. García Márquez loved poetry from the Spanish Golden Age to Pablo Neruda and the Colombian master Pablo de Greif. In *Living to Tell the Tale*, he describes his early passion: "We not only believed in poetry, and would have died for it, but we also knew with certainty—as Luis Cardoza y Aragón wrote—that 'poetry is the only concrete proof of the existence of man'" (252) ("No sólo creíamos en la poesía, y nos moríamos por ella, sino que sabíamos con certeza—como lo escribió Luis Cardoza y Aragón—que la 'poesía es la única prueba concreta dela existencia del hombre" [*Vivir para contarla* 304]).

16.　"—¿Leíste Doña Bárbara? —Por supuesto —le contesté—, y casi todo lo demás de Rómulo Gallegos. . . . La verdad es que en aquel momento, con mi fiebre de cuarenta grados por las sagas del Misisipí, empezaba a verle las costuras a la novela vernácula." (García Márquez, *Vivir para contarla* 35).

17.　In 1950 García Márquez wrote in the column "Otra vez el Premio Nobel": "Everything seems to indicate that Rómulo Gallegos will be the Nobel Prize in Literature in 1950. A significant number of (Latin) American intellectuals are satisfied with his candidacy, that is, moreover, backed by a widely disseminated and serious body of work, though its also understandably overrated" ("Todo parece indicar que Rómulo Gallegos será Premio Nobel de Literatura en 1950. Un respetable sector de la inteligencia americana se muestra satisfecho con esa candidatura que está, además, respaldada por una obra seria, justamente divulgada, aunque también explicablemente sobreestimada") (194).

18. "Admiradores precoces de Jorge Luis Borges, de Julio Cortázar, de Felisberto Hernández" (García Márquez, *Vivir para contarla* 135).

19. "El insólito cuentista uruguayo" (García Márquez, *Vivir para contarla* 425).

20. "El primer mensaje esperanzador de una España remota silenciada por dos guerras" (García Márquez, *Vivir para contarla* 135).

21. "Los novelistas ingleses y norteamericanos bien traducidos por la cuadrilla de Victoria Ocampo" (García Márquez, *Vivir para contarla* 135).

22. In a 1949 article on the occasion of William Faulkner being granted the Nobel Prize, a young García Márquez expressed his admiration for the author of *The Sound and the Fury* and his negative views on Thomas Mann: "The intransigent admirers of Faulkner find it uncomfortable to see the master seated at the same table with Mrs. Buck, Herman Hesse, and Thomas Mann" ("A los intransigentes admiradores de Faulkner nos resulta por lo menos incómodo ver al maestro sentado en la misma mesa con la señora Buck, con

Herman Hesse, con Thomas Mann") ("Faulkner, Premio Nobel" 495).

23. "Más tarde, cuando empecé a leer a Faulkner, también los pueblos de sus novelas me parecían iguales a los nuestros. Y no era sorprendente, pues éstos habían sido construidos bajo la inspiración mesiánica de la United Fruit Company, y con su mismo estilo provisional de campamento de paso" (García Márquez, *Vivir para contarla* 21).

24. "Entonces tomé conciencia de que mi aventura de leer *Ulises* a los veinte años, y más tarde *El sonido y la furia*, eran dos audacias prematuras sin futuro, y decidí releerlos con una óptica menos prevenida. En efecto, mucho de lo que me había parecido pedante o hermético en Joyce y Faulkner se me reveló entonces con una belleza y una sencillez aterradoras" (García Márquez, *Vivir para contarla* 441)

25. "La metamorfosis de Franz Kafka . . . definió un camino nuevo para mi vida desde la primera línea, y que hoy es una de las divisas grandes de la literatura universal: «Al despertar Gregorio Samsa una mañana, tras un sueño intranquilo, encontróse en su cama convertido en un monstruoso insecto». Eran libros misteriosos, cuyos desfiladeros no eran sólo distintos sino muchas veces contrarios a todo lo que conocía hasta entonces. No era necesario demostrar los hechos: bastaba con que el autor lo hubiera escrito para que fuera verdad, sin más pruebas que el poder de su talento y la autoridad de su voz" (García Márquez, *Vivir para contarla* 298).

26. "Las sobremesas . . . no fueron entonces con poemas del Siglo de Oro y los *Veinte poemas de amor* de Neruda, sino con párrafos de *La señora Dalloway* y los delirios de su personaje desgarrado, Septimus Warren Smith" (García Márquez, *Vivir para contarla* 409).

27. "Mis dos maestros mayores eran los dos novelistas norteamericanos que parecían tener menos cosas en común. Había leído todo lo que ellos habían publicado hasta entonces, pero no como lecturas complementarias, sino todo lo contrario: como dos formas distintas y casi excluyentes de concebir la literatura. Uno de ellos era William Faulkner . . . El otro era aquel hombre efímero que acababa de decirme adiós desde la otra acera, y me había dejado la impresión de que algo había ocurrido en mi vida, y que había ocurrido para siempre" (García Márquez, "Mi Hemingway personal" 286).

28. "La lectura inesperada de *El viejo y el mar*, de Hemingway, que llegó de sorpresa en la revista *Life en Español*, acabó de restablecerme de mis quebrantos" (García Márquez, "Mi Hemingway personal" 502).

29. "Por debajo de Dos Passos, de Steinbeck y, desde luego, del creador más extraordinario y vital del mundo moderno, William Faulkner" (García Márquez, "Al otro lado del río entre los árboles" 289).

30. In *Living to Tell the Tale*, a young García Márquez, living with his parents, receives a parcel with books from his Cartagena friends: "There were twenty-three distinguished works by contemporary authors, all of them in Spanish and selected with the evident intention that they be read for the sole purpose of learning to write." In addition to works by Faulkner, Borges, and Hernández, the list included "*Mrs. Dalloway*, by Mrs. Woolf, and *Point Counter Point*, by Aldous Huxley . . . Also *Manhattan Transfer* and perhaps another by John Dos Passos; *Orlando*, by Virginia Woolf; John Steinbeck's *Of Mice and Men* and *The Grapes of Wrath*; *Portrait of Jenny*, by Robert Nathan, and *Tobacco Road*, by Erskine Caldwell. Among the titles I do not remember at a distance of half a century, there was at least one by Hemingway, perhaps a book of short stories, which was the work of his the three in Barranquilla liked best" (*Living to Tell the Tale* 387) ("Eran veintitrés obras distinguidas de autores contemporáneos, todas en español y escogidas con la intención evidente de que fueran leídas con el propósito único de aprender a escribir . . . Sólo había leído dos: *La señora Dalloway*, de la señora Woolf, y *Contrapunto*, de Aldous Huxley . . . También *Manhattan Transfer* y tal vez otro, de John Dos Passos; *Orlando*, de Virginia Woolf; *De ratones y de hombres y Las viñas de la ira*, de John Steinbeck; *El retrato de Jenny*, de Robert Nathan, y *La ruta del tabaco*, de Erskine Caldwell. Entre los títulos que no recuerdo a la distancia de medio siglo había por lo menos uno de Hemingway, tal vez de cuentos" (*Vivir para contarla* 425).

31. The contrast between García Márquez's "Caribbean culture" (*Living*

to *Tell the Tale* 37, 116, 428) ("cultura caribe" [*Vivir para contarla* 40, 127, 469] "Caribbean localisms" (*Living to Tell the Tale* 71) ("localismos Caribe *Vivir para contarla* 78]), and "Caribbean dialect" (*Living to Tell the Tale* 256) ("dialecto caribe" [*Vivir para contarla* 28]], and the language and culture of Bogota is a constant in his writing. In *One Hundred Years of Solitude* this cultural distance is thematized in the character of Fernanda, who is "born and raised in a city six hundred miles away, a gloomy city where on ghostly nights the coaches of the viceroys still rattled through the cobbled streets" (205) ("Había nacido y crecido a mil kilómetros del mar, en una ciudad lúgubre por cuyas callejuelas de piedra traqueteaban todavía, en noches de espantos, las carrozas de los virreyes," *Cien años de soledad*, 237). Fernanda was educated in a convent, where "after having learned to write Latin poetry, play the clavichord, talk about falconry with gentlemen and apologetics, with archbishops, discuss affairs of state with foreign rulers and affairs of God with the Pope, she returned to her parents' home to weave funeral wreaths" (206) ("habiendo aprendido a versificar en latín, a tocar el clavicordio, a conversar de cetrería con los caballeros y de apologética con los arzobispos, a dilucidar asuntos de estado con los gobernantes extranjeros y asuntos de Dios con el Papa, volvió a casa de sus padres a tejer palmas fúnebres" 239).

32. "Todavía no se ha escrito en Colombia la novela que esté indubable y afortunadamente influida por los Joyce, por Faulkner o por Virginia Woolf. Y he dicho 'afortunadamente', porque no creo que podríamos los colombianos ser, por el momento, una excepción al juego de las influencias. En su prólogo a *Orlando*, Virginia confiesa sus influencias. Faulkner mismo no podría negar la que ha ejercido sobre él el mismo Joyce ... Franz Kafka y Proust andan sueltos por la literatura del mundo moderno" (García Márquez, "¿Problemas de la novela?" 269).

33. "Haber descubierto por esa época al autor de la saga de Yoknapatawpha County, el que, desde la primera novela que leí de él —*Las palmeras salvajes*, en la traducción de Borges—, me produjo un deslumbramiento que aún no ha cesado. Fue el primer escritor que estudié con papel y lápiz a la mano, tomando notas para no extraviarme en sus laberintos genealógicos y mudas de tiempo y de puntos de vista, y, también, tratando de desentrañar los secretos de la barroca construcción que era cada una de sus historias" (Vargas Llosa, *El pez en el agua*, 313).

34. Throughout his career, Bolaño criticized "imitators of a magic realism made for the consumption of zombies" ("Vienna and the Shadow of a Woman" 271) ("epígonos de un realismo mágico hecho para el consumo de zombis" ("Viena y la sombra de una mujer" 251). Regarding the rejection of this "magical realist imperative" in recent Mexican narrative, see Ignacio Sánchez Prado's *Strategic Occidentalism*, especially the chapter "The Crack Group contra the Magical Realist Imperative."

35. Molloy writes: "Departments of literature and/or comparative literature in the United States, [are]

intent, if not on 'exoticizing' Latin America, at least on acritically, even ahistorically, 'postcolonizing' it and channeling it through magic realism" (371).

36. "Tal es la locura latina que el editor de una prestigiosa revista literaria se da cuenta que, a cuadras de su oficina, en pleno campus, deambulan tres jóvenes escritores latinoamericanos. El señor se presenta y, sin más ni más, establece

un literary-lunch semanal en la cafetería que mira el río. La idea, dice, es armar un número especial de su prestigiosa revista literaria centrado en el fenómeno latino" (Fuguet and Gómez, 9).

37. "Pues bien, el editor lee los textos hispanos y rechaza dos. Los que desecha poseen el estigma de carecer de realismo mágico" (Fuguet and Gómez, 10).

CHAPTER 6

1. Bolaño, who was not beyond self-contradiction, on occasion referred negatively to García Márquez: "Who are the official inheritors of García Márquez? Isabel Allende, Laura Restrepo, Luis Sepúlveda, and others. Everyday García Márquez seems to me to resemble more and more Santos Chocano or Lugones" (Por ejemplo, ¿quiénes son los herederos oficiales de García Márquez?, pues Isabel Allende, Laura Restrepo, Luis Sepúlveda y algún otro. A mí García Márquez cada día me resulta más semejante a Santos Chocano o en el mejor de los casos a Lugones." "Entrevista con Roberto Bolaño"). Bolaño and Eltit had a feud that originated in his telling details about a dinner at her house that ended by insinuating Eltit had participated in the literary soirees at Mariana Callejas's house, where, mostly unbeknownst to the guests, victims of the Pinochet regime were tortured. Bolaño fictionalized the Callejas story in *Nocturno de Chile*

(*By Night in Chile*, 2003), the last novel published during his life.

2. "Me gustaban los formularios de lecturas de poesía, cócteles, esas cosas absurdas llenas de códigos que de alguna manera me sujetaban, y ustedes eran los terroristas también de estos formularios. Antes de comenzar mi primera lectura de poemas, en la Librería Gandhi, en el remoto año de 1974, me encomendé a Dios—en quien no creía por lo regular, pero a quien tenía que pedírselo—para que por favor no fueran a aparecer los infras. . . . Me daba horror leer en público —me parecía que eso era verdaderamente de payasos—, pero al temor de la tímida se pegaba el pánico del ridículo: los infras podrían aparecer, irrumpir a media sesión y llamarme tonta" (Bolaño, "Carmen Boullosa entrevista a Roberto Bolaño" 112).

3. Bolaño's reality may have been very different from the myth. As López-Calvo notes, "In any case, all this speculation has added to the so-called Bolaño myth by increasing the

bohemian and radical aura of an author who actually spent many years of his life as a devoted family man, quietly writing in his apartment in the Costa Brava" (23).

4. "[Bolaño] realiza sin complicaciones una defenestración del canon de la literatura en lengua española" (Manzoni 351).

5. "Trastoca las verticalidades impuestas por el canon occidental, pero al mismo tiempo somete a la tradición literaria moderna hispanoamericana a ese mismo impulso desestabilizador" (Zavala 60).

6. "Una profecía canónica en la que resuena el eco de la que animó la controversial reflexión del crítico norteamericano Harold Bloom" (336). And: "Una clasificación más cercana al absurdo de la enciclopedia china de Jorge Luis Borges que a la pretensión científica de Bloom" (336).

7. Giving some credence to Hoyos's belief that "the key thinker behind Bolaño's writing is the earlier figure, Bataille," there is one brief mention of the French pre-postmodernist in all of the Chilean's criticism. In his untranslated "En la sala de lectura del infierno," Bolaño describes the queer Spanish poet Leopoldo María Panero: "Sympathetic and monstruous (as he, in his moments of weakness, would like to be read) is the communication of that which he understands as political solidarity, at the same level of tears, that strange, language of limits, which Bataille speaks about" ("Simpático y monstruoso (como tal vez, en sus momentos de debilidad, le gustaría ser leído) es la comunicación aquello que entiende por solidaridad política, en el mismo nivel que las lágrimas, ese lenguaje extraño, limítrofe, del que nos habla Bataille"). In the same article, there is a footnote that references Bataille's *Literature and Evil*. It is worth noting that in "Roberto Bolaño: Solar Anus of World Literature," Hoyos does not to refer to this or any of Bolaño's other essays or interviews. Bataille is also mentioned in Bolaño's "Carnet de baile" (Dance Card).

8. "Para mí, un crítico notable, aunque estoy generalmente en desacuerdo con él y me hace rabiar pero me gusta leerlo, es Harold Bloom" ("Posturas son posturas" 43). Bolaño refers explicitly to Bloom in a few essays and interviews. For instance, when insisting on the importance of Cormac McCarthy's *Blood Meridian*, Bolaño notes: "According to the distinguished Harold Bloom, *Blood Meridian* is one of the best American novels of the twentieth century" (202). In his interview with Boullosa, he brings up Bloom as an authority he significantly contrasts with Nicanor Parra, a poet he held in the highest esteem: "Nicanor Parra says that the best novels are written in meter. And Harold Bloom says that the best poetry of the twentieth century is written in prose. I agree with both."

9. Valerie Miles asked Bloom, "What is your opinion on the work of Bolaño, with whom you exchanged correspondence?" He answered: "There's something there. We'll see. We had our differences, though he

claimed that I influenced him" ("¿Y qué piensa de la obra de Bolaño, con el que mantuvo correspondencia? "Hay algo ahí, ya veremos. Tuvimos nuestras diferencias, aunque dijo que ejercí influencia sobre él") ("Todos los días recibo correos con el mismo lamento").

10. The novel comments on this graphic: "What said it all was the appearance at opposite ends of the horizontal axis of Vladimir Smirnov, who disappeared in Stalin's concentration camps in 1938 (not to be confused with Ivan Nikitich Smirnov, executed by the Stalinists in 1936 after the first Moscow show trial), and Suslov, party ideologue, prepared to countenance any atrocity or crime. But the intersection of the horizontal by two slanted lines, reading Bunge and Revel above and Harold Bloom and Allan Bloom below, was something like a joke. And yet it was a joke. Amalfitano didn't understand, especially the appearance of the two Blooms. There had to be something funny about it, but whatever it might be, he couldn't put his finger on it, no matter how he tried" (Bolaño, *2666* 194). ("El que en un lado de la horizontal apareciera Vladímir Smirnov, desaparecido en los campos de concentración de Stalin en 1938, y al que no hay que confundir con Iván Nikitich Smirnov, fusilado por los estalinistas en 1936 tras el primer proceso de Moscú, mientras en el otro lado de la horizontal aparecía el nombre de Suslov, ideólogo del aparato, dispuesto a tragarse todas las infamias y crímenes, no podía ser más elocuente. Pero el que la horizontal estuviera

atravesada por dos líneas inclinadas, en las cuales se leían los nombres de Bunge y Revel, en la parte posterior, y de Harold Bloom y Allan Bloom en la inferior, resultaba muy semejante a un chiste. Un chiste que por otra parte Amalfitano no comprendió, sobre todo por la aparición de los dos Bloom, en donde seguro que debía de residir la gracia, una gracia que, sin embargo, por más que la acechaba no conseguía pillar" [Bolaño, *2666* 249–50]).

11. "Creo que Bloom está errado, como en tantas otras cosas, así como en tantas otras es probablemente el mejor ensayista literario de nuestro continente. Es cierto que todos los poetas americanos, para bien o para mal, tarde o temprano tienen que enfrentarse a Whitman. Neruda lo hace, siempre, como el hijo obediente. Vallejo lo hace como el hijo desobediente o como el hijo pródigo. Borges, y aquí radica su originalidad y su pulso que jamás tiembla, lo hace como un sobrino, ni siquiera muy cercano, un sobrino cuya curiosidad oscila entre la frialdad del entomólogo y el resignado ardor del amante. Nada más lejos de él que la búsqueda del asombro o la admiración. Nadie más indiferente que él ante las amplias masas en marcha de América, aunque en alguna parte de su obra dejó escrito que las cosas que le ocurren a un hombre le ocurren a todos" (Bolaño, "El libro que sobrevive" 186).

12. See Chapter 1, "Bloom in Latin America."

13. While Bolaño has claimed to be primarily a Latin American author

and has been seen as the "last Latin American" ("el último latinoamericano") (Volpi 191), in this and other texts he insists on a hemispheric literary identity. As Nicholas Birns has reminded us, Bolaño states this explicitly in his essay on Twain and Melville: "All American writers drink of these two galloping streams. All of us search these two forests, each looking for his own lost face" ("Our Guide to the Abyss" 292). ("Todos los escritores americanos beben en esos dos pozos relampagueantes. Todos buscan en esas dos selvas su propio rostro perdido" ["Nuestro guía en el desfiladero" 270]). Rather than implying an evolution or change on the part of Bolaño, it is necessary to see these changing locational identities as overlapping and representing different aspects of his writing and thinking. It may be worth mentioning that a stress on a hemispheric, rather than a Latin American, identity was a characteristic gesture of liberal pro-US Cold War warriors, such as Luis Alberto Sánchez or Germán Arciniegas. For a sympathetic take on Bolaño's pan-Americanism, see Birn's "Black Dawn."

14. In addition to these poets included in Bloom's canon, these, together with Vicente Huidobro, are often seen as the major Latin American poets as evidenced by, among many other sources, the title of Saul Yurkievich's influential *Fundadores de la poesía latinoamericana: Vallejo, Huidobro, Borges, Neruda, Paz* (1971).

15. Ángela Blanco notes regarding Borges: "the evolution of his poetry towards tradition, regarding rhythms, rhyme, and measure" ("la evolución de su poesía hacia lo tradicional, en cuanto a ritmos, rima, y medida" (102).

16. "Su poesía, sin embargo, es la más whitmaniana de todas: por sus versos circulan los temas de Whitman, sin excepción, y también sus reflejos y contrapartidas, el reverso y el anverso de la historia, la cara y la cruz de esa amalgama que es América y cuyo éxito o fracaso aún está por decidir. Y nada de esto lo agota, que no es poco admirable" (Bolaño, "El libro que sobrevive" 186).

17. Bolaño, an admirer of Piglia, is referring to the following passage: "the Russian critic, Yuri Tynianov, declares that literature evolves from uncle to nephew (and not from fathers to sons)" (Piglia, *Artificial Respiration* 17) ("El crítico ruso Iuri Tinianov, afirma que la literatura evoluciona de tío a sobrino (y no de padres a hijos" (*Respiración artificial* 21). Piglia is, however, mistaken. Shklovsky made this comparison in his article on Rozanov: "in the succession of literary schools, inheritance is not passed from fathers to sons, but from uncles to nephews" ("en el curso de la sucesión de las escuelas literarias la herencia no pasa de padres a hijos, sino de tíos a sobrinos" ("Rozanov: La obra y la evolución literaria" 172). Given Piglia's erudition, this mistaken attribution is surely deliberate.

18. This passage from *The Western Canon* is a close paraphrase of the beginning of *The Anxiety of Influence*: "Poetic history . . . is held to

be indistinguishable from poetic influence, since strong poets make that history by misreading one another, so as to clear imaginative space for themselves" (5).

19. With the exception of Bayly, most of the novelists Bolaño reviews are still considered among the most important in the Hispanic world, such as Juan Villoro, Pedro Lemebel, or the Spaniard Enrique Vila-Matas. Regarding Bayly, when comparing him with his predecessor Alfredo Bryce Echenique, Bolaño notes: "another similarity occurs to me: tenderness, a kind of compassionate gaze that some see in Bryce but refuse to see in Bayly" (327) ("otro punto en donde son semejantes: la ternura, una cierta mirada compasiva que algunos reconocen en Bryce pero no quieren reconocer en Bayly" [303]). One must note that Bolaño also celebrates Bayly's exploration of queer topics.

20. "Para mí, Parra es desde hace mucho el mejor poeta vivo en lengua española" (*Entre paréntesis* 69).

21. However, Bolaño's public celebration of Parra may have played a role in his receiving the Cervantes Award in 2012, the most important prize given to Spanish-language writers. In fact, Ignacio Echevarría, a close friend of Bolaño and editor of many of his posthumous works, edited Parra's *Obras completas & algo más* (2006) at Bolaño's suggestion.

22. "Sobre mi canon, no sé, el de todos, a mí hasta me da vergüenza decirlo de tan obvio que es. Aldana, Marnique, Cervantes, los cronistas de Indias, Sor Juana, Fray Servando, Teresa de Mier, Pedro Henríquez Ureña,

Rubén Darío, Alfonso Reyes, Borges, por nombrar sólo unos pocos y sin salir del territorio de nuestra lengua" (Bolaño, "Carmen Boullosa entrevista a Roberto Bolaño" 109)

23. "También me interesa la literatura norteamericana del ochocientos, sobre todo Twain y Melville, y la poesía de Emily Dickinson y Whitman" (Bolaño, "Carmen Boulllosa entrevista a Roberto Bolaño" 110).

24. "En fin, me interesa y creo que conozco un poco de toda la literatura occidental" (Bolaño, "Carmen Boullosa entrevista a Roberto Bolaño" 110).

25. "Borges es o debería ser el centro de nuestro canon" (Bolaño, "Sevilla me mata" 312).

26. The process of hypercanonization of Borges in Latin America was already at work, not only among critics such as Sarlo (1993) but also among the Boom writers. In 1970, Vargas Llosa, in an essay that attempts to introduce the Latin American novel of the late 1960s to US readers, singles out Borges as the writer who "best symbolizes the end of Latin America's inferiority complex vis-à-vis Europe" (9); and claims that "it is no longer surprising . . . to discover in the pages of *Tel Quel* of Paris that a French essayist repeats as his own the literary opinions Borges formulated ten years ago" (11). (Bolaño will himself savage the *Tel Quel* group and, arguably, through them French theory, in his short fiction "Labyrinth" ["Laberinto"]. In a 1987 text (included in his 2020 *Medio siglo con Borges*), Vargas Llosa makes clear the importance of Borges for

him: "Sé lo transeúntes que pueden
ser las valoraciones artísticas; pero
creo que en su caso no es arriesgado
afirmar que Borges ha sido lo más
importante que le ocurrió a la literatura en lengua española moderna
y uno de los artistas contemporáneos más memorables" ("I know
how temporary artistic values can be,
but I don't think it is risky to state
that Borges is the most important
thing to happen to modern Spanish language literatura, and one of
the most memorable contemporary
artists").

27. "La obra de Bolaño debe leerse sobre todo como reapropriación y ago-
tamiento del legado borgeano en la
modernidad continental" (Zavala
30–31).

28. "¿Qué es lo que hace que un autor
tan apreciado por quienes hablamos
español sea un autor de segunda o
tercera fila, cuando no un absoluto
desconocido, entre quienes se comu-
nican en otras lenguas? El caso de
Quevedo, recordaba Borges, tal vez
sea el más flagrante. ¿Por qué Quevedo no es un poeta vivo, es decir
digno de relecturas y reinterpreta-
ciones y ramificaciones, en ámbitos
foráneos a la lengua española? Lo
que lleva directamente a otra pregunta: ¿por qué consideramos nosotros a Quevedo nuestro más alto
poeta? ¿O por qué Quevedo y Góngora son nuestros dos más altos poetas?" (Bolaño, "La traducción es un
yunque" 222).

29. "Lo portentoso —y sin embargo
natural, en este caso— es que esas
traducciones, buenas o no, supie-
ron transmitir lo que en el caso de

Quevedo o de Góngora no supie-
ron ni probablemente jamás sabrán:
aquello que distingue una obra maestra absoluta de una obra maestra
a secas, o, si es posible decirlo, una
literatura viva, una literatura patrimonio de todos los hombres, de una
literatura que sólo es patrimonio de
determinada tribu o de un segmento
de determinada tribu" (Bolaño, "La
traducción es un yunque" 223).

30. "Ningún problema tan consustan-
cial con las letras y con su modesto
misterio como el que propone una
traducción" (Borges, "Las versiones
homéricas" 239).

31. "¿Cómo reconocer una obra de arte?
¿Cómo separarla, aunque sólo sea
un momento, de su aparato crítico,
de sus exégetas, de sus incansables
plagiarios, de sus ninguneadores, de
su final destino de soledad? Es fácil.
Hay que traducirla. Que el traductor
no sea una lumbrera. Hay que arran-
carle páginas al azar. Hay que dejarla
tirada en un desván. Si después de
todo esto aparece un joven y la lee,
y tras leerla la hace suya, y le es fiel
(o infiel, qué más da) y la reinter-
preta y la acompaña en su viaje a los
límites y ambos se enriquecen y el
joven añade un gramo de valor a su
valor natural, estamos ante algo, una
máquina o un libro, capaz de hablar
a todos los seres humanos" (Bolaño, "La traducción es un yunque"
223–24).

32. "¿Por qué consideramos nosotros
a Quevedo nuestro más alto poeta? ¿O por qué Quevedo y Góngora son nuestros dos más altos poetas?" (Bolaño, "La traducción es un
yunque" 222).

33. "¿Por qué un autor se convierte en un clásico? Ciertamente, no por lo bien que escribe; de ser así el mundo de la literatura estaría superpoblado de clásicos" ("Jonathan Swift" 166).

34. Zavala has correctly noted: "Bolaño literally articulates a condescending look at the influential Tel Quel group, transforming its members into fictional characters to whom literature— that is, Bolaño's literature—concedes the grace of approaching them, despite their incapacity of being of this fact. In other words, Bolaño assigns himself the power to authorize the literary condition of the most important French intelectual circle of the second half of the twentieth century" ("Desde su espacio literario, Bolaño articula una mirada literalmente condescendiente con el influyente grupo Tel Quel, convirtiendo a sus miembros en personajes de una ficción en la cual la 'literatura'—es decir, la literatura de Bolaño—les concede la gracia de acercárseles pese a su incapacidad de estar conscientes de ello. En otras palabras, Bolaño se autodesigna el poder de autorizar la condición literaria del círculo intelectual francés más relevante de la segunda mitad del siglo XX") (50). While Zavala sees Bolaño's treatment of the Tel Quel group in his posthumous short text "Laberinto" ("Labyrinth") as an example of how he undermines center-periphery cultural and literary hierarchies, it is also an example of a master writer's disdain toward critics (at least those who she does not admire).

35. It is almost certain that Bolaño was familiar with T. S. Eliot's ideas, even though he was not fluent in English. Bolaño mentions Eliot the poet, even as he claims to prefer Joyce and Pound over him ("The End: Distant Star" 357; "Final: Estrella Distante" 332). Given that Eliot's essays began to be translated in 1932, Bolaño must have been familiar with the Anglo-British poet's prose. Regarding his lack of English-language skills, Bolaño begins his essay "Literature and Exile": "I've been invited to talk about exile. The invitation I received was in English, and I don't speak English. There was a time when I did or thought I did, or at least there was a time, in my adolescence, when I thought I could read English almost as well, or as poorly, as Spanish. Sadly, that time has passed. I can't read English" (38). ("He sido invitado para hablar del exilio. La invitación me llegó escrita en inglés y yo no sé hablar inglés. Hubo una época en que sí sabía o creía que sabía, en cualquier caso hubo una época, cuando yo era adolescente, en que creía que podía leer el inglés casi tan bien, o tan mal, como el español. Esa época desdichadamente ya pasó. No sé leer inglés" [40]).

36. While there is no reference to the term *classic* in Eliot's essay, *canon* appears once. Eliot argues about the poet or writer: "In a peculiar sense he will be aware also that he must inevitably be judged by the standards of the past. I say judged, not amputated, by them; not judged to be as good as, or worse or better than, the dead; and certainly not judged by the canons of dead critics" (526).

Canon here seems to refer to, according to *Webster's*, "a general rule, fundamental principle, aphorism, or axiom governing the systematic or scientific treatment of a subject; e.g., canons of descent or inheritance; a logical, grammatical, or metrical canon; canons of criticism, taste, art."

37. "Un clásico, en su acepción más generalizada, es aquel escritor o aquel texto que no sólo contiene múltiples lecturas, sino que se adentra por territorios hasta entonces desconocidos y que de alguna manera enriquece (es decir, alumbra) el árbol de la literatura y allana el camino para los que vendrán después. Clásico es aquel que sabe interpretar y sabe reordenar el canon. Normalmente su lectura, según los bobitos, no es considerada urgente. También hay otros clásicos cuya principal virtud, cuya elegancia y vigencia, está simbolizada por la bomba de relojería, una bomba que no sólo recorre peligrosamente su tiempo sino que es capaz de proyectarse hacia el futuro" (Bolaño, "Jonathan Swift" 166).

38. This quotation from our cowritten "Introduction: Fractured Masterpieces," and the others in this chapter, come from passages mainly written by Nicholas Birns.

39. Gutiérrez-Mouat is quoting from a passage in the Spanish version of *The Savage Detectives* in which García Madero reflects on the position of the "visceral realists" in Mexican poetry: "Nuestra situación (según me pareció entender) es insostenible, entre el imperio de Octavio Paz y el imperio de Pablo Neruda. Es decir: entre la espada y la pared" (30). The English version renders *imperio*,

that is, *empire*, as "reign": "Our situation (as far as I could understand) is unsustainable, trapped as we are between the reign of Octavio Paz and the reign of Pablo Neruda. In other words, between a rock and a hard place" (19).

40. While nearly all of Paz's poetry has been translated, there is no standalone English-language version of the collection *Libertad bajo palabra*. The title means "freedom under (one's) word," the term used in Spanish for *parole*.

41. "El único poeta mexicano que sabe de memoria estas cosas es Octavio Paz (nuestro gran enemigo), el resto no tiene ni idea, al menos eso fue lo que me dijo Ulises Lima minutos después de que yo me sumara y fuera amistosamente aceptado en las filas del realismo visceral" (Bolaño, *Los detectives salvajes* 14).

42. "Por un momento, no lo niego, se me pasó por la cabeza la idea de una acción terrorista, vi a los real visceralistas preparando el secuestro de Octavio Paz, los vi asaltando su casa (pobre Marie-José, qué desastre de porcelanas rotas), los vi saliendo con Octavio Paz amordazado, atado de pies y manos y llevado en volandas o como una alfombra, incluso los vi perdiéndose por los arrabales de Netzahualcóyotl en un destartalado Cadillac negro con Octavio Paz dando botes en el maletero" (Bolaño, *Los detectives salvajes*, 171).

43. "Una selva donde campean los ladrones y los violadores, los teporochos y las mujeres de la mala vida" (Bolaño, *Los detectives salvajes* 504).

44. "Un grupo de energúmenos de la extrema izquierda [que] planearon

secuestrarme" (Bolaño, *Los detectives salvajes* 507).

45. "Poeta real visceralista, el penúltimo poeta real visceralista que queda en México" (Bolaño, *Los detectives salvajes* 509).

46. "Real visceralista (como si el nombre le sonara de algo), ¿no fue ése el grupo poético de Cesárea Tinajero?" (Bolaño, *Los detectives salvajes* 509).

47. "Que Neruda era una mierda y que Nicanor Parra era el gran poeta de la lengua española" (Bolaño, *Los detectives salvajes* 164).

48. *Last Evenings on Earth* is an English-language anthology that includes stories from two short-story collections by Bolaño, *Putas asesinas* (2001) and *Llamadas telefónicas* (1997).

49. "Un único libro: *Veinte poemas de amor y una canción desesperada*, Editorial Losada, Buenos Aires, 1961" (Bolaño, "Carnet de baile" 205).

50. "Neruda ya no me gustaba. ¡Y menos aún los *Veinte poemas de amor!*" (Bolaño, "Carnet de baile" 206).

51. "Quince días después Hitler se esfumó y yo pensé que el siguiente en aparecer sería Stalin. Pero Stalin no apareció. 50. Fue Neruda el que se instaló en mi pasillo. No quince días, como Hitler, sino tres, un tiempo considerablemente más corto, señal de que la depresión amenguaba. 51. En contrapartida, Neruda hacía ruidos (Hitler era silencioso como un trozo de hielo a la deriva), se quejaba, murmuraba palabras incomprensibles, sus manos se alargaban, sus pulmones sorbían el aire del pasillo (de ese frío pasillo europeo) con fruición, sus gestos de dolor y sus modales de mendigo de la primera noche fueron cambiando de tal manera que al final el fantasma parecía recompuesto, otro, un poeta cortesano, digno y solemne. 52. A la tercera y última noche, al pasar por delante de mi puerta, se detuvo y me miró (Hitler nunca me había mirado) y, esto es lo más extraordinario, intentó hablar, no pudo, manoteó su impotencia y finalmente, antes de desaparecer con las primeras luces del día, me sonrió (¿como diciéndome que toda comunicación es imposible pero que, sin embargo, se debe hacer el intento?)" (Bolaño, "Carnet de baile" 211–12).

52. "Belano-Bolaño ubica al Neruda de la alucinación en el dilema del siglo XX, el del fascismo y la contrapartida feroz del estalinismo, el cual se hilvana con la violencia que en el presente sufren en carne propia los miembros de su propia generación" (Fischer).

53. "Viejitos que bajan de los autocares con el puño en alto" (Bolaño, "Carnet de baile" 212).

54. "Pienso en Beltrán Morales, pienso en Rodrigo Lira, pienso en Mario Santiago, pienso en Reinaldo Arenas. Pienso en los poetas muertos en el potro de tortura, en los muertos de sida, de sobredosis, en todos los que creyeron en el paraíso latinoamericano y murieron en el infierno latinoamericano. Pienso en esas obras que acaso permitan a la izquierda salir del foso de la vergüenza y la inoperancia" (Bolaño, "Carnet de baile" 212).

55. "66. ¿Como a la Cruz, hemos de volver a Neruda con las rodillas sangrantes, los pulmones agujereados, los ojos llenos de lágrimas? 67.

Cuando nuestros nombres ya nada signifiquen, su nombre seguirá brillando, seguirá planeando sobre una literatura imaginaria llamada literatura chilena. 68. Todos los poetas, entonces, vivirán en comunas artísticas llamadas cárceles o manicomios. 69. Nuestra casa imaginaria, nuestra casa común" (Bolaño, "Carnet de baile" 213).

56. In Erik Hasnoot's documentary *Bolaño cercano*, the Spanish writer Enrique Vila-Matas, one of Bolaño's best friends, recounts that on one of the last occasions the two writers met, Vila-Matas criticized then president George W. Bush, only to be surprised by Bolaño's defense of the US administration. Vila-Matas agrees with the statement by Bolaño's widow, Carolina López, "He loved polemics, he loved discussions."

57. "Los cuatro grandes poetas de Chile / son tres: / Alonso de Ercilla y Rubén Darío" (qtd. In Bolaño, "Literatura y exilio" 44).Alonso de Ercilla (1533–1594) was a Spanish conquistador who wrote *La Araucana*, an epic poem about the struggles between the Spaniards and the Araucans in what today is Chile. Rubén Darío (1867–1916) was a Nicaraguan poet, generally considered among the very greatest in the Spanish language, who lived in Chile from 1886 to 1887.

58. The archetypal example of the 1960s rejection of pan-Americanism is found in Fidel Castro: "Instead of the hypocritical pan-Americanism that only represents the predominance of Yankee monopolies over the interests of our peoples. . . the Assembly of the People of Cuba proclaims the liberating Latin Americanism found in the thought of Benito Juárez and José Martí" ("frente al hipócrita panamericanismo que es sólo predominio de los monopolios yanquis sobre los intereses de nuestros pueblos . . . la Asamblea del Pueblo de Cuba proclama latinoamericanismo liberador que late en el pensamiento de Benito Juárez y José Martí") ("Discurso pronunciado en la Magna Asamblea Popular celebrada por el pueblo de Cuba" 231).

59. Notably, his fiction presents a darker view of cosmopolitanism than his essays. Thus, Mariano Siskind has argued that Bolaño's version of cosmopolitanism, of world flatness, "precisely, tries to name this universalization of loss that is constitutive of the experience of the displacement of refugees, migrants, the homeless and the errant orphans for whom there no longer is a world underfoot and who can only afford to dwell in the time and place of their own dislocation" (227). Although it is, in my opinion, impossible not to share Siskind's despair about the state of the world, or his sense that Bolaño's works reflect our current dismal condition, in politics or ecology, the question that remains is whether the Chilean writer's sense of universal loss—in many ways the mirror image of the joyous cosmopolitanism characteristic of neoliberalism—is ultimately not also compatible with our contemporary world structures, whether cultural or political.

CHAPTER 7

1. Regarding the titles in Spanish and English, Tom McEnaney notes that "the emphasis on political consciousness raising in Spanish to the focus on ethnic identity in English" (398n1).

2. Among the inexactitudes pointed out by Stoll, he proves that she learned Spanish much earlier than she claimed, that her family had been involved in intra-indigenous squabbles, and that her brother had not been burned alive but shot.

3. According to Katherine Isbester, "Menchú's efforts were one of the reasons for the international pressure that eventually democratized Guatemala and led to its UN-brokered peace accords [1996]" (131).

4. There have always been important testimonial texts in Latin America, including *Juan Pérez Jolote* (1952), compiled by the Mexican Ricardo Pozas; the Cuban *Biografía de un cimarrón* (*Biography of a Runaway Slave*, 1966), the former slave Esteban Montejo's *testimonio* compiled by Miguel Barnet; and *Hasta no verte Jesús mío* (*Here's to You, Jesusa*, 1969), edited and rewritten by the Mexican novelist Elena Poniatowska. The *testimonio*, however, began to be considered a literary genre when the Cuban Casa de las Américas began awarding the best work in the genre in 1970. However, although *I, Rigoberta Menchú*, won the award, in 1982, it was given to Elizabeth Burgos-Debray, who was considered the author. At the time, it was the interviewer and editor (*gestor*), not the person interviewed, in this case, Menchú, who was considered the author of a *testimonio*.

5. The English translation of Menchú's *testimonio* is unusually free.

6. With some exaggeration, Roberto González Echevarría noted in 2010: "And works that in their moment were acclaimed for political reasons, such as *I, Rigoberta Menchú*, are falling into the oblivion they deserve" ("Y obras que en un momento fueron aclamadas por razones políticas, como *Me llamo Rigoberta Menchú*, van cayendo en el olvido que se merecían") (118).

7. An example of this boom in indigenous literature is that Elicura Chihuailaf, a Mapuche writer, was awarded in 2020 the prestigious Premio Nacional de Literatura in Chile.

8. "El libro en que Lurgio Gavilán Sánchez cuenta su historia es conmovedor, un documento humano que se lee en estado de trance por la experiencia terrible que comunica, por su evidente sinceridad y limpieza moral" (Vargas Llosa, "*El soldado desconocido*").

9. The Shining Path, a loosely Maoist guerrilla group, originally based in the southern Peruvian Andes and led by the charismatic and dogmatic former philosophy professor Abimael Guzmán, unleashed a brutal total war on Peruvian society in its attempt to take power from 1983 until 1992, when Guzmán was captured.

10. According to Ulises Zevallos, "Although it is called a *memoria* in its title, the book can still be considered as a testimonio for two reasons. First, a bilingual Quechua person is giving

testimony of his participation in Peru's internal war between 1980 and 1985. The second is that it is a supervised autobiography. Yerko Castro Neira's, his [Gavilán's] graduate studies advisor, participation was so important that he received credit on the cover of the book" ("A pesar de que lleva el título de memoria, el libro puede seguir siendo considerado como testimonio por dos razones. Primero, un quechua bilingüe da testimonio sobre su involucramiento en la guerra interna que tuvo lugar en el Perú entre 1980 y 1995. Segundo, es una autobiografía tutelada. La participación en la edición del manuscrito de su asesor en sus estudios de doctorado en antropología, Castro Neira, fue tan grande que tuvo que darle crédito en la tapa del libro) (231).

11. For instance, limiting myself to Andean *testimonios*, in the case of *Gregorio Condori Mamani: Autobiografía* (1977) (translated and expanded as *Andean Lives: Gregorio Condori Mamani and Asunta Quispe Huamán* in 1996), Gregorio Condori Mamani was illiterate.

12. "Aprended a cuidaros, guardando nuestro secreto" (Menchú/Burgos 27).

13. "Burgos chose epigraphs for each chapter, taken chiefly from three sources: statements by Menchú herself; passages from Asturias's novels depicting native culture; and quotations from the Popol Vuh, the classic Mayan story of creation and early history. This is, however, a text that Menchú herself never mentions and seems never to have seen" (Damrosch, 244).

14. "Todo eso ha contribuido a que nosotros guardemos muchas cosas y que la comunidad no quiere que se cuente eso" (Menchú, *Me llamo Rigoberta Menchú* 29). And: "Por ejemplo, nuestras costumbres" (Menchú, *Me llamo Rigoberta Menchú* 29).

15. "Nosotros los indígenas hemos ocultado nuestra identidad, hemos guardado muchos secretos, por eso somos discriminados. Para nosotros es bastante difícil muchas veces decir algo que se relaciona con uno mismo porque uno sabe que tiene que ocultar esto hasta que garantice que va a seguir como una cultura indígena, que nadie nos puede quitar. Por eso no puedo explicar el nahual pero hay ciertas cosas que puedo decir a grandes rasgos. Yo no puedo decir cuál es mi nahual porque es uno de nuestros secretos" (Menchú, *Me llamo Rigoberta Menchú* 41).

16. "Ahí es cuando precisamente se le dice al niño que no hay que abusarse de su dignidad, que los antepasados nunca abusaron de su dignidad y es cuando se les hace recordar que nuestros antepasados fueron violados por medio de los blancos y de la colonia. Pero no lo dicen como está escrito sino a través de las recomendaciones que han venido dando nuestros abuelos y nuestros antepasados. Porque la mayor parte del pueblo no sabe leer ni escribir ni sabe que existe un documento para el indígena. Pero se dice que los españoles violaron a los mejores hijos de los antepasados, a las gentes más humildes y en honor a esas gentes más humildes nosotros tenemos

que seguir guardando nuestros secretos. Y esos secretos nadie podrá descubrir más que nosotros los indígenas. Un montonón de cosas de esas" (Menchú, *Me llamo Rigoberta Menchú* 34).

17. "Por ejemplo, cuando se trata de explorar las relaciones de letrados y subalternos, casi siempre se toma como objeto de estudio a *Me llamo Rigoberta Menchú y así me nació la conciencia* . . . y se llegan a conclusiones que no se aplican a un buen número de testimonios latinoamericanos. Por un lado, *Me llamo Rigoberta* . . . es el resultado de entrevistas realizadas en un corto tiempo (ocho días) y en la lengua materna (castellano) y el lugar de residencia de la entrevistadora, Elizabeth Burgos (París). Por otro lado, las diferencias culturales, económicas y sociales que existen entre Elizabeth Burgos y Rigoberta Menchú hacen que la entrevistada mantenga secretos de su cultura indígena cuando hace declaraciones a su entrevistadora" (Zevallos 213).

18. "No quedaba otra opción que subirse al arca de SL [Sendero Luminoso] o unirse a la agrupación de rondas campesinas" (Gavilán, *Memorias de un soldado desconocido*).

19. "No es una historia de violencia, sino relatos de la vida cotidiana que me tocó vivir, carentes de dramatismo y victimización" (Gavilán, *Memorias de un soldado desconocido*).

20. A more complete quotation: "las primeras gotas de lluvia dieron esperanzas de vida, justicia social, pero las lluvias cada día se prolongaron y vino el miedo, porque 'las aguas'

comenzaron a destruir y limpiar 'todo lo viejo'. Entonces se empezó a vivir el 'diluvio'" (Gavilán, *Memorias de un soldado desconocido*).

21. "Así, harapientos, aún teníamos fe en nuestro presidente Gonzalo, que tal vez podría aparecer con cachicachis y arrear a los militares. Pero no, nunca apareció" (Gavilán, *Memorias de un soldado desconocido*).

22. Uchuraccay was the location of a massacre of journalists on the part of agrarian commune members who thought they were Shining Path. Mario Vargas Llosa wrote a report on the event at the bequest of then president Fernando Belaúnde Terry.

23. "Perú es un país plural, diverso — como insistió José María Arguedas—, de todas las sangres, una amalgama de culturas con una idiosincrasia discriminatoria. ¿Cuándo hemos sido un solo Perú, un país unificado? o ¿cuándo hemos aprendido a vivir en la diversidad?" (Gavilán, *Memorias de un soldado desconocido* n.p.).

24. "Los toros bravos vienen sujetos de los cuernos con varias sogas, como cuando los reclutas eran llevados en los años cincuenta y sesenta atados para 'servir a la patria', o como era llevado el Misitu para el Yawar fiesta. Ese día era la fiesta de Ccarhuapampa" (Gavilán, *Memorias de un soldado desconocido* n.p.).

25. "Yo soñaba con harta comida: papa, yuca, arroz, como cuando comía al lado de mi madre, pero al despertarme solo sonaba mi estómago. Y nos mirábamos como esos perros escuálidos del cuento de Ciro Alegría. Pero el partido estaba ahí, siempre

adelante" (Gavilán, *Memorias de un soldado desconocido* n.p.).

26. "Me quedo con esta frase del santo de Asís, Francisco: 'Comencemos hermanos, poco o nada hemos hecho', o con la sentencia de César Vallejo Mendoza, poeta universal: 'y desgraciadamente hombres humanos . . . hay hermanos muchísimo qué hacer'" (Gavilán, *Memorias de un soldado desconocido* n.p.).

27. "¿Para qué serviría? Ahora prefiero, mejor —como dice el maestro José Carlos Mariátegui—, que la obra se encargue de justificarme" (Gavilán, *Memorias de un soldado desconocido* n.p.). (It is worth noting that the reference to Mariátegui as "teacher" or "master' is not found in the English translation).

28. "Kafka showed us Gregor Samsa as a hardworking and honest man, but one morning, after bad dreams, he woke up transformed into a monstruous insect and life for him, and those around him, began to change. Abimael Guzmán was a university professor who taught young people in one of the poorest regions of the country. Even though he liked to wear a suit and tie, according to those who knew him, he was a simple man who would even repair the shirts of his students, and he walked down the streets of Ayacucho thinking about the future of the people. But suddenly, his thought became charged with hate and with the hope of destroying anyone who became an obstacle on the path to revolution." ("Kafka nos presentaba a Gregorio Samsa como un hombre trabajador y honesto, pero una mañana después de un sueño intranquilo se despierta convertido en un monstruoso insecto y la vida para él y para todos los que estaban a su alrededor empieza a cambiar; Abimael Guzmán fue un catedrático que formaba a jóvenes en una de las regiones más pobres del país; aunque le gustaba usar saco y corbata —según los que conocieron— era gente sencilla que zurcía la camisa de sus estudiantes y caminaba por las calles de Ayacucho pensando en el porvenir del pueblo, pero de pronto se encarnó ese pensamiento de odio revestido de una esperanza de vida para aniquilar a todo aquel que se ponga como obstáculo en el camino de la revolución") (Gavilán, "Reflexiones del soldado desconocido).

29. "Desde que empecé con el manuscrito pensaba en ellos, nosotros. Éramos niños y adolescentes que habíamos sido capturados o rescatados de las filas de Sendero Luminoso, vivíamos en el cuartel y nos llamaban los cabitos: pioneros —junto con los soldados y oficiales— en la lucha por la pacificación del Estado peruano, a pesar de nuestra corta edad" (Gavilán, *Memorias de un soldado desconocido*).

30. "Quizás la insistencia en la decisión individual atrajo el interés de Vargas Llosa. El escritor peruano ha sido el gran impulsor del neoliberalismo y promueve el valor del individuo que se hace a sí mismo como solución a los problemas sociales" (Zevallos 233).

31. "Por estos lugares andaba yo en 1983. Entonces la gente era conversadora y cariñosa. Ahora las personas se

muestran indiferentes, te miran de pies a cabeza como si fueses algún enemigo, algún bicho extraño. De todo desconfían. Siguen en la pobreza como en aquella época, no han cambiado económicamente, siguen cultivando sus tubérculos, sus arvejitas, su maíz. Si se hubiesen hecho realidad los discursos del PCP sobre la igualdad, que nadie sea rico ni pobre, que todos tuviéramos las mismas oportunidades sin egoísmo, sin explotación del hombre por el hombre, o si el Estado estuviese interesado en los campesinos, en su

agricultura, en educar a sus niños como predican en las elecciones presidenciales, de seguro estos hombres no estarían arañando estas tierras para sobrevivir como yo he arañado en mi vida para contar lo sucedido" (Gavilán, *Memorias de un soldado desconocido*).

32. "Ninguno de los dos bandos ha cumplido las promesas. Poco se ha transformado y continúan las carencias en las provincias. Lo poco que ha cambiado es la actitud de la gente" (Zevallos 234).

EPILOGUE

1. According to Boyd, less than 1 percent of all literary books published in the US are translations, and Spanish ranks fourth as source language, after French, German, and English (translated into other languages). Even assuming the by now obsolete percentage of 3 percent for all translations—including nonfiction and technical book—this pales in comparison with the fact 21 percent of all books published in Spain are translations ("Las traducciones en España suponen el 21%").

WORKS CITED

Aboul-Ela, Hosam. *Other South: Faulkner, Coloniality and the Mariátegui Tradition.* U of Pittsburgh P, 2007.

Aizenberg, Edna. *Books and Bombs in Buenos Aires: Borges, Gerchunoff, and Argentine-Jewish Writing.* UP of New England, 2002.

Alberca, Manuel. "¿Existe la autoficción hispanoamericana?" *Cuadernos del CILHA*, vol. 7, no. 8, 2005, pp. 115–127.

Almond, Ian. "Borges, the Post-Orientalist: Images of Islam from the Edge of the West." *Modern Fiction Studies*, vol. 50, no. 2, 2004, pp. 435–59.

Álvarez, Julia. *Yo!* Plume, 1997.

Arias, Arturo. *Taking Their Word: Literature and Signs of Central America.* U of Minnesota P, 2007.

Armino, Mauro. "Tragarse las palabras: De Octavio Paz a Léon Blum." *El siglo de Europa*, no. 1057, 2014, pp. 50–51.

Avelar, Idelber. "Como respiran los ausentes: La narrativa de Ricardo Piglia." *MLN*, vol. 110, no. 2, 1995, pp. 416–32.

Balderston, Daniel. "Detalles circunstanciales: Sobre dos borradores de 'El escritor argentino y la tradición'." *Cuaderno Lírico: Revista de la red interuniversitaria de estudios sobre las literaturas rioplatenses contemporañeas en Francia*, no. 9, 2013. http://journals.openedition.org/lirico/1111.

———. "Introduction." *Artificial Respiration*, by Ricardo Piglia, translated by Daniel Balderston, Duke UP, 1994.

Baldick, Chris. *The Concise Oxford Dictionary of Literary Terms.* Oxford UP, 2001.

Beasley Murray, Jon. "Conundrum." *Posthegemony*, 14 May 2006, https://posthegemony.wordpress.com/2006/05/14/conundrum.

Berman, Carolyn Vellenga. *Creole Crossings: Domestic Fiction and the Reform of Colonial Slavery.* Cornell UP, 2006.

Beverley, John. *The Failure of Latin America: Postcolonialism in Bad Times.* U of Pittsburgh P, 2019.

Bhabha, Homi. "Introduction." *Nation and Narration*, edited by Homi Bhabha, Routledge, 1990, pp. 1–7.

Birns, Nicholas. "Black Dawn: Roberto Bolaño as (North) American Writer." *Roberto Bolaño as World Literature*, edited by Nicholas Birns and Juan E. De Castro, Bloomsbury, 2017, pp. 183–202.

———. *Theory after Theory: An Intellectual History of Literary History from 1950 to the Early 21st Century*. Broadview, 2010.

Birns, Nicholas, and Juan E. De Castro. "Introduction: Fractured Master-pieces." *Roberto Bolaño as World Literature*, edited by Nicholas Birns and Juan E. De Castro, Bloomsbury, 2017, pp. 1–19

Blanco Amores de Pagella, Ángela. "Los temas esenciales." *Expliquémonos a Borges como poeta*, edited by Ángel Flores, Siglo XXI, 1984, pp. 89–108.

Bloom, Allan. *The Closing of the American Mind: How Higher Education Has Failed Democracy and Impoverished the Soul of Today's Students*. Simon & Schuster, 1987.

Bloom, Harold. "According to Harold Bloom, What We Are Seeing Is the Fall of America." Interview by Eva Sohlman. *The Women's International Perspective*, 17 January 2008. https://www.commondreams.org/views/2008/01/17/according-harold-bloom-what-we are-seeing-isacaathe-fall-america.

———. *The Anxiety of Influence: A Theory of Poetry*. 2nd ed. Oxford UP, 1997.

———. "Para Harold Bloom, Donald Trump es 'un monstruo, un anticristo, una bestia del mal." Interview. *Infobae*, 11 Apr. 2017. https://www.infobae.com/cultura/2017/04/22/para-harold-bloom-donald-trump-es-un-monstruo-un-anticristo-una-bestia-del-mal/.

———. *The Western Canon: The Books and School of the Ages*. New York: Harcourt Brace, 1994.

———. "Todos los días recibo correos con el mismo lamento: Leemos basura." Interview with Valerie Miles. *El País*. https://elpais.com/cultura/2014/12/08/actualidad/1418055903_266402.html

Bolaño, Roberto. "Bolaño a la vuelta de la esquina." Interview with Rodrigo Pinto. *Últimas Noticias*, 22 Jan. 2001. http://www.letras.mysite.com/bolao1.htm

———. "The Book That Survives." *Between Parentheses: Essays, Articles, and Speeches, 1998 2003*, edited by Ignacio Echeverría, translated by Natasha Wimmer, New Directions, 2004, pp. 198–200.

———. "Carmen Boullosa entrevista a Roberto Bolaño." Interview with Carmen Boullosa. *Roberto Bolaño: La escritura como tauromaquia*, edited by Celina Manzoni, *El corregidor*, 2006, pp. 105–13.

———. "Carnet de baile." *Putas asesinas*, Vintage Español, 2017, pp. 205–13.

———. "Dance Card." *Last Evenings on Earth*, New Directions, 2006, pp. 210–19.

———. *Los detectives salvajes*. Anagrama, 2006.

———. "El libro que sobrevive." *Entre paréntesis: Ensayos, artículos y discur-*

sos (1998–2003), edited by Ignacio Echeverría, Anagrama, 2012, pp. 184–86.

———. "The End: Distant Star. (Interview with Monica Maristain)." *Between Parentheses: Essays, Articles, and Speeches, 1998–2003*, edited by Ignacio Echeverría, translated by Natasha Wimmer, New Directions, 2004, pp. 354–69.

———. "Entrevista con Roberto Bolaño." Interview with Luis García Santillán. *Crítica.cl: Revista Latinoamericana de Ensayo*. 4 Apr. 2002. http://critica.cl/entrevistas/entrevista-con-roberto-bolano.

———. "Final: 'Estrella distante' (entrevista de Mónica Maristain)." *Entre paréntesis: Ensayos, artículos y discursos (1998–2003)*, edited by Ignacio Echeverría, Anagrama, 2012, pp. 329–43.

———. "Jonathan Swift." *Entre paréntesis: Ensayos, artículos y discursos (1998–2003)*, edited by Ignacio Echeverría, Anagrama, 2012, pp. 166–68.

———. "Jonathan Swift." *Between Parentheses: Essays, Articles, and Speeches, 1998–2003*, edited by Ignacio Echeverría and translated by Natasha Wimmer, New Directions, 2011, pp. 179–81.

———. "La traducción es un yunque." *Entre paréntesis: Ensayos, artículos y discursos (1998 2003)*, edited by Ignacio Echeverría, Anagrama, 2012, pp. 222–24.

———. "Literatura y exilio." *Entre paréntesis: Ensayos, artículos y discursos (1998–2003)*, edited by Ignacio Echeverría, Anagrama, 2012, pp. 40–46.

———. "Literature and Exile." *Between Parentheses: Essays, Articles, and Speeches, 1998–2003*, edited by Ignacio Echeverría, translated by Natasha Wimmer, New Directions, 2011, pp. 38–46.

———. "Nuestra guía en el desfiladero." *Entre paréntesis: Ensayos, artículos y discursos (1998 2003)*, edited by Ignacio Echeverría, Anagrama, 2012, pp. 269–80.

———. "Our Guide to the Abyss." *Between Parentheses: Essays, Articles, and Speeches, 1998 2003*, edited by Ignacio Echeverría, translated by Natasha Wimmer, New Directions, 2011, pp. 291–302.

———. "Roberto Bolaño by Carmen Boullosa." Interview by Carmen Boullosa. *BOMB*, 1 Jan. 2002. https://bombmagazine.org/articles/roberto-bolaño/

———. *The Savage Detectives*. Translated by Natasha Wimmer, Farrar Straus & Giroux, 2007.

———. "Positions Are Positions and Sex Is Sex." Interview by Eliseo Álvarez. *Roberto Bolaño: The Last Interview & Other Conversations*, translated by Sybyl Perez, Melville House, 2009, pp. 69–91.

———. "Las posturas son posturas y el sexo es el sexo." Interview by Eliseo Álvarez. *Bolaño por si mismo—entrevistas escogidas*, 2nd edition, edited by Andrés Braithwaite, Universidad Diego Portales, 2008, pp. 34–45.

———. *The Savage Detectives: A Novel.* Translated by Natasha Wimmer, Picador, 2007.

———. "Sevilla Kills Me." *Between Parentheses: Essays, Articles, and Speeches,*

1998–2003, edited by Ignacio Echeve-rría, translated by Natasha Wimmer, New Directions, 2011, pp, 336–39.

———. "Sevilla me mata." *Entre paréntesis: Ensayos, artículos y discursos (1998–2003)*, edited by Ignacio Echeverría, Anagrama, 2012, pp. 311–14.

———. "Translation Is an Anvil." *Between Parentheses: Essays, Articles, and Speeches, 1998-2003*, edited by Ignacio Echeverría, translated by Natasha Wimmer, New Directions, 2011, pp. 239–241.

———. *2666*. Vintage Español, 2004.

———. *2666: A Novel*. Translated by Natasha Wimmer, Picador, 2009.

———. "Vienna and the Shadow of a Woman." *Between Parentheses: Essays, Articles and Speeches, 1988–2003*, edited by Ignacio Echeverría, translated by Natasha Wimmer, New Directions, 2011, pp. 270–74.

———. "Viena y la sombra de una mujer." *Entre paréntesis: Ensayos, artículos y discursos, 1988–2003*, edited by Ignacio Echevarría, Anagrama, 2012, pp. 250–53.

Borges, Jorge Luis. "The Argentine Writer and Tradition." *Selected Non-Fiction*, edited by Eliot Weinberger, translated by Esther Allen, Viking, 1999, pp. 420–27.

———. "Bartleby." *Obras completas 4 1975–1988*, Emecé, 1996, pp. 118–20.

———. "Bartleby, the Scrivener." *Selected Non-Fiction*, edited by Eliot Weinberger, translated by Suzanne Jill Levine, Viking, 1999, pp. 245–46.

———. "Darío." *Textos recobrados III (1956–1986)*, Penguin Random House, 2015, pp. 125–26.

———. "El cuento policial." *Borges oral*, Buenos Aires: Emecé, 1979, pp. 63–80.

———. "The Detective Story." *Selected Non-Fiction*, edited by Eliot Weinberger, translated by Esther Allen, Viking, 1999, pp. 491–99.

———. "El escritor argentino y la tradición." *Obras completas 1923–1972*, Emecé, 1974, pp. 267–74.

———. "The Homeric Versions." *Selected Non-Fiction*, edited and translated by Eliot Weinberger, Viking, 1999, pp. 69–74.

———. "Kafka and His Precursors." *Other Inquisitions. 1937–1952*, translated by Ruth L. Simms, U of Texas P, 1965, pp. 106–8.

———. "Kafka y sus precursores." *Obras completas 1923–1972*, Emecé, 1974, pp. 710–12.

———. "La biblioteca de Babel." *Ficciones*, in *Obras completas 1923–1972*, Emecé, 1974, pp. 465–71.

———. "The Library of Babel." *Collected Fictions*, edited and translated by Andrew Hurley, Penguin, 1999, pp. 112–18.

———. "La lotería en Babilonia." *Obras completas 1923–1972*, Emecé, 1974, pp. 456–60.

———. "The Lottery in Babylon." *Collected Fictions*, edited and translated by Andrew Hurley, Penguin, 1999, pp. 101–06.

———. "Nathaniel Hawthorne." *Obras completas 1923–1972*, Emecé, 1974, pp. 670–85.

———. "Nathaniel Hawthorne". *Other Inquisitions. 1937–1952*, U of Texas P, 1965, pp. 47–65.

———. "Nostalgia del latín." *Textos recobrados III (1956–1986)*, Penguin

Random House, 2015, pp. 219–24.

———. "Nota de un mal lector." *Textos recobrados III (1956–1986)*, Penguin Random House, 2015, pp. 11–12.

———. "Quevedo." *Other Inquisitions: 1937–1952*, U of Texas P, 1965, pp. 36–42.

———. "Quevedo." *Obras completas 1923–1972*, Emecé, 1974, pp. 660–66.

———. "Rabindranath Tagore." *Collected Poems and Plays: Selected Non-Fiction*, edited and translated by Eliot Weinberger, Viking, 1999, pp. 180–81.

———. "Las versiones homéricas." *Obras completas 1923–1972*, Emecé, 1974, pp. 239–43.

———. "Un sueño eterno." *Textos recobrados III. (1956–1986)*, Penguin, 2015, pp. 231–33.

Boyd, Martin. "The Infamous Three Percent." 9 Apr. 2016. https://dialogos.ca/2016/04/the-infamous-three-percent/.

Briggs, Ronald. *The Moral Electricity of Print: Transatlantic Education and the Lima Women's Circuit, 1876–1910.* Vanderbilt UP, 2017.

Brooks, Van Wyck. "On Creating a Usable Past." *The Dial: A Fortnightly Journal of Literature and the Arts*, no. 64, 3 Jan.–6 June 1918, pp. 337–41.

Cabello de Carbonera, Mercedes. *El conde Tolstoi.* Lima: Imprenta de El Diario Judicial, 1896.

———. "La novela moderna." *El Perú ilustrado: Semanario para las familias* no. 232, 17 October 1891, pp. 4373–4375; no. 233, 24 October 1891, pp. 5013–5019, no. 234, 31 October 1891, pp. 5053–5057; no. 235, 7 November 1891, pp. 5093–5095.

Carpentier, Alejo. "Prólogo." *Obras escogidas*, 25–140, Editorial Andrés Bello, 1993, pp. 25–31.

———. "Prologue: *The Kingdom of this World.*" *The Oxford Book of Latin American Essays*, edited by Ilan Stavans, translated by Alfred MacAdam, Oxford UP, 1997, pp. 194–98.

Casanova, Pascale. *The World Republic of Letters.* Harvard UP, 2004.

Castellanos, Rosario. *Juicios sumarios: Ensayos sobre literatura II.* Fondo de Cultura Económica, 2017. Google Play.

Castilho, Celso Thomas. "*La cabaña del Tío Tom (Uncle Tom's Cabin)*, la esclavitud atlántica y la racialización de la esfera pública en la ciudad de México de mediados del siglo XIX." *Historia mexicana*, vol. 69, no. 2, pp. 789–835.

Castro, Fidel. "Discurso pronunciado en la Segunda Asamblea Nacional del Pueblo de Cuba." *Fidel Castro: La historia me absolverá y otros discursos*, 239–84. Ministerio de Poder Popular (Venezuela), 2009, pp. 239–84.

Castro-Klarén, Sara. "Posting Letters: Writing in the Andes and the Paradoxes of the Postcolonial Debate." *Coloniality at Large: Latin America and the Postcolonial*, edited by Mabel Moraña, Enrique Dussel, and Carlos A. Jaúregui, Duke UP, 2008, pp. 130–57.

Cella, Susana. "Canon y otras cuestiones." *Dominios de la literatura: Acerca del canon*, edited by Susana Cella, Losada, 1998, pp. 7–16.

Chanady, Amaryll. "Magical Realism and the Marvelous Real in the Novel." *The Oxford Handbook of the Latin American Novel*, edited by Juan E. De Castro and Ignacio López Calvo. Oxford UP, forthcoming.

Chandler Caldwell, Roy, Jr. "Mascarita's Metamorphosis: Vargas Llosa and Kafka." *The Comparatist*, vol. 25, 2001, pp. 50–68.

Cheng, Vincent J. *Joyce, Race, and Empire.* Cambridge UP, 1995.

Clayton, Michelle. *Poetry in Pieces: César Vallejo and Lyric Modernity.* U of California P, 2011.

"Colombia, Realismo Mágico." 10 Apr. 2013. https://procolombia.co/archivo/colombia-realismo-magico.

Cornejo Polar, Antonio. "Literatura peruana: Totalidad contradictoria." *Revista de crítica literaria latinoamericana*, vol. 9, no. 18, 1983, pp. 37–50.

———. "Mestizaje e hibridez: Los riesgos de las metáforas. Apuntes." *Revista Iberoamericana*, vol. 63, no. 180, 1997, pp. 341-44.

Cortázar, Julio. "Roberto Arlt: Apuntes de relectura." *Obra crítica III*, edited by Saúl Sosnowski. Alfaguara, 2018. Kindle.

Couto, Mia. "Entrevista a Mia Couto, escritor y poeta mozambiqueño: 'África está llena de Macondos, de pueblos así, como el de Gabo." http://2014.kaosenlared.net/component/k2/55831-entrevista-a-mia-couto-escritor-y-poeta-mozambiqueño-áfrica-está-llena-de-macondos-de-pueblos-as%C3%AD-como-el-de-gabo.

Cruz, Sor Juana Inés de la. *Obra selecta.* Biblioteca Ayacucho, 1994.

———. *Obra selecta: Tomo II.* Biblioteca Ayacucho, 1994.

———. *Selected Works.* Translated by Edith Grossman. Norton, 2014.

Damrosch, David. *What Is World Literature.* Princeton UP, 2003.

Danticat, Edwidge. "Gabriel García Márquez: An Appreciation." *New Yorker*, 11 Apr. 2014. https://www.newyorker.com/books/page-turner/gabriel-garca-mrquez-an-appreciation.

Darío, Rubén. "Los colores del estandarte." *Nosotros: Revista Mensual de Letras*, vol. 10, February 1916, pp. 161–67.

Deleuze, Gilles, and Félix Guattari. *Kafka: Toward a Minor Literature.* U of Minnesota P, 1986.

Deresiewicz, William. "The Literary World System." *The Nation*, 16 Dec. 2004. https://www.thenation.com/article/archive/literary-world-system/.

De Castro, Juan E. *Mestizo Nations: Culture, Race, and Conformity in Latin American Literature.* U of Arizona P, 2002.

———. *The Spaces of Latin American Literature: Tradition, Globalization and Cultural Production.* Palgrave, 2008.

Del Aguila, Rocío. "(A)filiaciones femeninas: Gorriti y la genealogía de la escritura en Lima." *Decimonónica: Journal of Nineteenth Century Hispanic Cultural Production*, vol. 10, no. 1, 2013, pp. 45–61.

De Man, Paul. "A Modern Master." *Critical Writings, 1953–1978*, edited by Lindsay Waters, U of Minnesota P, 1989, pp. 123–29.

Derrida, Jacques. "From *Des tours de Babel*." Translated by Joseph F. Graham, *A Derrida Reader: Between the Blinds*, edited by Peggy Kamuf, Columbia UP, 1991, pp. 243–253.

Domínguez Michael, Christopher. "Observaciones sobre el canon de Bloom." *Vuelta*, June 1997, pp. 57–59.

D'Souza, Dinesh. *Illiberal Education: The Politics of Race and Sex on Campus.* Simon and Schuster, 1991.

Eliot, T. S. "Tradition and the Individual Talent." *Criticism: The Major Texts,* edited by W. J. Bate, Harcourt, 1990, pp. 525–29.

Finchelstein, Federico. "An Argentine Experience: Borges, Judaism and the Holocaust." *The New Jewish Argentina,* edited by Adriana Brodsky and Raanan Rein, Brill, 2013, pp. 147–78.

Fiol-Matta, Licia. *A Queer Mother for the Nation: The State and Gabriela Mistral.* U of Minnesota P, 2002.

Fischer, María Luisa. "Los territorios de la poesía en Roberto Bolaño." *Ciberletras,* vol. 30, 2013. https://www.lehman.cuny.edu/ciberletras/v30/fischerml.html.

Franco, Jean. "¿La historia de quién? La piratería postmoderna." *Revista de crítica literaria latinoamericana,* vol. 17, no. 33, 1991, pp. 11–20.

———. "From Romance to Refractory Aesthetic." *Critical Passions: Selected Essays,* edited by Mary Louise Pratt and Kathleen Newman, Duke UP, 1999, pp. 97–108.

Fuguet, Alberto, and Sergio Gómez. "Presentación del país McOndo." *McOndo,* edited by Alberto Fuguet and Sergio Gómez, Grijalbo Mondadori, 1996, pp. 9–18.

García Márquez, Gabriel. "Al otro lado del río entre los árboles." *Obra periodística I: Textos costeños (1948–1952),* edited by Jacques Girard, vol. 1, Oveja Negra, 1983, pp. 288–90.

———. *Cien años de soledad: Edición conmemorativa.* Real Academia Española, 2007.

———. "Faulkner premio Nobel." *Obra periodística I: Textos costeños (1948–1952),* edited by Jacques Girard, Oveja Negra, 1983, pp. 494–96.

———. *Living to Tell the Tale.* Vintage, 2004.

———. "Mi Hemingway personal." *El escándalo del siglo: Textos en prensa y revistas (1950–1984),* edited by Cristóbal Pera, Vintage Español, 2018, pp. 287–90.

———. "My Personal Hemingway." *The Scandal of the Century and Other Writings,* translated by Anne McLean, Knopf, 2019, pp. 236–41.

———. *One Hundred Years of Solitude.* Harper Perennial, 2006.

———. "Otra vez el premio Nobel." *Obra periodística I: Textos costeños (1948–1952),* edited by Jacques Girard, Oveja Negra, 1983, pp. 194–95.

———. "Playboy Interview: Gabriel García Márquez." Interview by Claudia Dreifus. *Conversations with Gabriel García Márquez,* edited by Gene Bell-Villada, U of Mississippi P, 2006, pp. 93–132.

———. "¿Problemas de la novela?" *Obra periodística I: Obra periodística I: Textos costeños (1948–1952),* edited by Jacques Girard, vol. 2, Oveja Negra, 1983, pp. 212–13.

———. "La soledad de América Latina: Nobel Lecture." https://www.nobelprize.org/prizes/literature/1982/marquez/25603-gabriel-garcia-marquez-nobel-lecture-spanish/.

———. "The Solitude of Latin America: Nobel Lecture." https://www.nobelprize.org/prizes/literature/1982/marquez/lecture/.

———. *Vivir para contarla.* Vintage Español, 2003.

Gavilán, Lurgio. *Memorias de un soldado desconocido*. 2nd ed., Instituto de Estudios Peruanos, 2017.

———. "Reflexiones del soldado desconocido: Pensamiento Gonzalo." Polemos.pe, 19 Sept. 2017. https://polemos.pe/reflexionedelsoldadodesconocidopensamiento-gonzalo/.

———. *When Rains Became Floods: A Child Soldier's Story*. Translated by Margaret Randall. Duke UP, 2015.

Gioia, Ted. *El canon del jazz: Los 250 temas imprescindibles*, translated by Víctor V. Úbeda. Turner, 2013.

———. *The Jazz Standards: A Guide to the Repertoire*. Oxford UP, 2012.

González Echevarría, Roberto. "*Nocturno de Chile* y el canon." *Acta Literaria*, vol. 41, 2010, pp. 117–28.

Gorak, Jan. *The Making of the Modern Canon: Genesis and Crisis of a Literary Idea*. Continuum, 1991.

Grandin, Greg. *The End of Myth: From the Frontier to the Border Wall in the Mind of America*. Henry Holt, 2019.

———. "Rigoberta Menchú Vindicated." *The Nation*, 21 Jan. 2015. https://www.thenation.com/article/archive/rigoberta-menchu-vindicated/.

Gugelberger, Georg. M. "Introduction: Institutionalization of Transgression: Testimonial Discourse and Beyond." *The Real Thing: Testimonial Discourse and Latin America*, Duke UP, 1995, pp. 1–19.

Guillory, John. "Canon." *Critical Terms for Literary Study*, edited by Frank Lentricchia and Thomas McLaughlin, 2nd ed., U of Chicago P, 1995.

———. *Cultural Capital: The Problem of Literary Canon Formation*. U of Chicago P, 1993.

Glantz, Margot. "Prólogo." *Sor Juana Inés de la Cruz: Obra selecta I*. Biblioteca Ayacucho, 1994, pp. xi–xc.

Gutiérrez-Mouat, Ricardo. *Understanding Roberto Bolaño*. U of South Carolina P, 2016.

Haasnoot, Erik. *Bolaño cercano*. Video. Candaya/UNAM. 2008.

Hecht, Valerie. "Guadalupe Nettel." *The Contemporary Spanish American Novel: Bolaño and After*, edited by Will H. Corral, Juan E. De Castro, and Nicholas Birns, Bloomsbury, 2013, pp. 50–54.

Henríquez Ureña, Pedro. *Seis ensayos en busca de nuestra expresión*. Editorial Nueva Nicaragua, 1986.

Herralde, Jorge. "Anagrama, 40 años creando prestigio." Interview by Josep Massot. *La Vanguardia*, 21 June 2009. https://www.lavanguardia.com/cultura/20090621/53727975839/anagrama-40-anos-creando-prestigio.html.

Hirsch, E. D. *Cultural Literacy: What Every American Needs to Know*. Random House, 1988.

Horswell, Michael J. "Baroque and Neo-Baroque Literary Tradition." 2013/2017. https://www.oxfordbibliographies.com/view/document/obo-9780199766581/obo-9780199766581-0004.xml.

Hoyos, Héctor. *Beyond Bolaño: The Global Latin American Novel*. Columbia UP, 2015.

———. "Roberto Bolaño, Solar Anus of World Literature." *A Companion to World Literature: 1920 to Early 21st Century*, edited by Ken Seigneurie et al., Wiley, 2020. https://doi.org/10.1002/9781118635193.ctwl0259.

Joon-ho, Bong. "Bong Joonho Talks True Crime, Steve Buscemi, Unlikely Success of Parasite." Interview by Jordan Mintzer. *Hollywood Reporter*, 18 Oct. 2019. https://www.hollywoodreporter.com/news/bong-joon-ho-parasite-success-true-crime-steve-buscemi-1248655.

Isbester, Katherine. "Guatemala: Ethnicity and the Shadow State." *The Paradox of Democracy in Latin America: Ten Country Studies of Division and Resilience*, edited by Katherine Isbester, U of Toronto P, 2011, pp. 131–56.

Kafka, Franz. "The Great Wall of China." *Selected Short Stories of Franz Kafka*, translated by Willa and Edwin Muir, Random House, 1952, pp. 129–146.

———. "The Metamorphosis." *Selected Short Stories of Franz Kafka*, translated by Willa and Edwin Muir, Random House, 1952, pp. 19–89.

Kerr, Lucille. *Reclaiming the Author.* Duke UP, 1992.

———. *Suspended Fictions: Reading Novels by Manuel Puig.* U of Illinois P, 1987.

Kristal, Efraín. *Invisible Work: Borges and Translation.* Vanderbilt UP, 2002.

———. *The Temptation of the Word: The Novels of Mario Vargas Llosa.* Vanderbilt UP, 1998.

"Las traducciones en España suponen el 21% de la producción editorial en España con 14,000 libros de media al año." *La Vanguardia*, 23 May 2018. https://www.lavanguardia.com/vida/20180523/443786087954/las-traducciones-en-espana-suponen-el-21-de-la-produccion-editorial-en-espana-con-14000-libros-de-media-al-ano.html.

Lago, Eduardo. "Muere a los 89 años Harold Bloom, el más influyente crítico literario." *El País*, 15 Oct. 2019. https://elpais.com/cultura/2019/10/14/actualidad/1571082354_799988.html.

Lépori, Roberto. "Borges contra la democracia. Una relectura paranoica de "La lotería en Babilonia." https://www.borges.pitt.edu/sites/default/files/lepori.pdf.

Liddicoat, Anthony J. "Translation as Intercultural Mediation: Setting the Scene." *Perspectives: Studies in Translation Theory and Practice*, vol. 24, no. 3, 2016, pp. 347–53.

López-Calvo, Ignacio. "On Magical Realism as an International Phenomenon in the Twenty First Century." *Critical Insights: Magical Realism*, edited by Ignacio López-Calvo, Salem Press, 2014, pp. xvi–xxx.

———. "On Roberto Bolaño: Poet and Vagabond." *Critical Insights: Roberto Bolaño*, editor Ignacio López-Calvo, Salem Press, 2015, pp. 3–24.

Loy, Benjamin. "Mocking World Literature and Canon Parodies in Roberto Bolaño's Fiction." *Roberto Bolaño as World Literature*, edited by Nicholas Birns and Juan E. De Castro, Bloomsbury, 2017, pp. 153–66.

Luiselli, Valeria. "El cuerpo escrito de Guadalupe Nettel." *Nexos*, 1 Dec 2011. https://www.nexos.com.mx/?p=14602.

Malpartida, Juan. "*El canon occidental: La escuela y los libros de todas las épocas* de Harold Bloom." *Vuelta*, May 1996, pp. 42–43.

Manzoni, Celina. "Ficción de futuro y lucha por el canon en la narrativa de Roberto Bolaño." *Bolaño salvaje,* edited by Edmundo Paz Soldán and Gustavo Faverón, Candaya, 2008, pp. 335–357.

Mariátegui, José Carlos. *7 ensayos de interpretación de la realidad peruana.* Editora Amauta, 1981.

———. "James Joyce." *El alma matinal y otras estaciones del hombre de hoy.* Editora Amauta, 1981, pp. 177–80.

———. "Nacionalismo y vanguardismo: En la literatura y el arte." *Peruanicemos al Perú,* Editora Amauta, 1981, pp. 76–79.

———. *Seven Interpretive Essays on Peruvian Reality.* Translated by Marjorie Urquidi, U of Texas P, 1971.

Martin, Gerald. *Gabriel García Márquez: A Life.* Bloomsbury, 2012.

Matto de Turner, Clorinda. *Leyendas y recortes.* Lima: La Equitativa, 1891.

McEnaney, Tom. "Rigoberta's Listener. The Significance of Sound in *Testimonio.*" *PMLA,* vol. 135, no. 2, 2020, pp. 393–400.

Menchú, Rigoberta and Elizabeth Burgos. *I, Rigoberta Menchú: An Indian Woman in Guatemala.* Translated by Ann Wright. Verso, 1984.

———. *Me llamo Rigoberta Menchú y así me nació la conciencia.* Siglo XXI, 2007.

Mistral, Gabriela. *Bendita sea mi lengua: Diario íntimo de Gabriela Mistral (1905–1956).* Edited by Jaime Quezada. Planeta/Ariel, 2002.

———. "Norah Borges, la argentina" (manuscrito). Biblioteca Nacional Digital. http://www.bibliotecanacionaldigital.gob.cl/bnd/623/w3-article-137964.html.

———. *Poesía y prosa.* Edited by Jaime Quezada. Biblioteca Ayacucho, 1993.

———. *Women.* Edited by Marjorie Agosín and Jacqueline Nanfito, and translated by Jacqueline Nanfito. White Pine Press, 2000.

Mistral, Gabriela and Victoria Ocampo. *Esta América nuestra: Correspondencia 1926–1956.* Edited by Elizabeth Horan and Doris Meyer. El Cuenco de Plata, 2007.

———. *This America of Ours: The Letters of Gabriela Mistral and Victoria Ocampo.* Edited and translated by Elizabeth Horan and Doris Meyer. U of Texas P, 2003.

Molina Foix, Vicente. "Un sorprendente 'hit parade' de la inmortalidad." *El País,* 12 Dec. 1994. https://elpais.com/diario/1994/12/24/cultura/788223612_850215.html.

Molloy, Silvia. "Postcolonial Latin America and the Magical Realist Imperative." *Nation, Language, and the Ethics of Translation,* edited by Sandra Bermann and Michael Wood, Princeton UP, 2005, pp. 370–79.

Murcia, Elizabeth. "Figura de autor e identidad marginal en *El cuerpo en que nací*, de Guadalupe Nettel." *Diseminaciones,* vol. 1, no. 2, 2018, pp. 71–88.

Nettel, Guadalupe. *The Body Where I was Born: A Novel.* Translated by J. T. Lichtenstein. *Seven Stories Press,* 2015.

———. *El cuerpo en que nací.* Anagrama, 2011. Kindle.

———. "Guerra en los basureros." *El matrimonio de los peces rojos,* Ediciones Páginas de Espuma, 2013, pp. 43–62.

———. "Guadalupe Nettel: 'Empecé a mirar lo que me avergüenza, todo lo doloroso de mi vida.'" Interview with

Natalia Blanc. *La Nación*, 15 May 2015. https://www.lanacion.com.ar/cultura/guadalupe-nettel-empece-a-mirar-lo-que-me-averguenza-todo-lo-doloroso-de-mi-vida-nid1792986/.

"The Nobel Prize in Literature 1982." https://www.nobelprize.org/prizes/literature/1982/summary/.

Olivera-Williams, María Rosa. "Boom, *Realismo mágico*—Boom and *Boomito*." *The Cambridge History of Latin American Women's Literature*, edited by Ileana Rodríguez and Mónica Szurmuk, Cambridge UP, 2015, pp. 278–95.

———. "Twentieth Century Women Writers and the Feminist Novel." *The Oxford Handbook of the Latin American Novel*, edited by Juan E. De Castro and Ignacio López-Calvo. Oxford UP, forthcoming.

Palapa Quijas, Fabiola. "Guadalupe Nettel se despoja del dolor de su niñez y escribe *El cuerpo en que nací*." *La Jornada*, 1 August 2011. https://www.jornada.com.mx/2011/08/01/cultura/a14n1cul.

Palou, Miguel Ángel. "La feria del Crack (Una Guía)." *Manifiesto del Crack (1996)*, by Palou et al. https://confabulario.eluniversal.com.mx/manifiesto-del-crack-1996/.

Pastor, Beatriz. "Polémicas en torno al canon: Implicaciones filosóficas, pedagógicas y políticas." *Casa de las Américas*, vol. 29, no. 171, 1988, pp. 78–87.

Paz, Octavio. *Sor Juana, or, The Traps of Faith*. Translated by Margaret Sayers Peden. Harvard UP, 1988.

Pestaña Castro, Cristina. "Intertextualidad de F. Kafka en J. L. Borges." *Es-péculo: Revista de Estudios Literarios*, vol. 7, 1997. http://webs.ucm.es/info/especulo/numero7/borg_kaf.htm.

Piglia, Ricardo. *Artificial Respiration*. Translated by Daniel Balderston, Duke UP, 1994.

———. "Clase 1 *Borges por Piglia*. Televisión Pública, Buenos Aires, 7 Sept. 2013. https://www.youtube.com/watch?v=im_kMvZQlv8; transcript: http://revistapenultima.com/borges-por-piglia-las-cuatro-clases-sin-cortes-y-sus-transcripciones-completas/.

———. "Clase 4 *Borges por Piglia*. Televisión Pública, Buenos Aires, 28 Sept. 2013. https://www.youtube.com/watch?v=5svf4mzbeTc; transcript: http://revistapenultima.com/borges-por-piglia-las-cuatro-clases-sin-cortes-y-sus-transcripciones-completas/.

———. *Respiración artificial*. Seix Barral, 2000.

———. "Vivencia literaria." *Dominios de la literatura: Acerca del canon*, edited by Susana Cella, Losada, 1998, pp. 155–57.

Pohl, Burkhard. "'Ruptura y continuidad': Jorge Volpi, el Crack, y la herencia del 68." *Revista de crítica literaria latinoamericana*, vol. 30, no. 59, 2004, pp. 53–70.

Pratt, Mary Louise. "'Don't Interrupt Me: The Gender Essay as Conversation and Countercanon." *Revista Brasileira de Literatura Comparada*, vol. 4, 1998, pp. 85–101.

Pulido Tirado, Genara. "Harold Bloom, El canon occidental y su repercusión en España." *The Grove*, vol. 6, 1999, pp. 193–204.

Quijano, Aníbal. "Modernidad, identidad y utopía en América Latina." *Modernidad, identidad y utopía en América Latina*. Sociedad y Política, 1988, pp. 45–69.

———. "Modernity, Identity and Utopia in Latin America." *The Postmodernism Debate in Latin America*, edited by John Beverley, Michael Aronna, and José Oviedo, Duke UP, 1995, pp. 201–16.

Rama, Ángel. *Transculturación narrativa en América Latina*. Ediciones El Andariego, 2008.

———. *Writing across Cultures: Narrative Transculturation in Latin America*. Edited and translated by David Fry, Duke UP, 2012.

Robbins, Timothy R. "From the Mexican Onda to McOndo: The Shifting Ideology of Mass Culture." *New Trends in Contemporary Latin American Narrative*, edited by Timothy R. Robbins and José Eduardo González, Palgrave Macmillan, 2014, pp. 15–38.

Robertson, Ritchie. *Kafka: A Very Short Introduction*. Oxford UP, 2004.

Rodríguez Monegal, Emir. *Borges: A Literary Biography*. Paragon, 1988.

Roger, Sarah. *Borges and Kafka: Sons and Writers*. Oxford UP, 2017.

Rowe, William. "Liberalism and Authority: The Case of Mario Vargas Llosa." *On Edge: The Crisis of Contemporary Latin American Culture*, edited by George Yúdice, Jean Franco, and Juan Flores, U of Minnesota P, 1992, pp. 45–64.

Rushdie, Salman. "Salman Rushdie on Gabriel García Márquez: His World Was Mine." *The Telegraph*, 25 Apr. 2014. https://www.telegraph.co.uk/culture/books/10787739/Salman-Rushdie-on-Gabriel-Garcia-Marquez-His-world-was-mine.html.

Sarlo, Beatriz. *Jorge Luis Borges: A Writer on the Edge*. Verso, 2007.

Sánchez Prado, Ignacio. *El canon y sus formas: La reinvención de Harold Bloom y sus lecturas hispanoamericanas*. Gobierno del Estado de Puebla, 2002.

———. "On Cosmopolitanism and the Love of Literature: Revisiting Harold Bloom through His Final Books." *Los Angeles Review of Books*, 2 Mar. 2021. https://lareviewofbooks.org/article/on-cosmopolitanism-and-the-love-of-literature-revisiting-harold-bloom-through-his-final-books.

———. "Repensar a Harold Bloom: Reflexiones personales a diez años de *El canon y sus formas*." *La influencia de Harold Bloom: Estudios y testimonios*, edited by Carlos X. Ardavín Trabanco and Antonio Lastra, La Torre del Virrey/Nexofía 2012, pp. 94–104.

———. *Strategic Occidentalism: On Mexican Fiction, the Neoliberal Book Market, and the Question of World Literature*. Northwestern UP, 2018.

Shklovski, Víktor. "Rozanov: La obra y la evolución literaria." *Antología del formalismo ruso y el grupo de Bajtín*, edited by Emil Volek, Fundamentos, 1992, pp. 171–76.

Siskind, Mariano. *Cosmopolitan Desires: Global Modernity and World Literature in Latin America*. Northwestern UP, 2014.

———. "Toward a Cosmopolitanism of Loss: An Essay about the End of the World." *World Literature, Cosmopolitanism, Globality: Beyond, Against, Post, Otherwise*, edited by Gesine

Müller and Mariano Siskind, De Gruyter, 2019, pp. 205–35.

Sommer, Doris. "Rigoberta's Secrets." *Latin American Perspectives*, vol. 18, no. 3, 1991, pp. 32–50.

Sorrentino, Fernando. "El kafkiano caso de la *Verwandlung* que Borges jamás tradujo." *Espéculo: Revista de Estudios Literarios*, vol. 10, 1998. http://webs.ucm.es/info/especulo/numero10/borg_tra.html.

Sosa, Francisco. *Escritores y poetas sud-americanos*. Mexico: Oficina Tipográfica del Ministerio de Fomento, 1890.

Starn, Orin. "Introduction." *When Rains Became Floods: A Child Soldier's Story*, translated by Margaret Randall, Duke UP, 2015, pp. xiii–xxiii.

Stavans, Ilan. "Willing Outcast: How a Chilean-Born Iconoclast Became a Great Mexican Novelist." *Washington Post*, 6 May 2007.

Steiner, George. "Tigers in the Mirror." *Extraterritorial*, Atheneum, 1971, pp. 22–24.

Stoll, David. *Rigoberta Menchú and the Story of All Poor Guatemalans*. Routledge, 1999.

Swanson, Philip. "Introduction." *The Cambridge Companion to Gabriel García Márquez*, edited by Philip Swanson, Cambridge UP, 2010, pp. 1–6.

Unruh, Vicky. "Mariátegui's Aesthetic Thought: A Critical Reading of the Avant-Gardes." *Latin American Research Review*, vol. 24, no. 3, 1989, pp. 45–69.

Updike, John. "The Author as Librarian." *Picked-Up Pieces*, Knopf, 1975, pp. 169–90.

Van Doren, Carl. "Toward a New Canon." *The Nation*, 13 Apr. 1932, pp. 429–30.

Vargas Llosa, Mario. *A Fish in the Water*. Translated by Helen Lange, Farrar, Straus & Giroux, 1994.

———. *La civilización del espectáculo*, Penguin Random House, 2012. Nook.

———. *Conversación en La Catedral*. Punto de Lectura, 2001.

———. *Conversación en Princeton: Con Rubén Gallo*. Alfaguara, 2017. Kindle.

———. *Conversation in the Cathedral*. Translated by Gregory Rabassa. Harper & Row, 1975.

———. "*Death in Venice*: The Call of the Abyss." *Touchstones: Essays on Literature, Art, and Politics*, edited and translated by John King, Farrar, Straus, & Giroux, 2011. Kindle.

———. *El hablador*. Seix Barral, 1991.

———. *El pez en el agua*. Alfaguara, 1993.

———. "El soldado desconocido." *El País*, 15 Dec. 2012. https://elpais.com/elpais/2012/12/13/opinion/1355421080_101974.html.

———. "Las ficciones de Borges." *Medio siglo con Borges*, Alfaguara, 2020. Kindle.

———. "*La muerte en Venecia*. El llamado del abismo." *La verdad de las mentiras: Ensayos sobre la novela moderna*, Peisa, 1993, pp. 19–26.

———. "La tumba de Kafka." *El País*, 18 May 2019. https://elpais.com/elpais/2019/05/17/opinion/1558109137_398362.html.

———. *Notes on the Death of Culture: Essays on Spectacle and Society*. Farrar, Straus & Giroux, 2015.

———. *The Storyteller*. Penguin, 1990.

Vásquez, Juan Gabriel. "Malentendidos alrededor de García Márquez." *El arte de la distorsión*, Alfaguara 2009. Kindle.

Villoro, Juan. "El rey duerme: Crónica hacia *Hamlet: De eso se trata ensayos literarios.*" Anagrama, 2008. http://www.cervantesvirtual.com/obra-visor/el-rey-duerme-cronica-hacia-hamlet--o/html/c7c71688–10b2–4552–9539–1693261a8e61_2.html.

Volpi, Jorge. "Bolaño epidemia." *Bolaño salvaje*, edited by Edmundo Paz Soldán and Gustavo Faverón, Candaya, 2008, pp. 191–207.

Zavala, Oswaldo. *La modernidad insufrible: Roberto Bolaño en los límites de la literatura latinoamericana contemporánea*. U of North Carolina P, 2016.

Zevallos, Ulíses Juan. "El testimonio. De la representación a la autorrepresentación (1974–2016)." *Contrapunto ideológico y perspectivas dramatúrgicas en el Perú contemporáneo*, edited by Juan E. De Castro and Leticia Robles-Moreno, PUCP, 2018, pp. 211–38.

INDEX